The Future of Black Studies

"Alkalimat's unique talent and skill, as a life-long teacher, is to unpack, make accessible, and organize layers of knowledge, turning it into academic coursework. Alkalimat is encyclopedic, radical, yet accommodative of all streams of Black Liberation. As Steve Biko said, 'students are firstly members of the Black community, where the struggle is waged'; for Alkalimat, Black Studies are about the history, the present and the future of Black Freedom."

—Vusi Mchunu a.k.a. Macingwane, South African poet, Chairperson of the Freedom Park Council

"Written by one of its African-American founding fathers, the book places Black Studies at the intersection of American history, progressive social movements, and academia. In tracing the emergence of Diaspora Studies and the role of African and Caribbean thinkers, Abdul Alkalimat builds on a life-long commitment, decades of research, and a global network to provide unique insights into little-known diasporic linkages that extend to countries as diverse as England, Germany, Ghana, and Jamaica."

—Nii Addy, German-Ghanaian Political Scientist

Praise for *The History of Black Studies*

"Abdul Alkalimat is one of the most rigorous and committed Black radical thinkers of our time."
—Barbara Ransby, award-winning author of *Ella Baker and the Black Freedom Movement*

"Magisterial [...] The most comprehensive history of the field of Black Studies. This landmark book will become a standard in the history of our field."
—Molefi Kete Asante, Professor at the Department of Africology, Temple University

"Abdul Alkalimat, one of the pioneers of Black Studies, has done a great service by providing a powerful, expansive, and compelling history of the field."
—Keisha N. Blain, award-winning author and co-editor of the #1 New York Times Bestseller *400 Souls*

"This is Alkalimat's magnum opus [...] a focal point for scholarship on the history of Africana thought in the academy. It is required reading for Black Studies scholars and intellectual historians."
—Fabio Rojas, Virginia L. Roberts Professor of Sociology Indiana University

"A visionary and a documentarian, Alkalimat has been a major figure in the Black Studies movement since its modern inception. This landmark book is indispensable."
Martha Biondi, author of *The Black Revolution on Campus*

"Stunning [...] a precious guide to a forgotten past as well as a valuable tool for future battles over the political direction of education against racism."
—Paul Gilroy, author of *There Ain't No Black in the Union Jack*

"A must-read chronicle of one of the most significant developments in US social movements, making more visible the role of Black women who have too often been footnotes in this history. Even veteran pioneers and Black Studies comrades will be wowed!"
—Beverly Guy-Sheftall, the Anna Julia Cooper Professor of Women's Studies at Spelman College

The Future of Black Studies

Abdul Alkalimat

First published 2022 by Pluto Press
New Wing, Somerset House, Strand, London WC2R 1LA

www.plutobooks.com

British Library Cataloguing in Publication Data
A catalogue record for this book is available from the British Library

ISBN 978 0 7453 4701 1 Hardback
ISBN 978 0 7453 4700 4 Paperback
ISBN 978 0 7453 4703 5 PDF
ISBN 978 0 7453 4702 8 EPUB

This book is printed on paper suitable for recycling and made from fully managed and sustained forest sources. Logging, pulping and manufacturing processes are expected to conform to the environmental standards of the country of origin.

Typeset by Stanford DTP Services, Northampton, England

Simultaneously printed in the United Kingdom and United States of America

To my wife Kate, who I will share my future with.

To my grandsons, niece and nephew for the future they will live:
Donis, Solomon, Lucie and Ben.

Contents

Figures

Tables

Introduction

This book is about the future of Black Studies.

One of the aspects of being human is the experience of time. Most cultures encode historical time in collective consciousness, including some sense of the past, the present, and the future. This is no less true for Africans and African descendants throughout the African Diaspora. We seek to remember Africa before the European invasion and takeover. We imagine a future beyond our oppression that makes colonization merely an interruption and not a permanent replacement of our own history. We work to recapture African history, to once again be driven by African agency in theory and in practice. African Americans, at every stage of the US experience of oppression and exploitation, have remembered our collective pain and its perpetrators, and imagined freedom, the absence of that pain, and the creation of a sustainable future of well-being and prosperity.

All this recommences with every advance in the progress of the freedom struggle. And this energizes Black Studies: "That beat has carried Black Studies from academic immigrancy to forceful, scholarly citizenship in the American University. And the new story of Black Studies is the amazing proliferation of its energies in a manner that makes avoidance or eradication impossible" (Baker 1993, 32). The future of Black Studies itself has long been debated, but after fifty years of development, contemporary Black Studies has established itself as a stable fixture in education, especially in higher education. Given this sustainability, it is important to look at today's innovation to see how Black Studies is actually moving into its future.

In the companion volume to this one, the *History of Black Studies*, I analyzed Black Studies in three ways: as intellectual history, as a social movement, and as an academic profession. Each of these ways had high points that were sequential, but together represent manifestations of the production and distribution of knowledge about the Black experience as acts of agency against the oppression and exploitation of Black people. Black Studies includes both theory and practice, science and art. It involves both campus and community (Alkalimat 2021).

Black Studies as intellectual history has its academic foundation in the scholarship of the first two generations of Black PhDs. This provided a treasure trove of intellectual faculty talent at historically Black colleges and universities (HBCUs), because of segregationist practices of mainstream institutions. Great periods of productivity of scholarship on the Black experience took place at such institutions as Howard University, Fisk University, and the Atlanta University Center. Intellectual and cultural creativity had origins in the institutions of the Black community as well. This is especially true in large regional cities with large Black populations, for example, New Orleans, New York, Chicago, and Los Angeles. The third source of Black Studies as intellectual history is the ideological development of the Black Freedom Movement.

We discussed Black Studies as social movement in six ways: the Freedom Movement, the Black Power Movement, the Black Arts Movement, the New Communist Movement, the Black Women's Movement, and the Black Student Movement. Each of these included education programs, mass education for the community, and cadre-level education for movement activists. A critical development was the new emergent institutions, often called Freedom Schools. These community-based freedom schools were based on curriculum development in Black history, Black culture, and ideologies of social justice protest.

Finally, the history of Black studies includes formal academic programs, especially in higher education. In the *History of Black Studies*, data from 2013 is presented that indicate 76 percent of institutions of higher education offer some sort of Black Studies, including 331 degree-granting units. By 2019, this number had increased to 356 (Alkalimat 2021, 235). There are now over a dozen units that grant the PhD degree in Black Studies. For the most part, these academic programs fit into the normative structure of their institutional context, from research universities to community colleges, in both private and public institutions. However, it must be noted that, in times of crisis, the activist social justice function latent in these programs comes to the fore. Academic programs in Black Studies have a continuing tie to the political life of the Black community, sometimes with the support of faculty and sometimes as a challenge to faculty.

The future of Black Studies has to take into consideration what is being projected as the future of the society in general, especially what is impacting the Black community. At the turn of the century, dystopian thinking began to come from the highest levels of society. Samuel Huntington, a former Harvard political scientist, has been a leading voice on a dystopian politics for the US future. He laid the basis for the war against Iraq and the current plague of Islamophobia with his book *Clash of Civilizations and the Remaking of World Order* (1996). This book argues that there can be no future coexistence of Christianity and Islam, thereby laying the basis for a holy war that the USA continues to fight today. He has also written a book that laid the ideological basis for the current immigration crisis, in which he projects conflict with people of Latino nationalities because they are not submitting to Anglo assimilationist transformation: *Who Are We? The Challenges to American National Identity* (2004). Huntington sees the future as a war against non-European descendant populations, Muslims and Latinos. This is an academic argument that produces white supremacist nationalism, and has a direct negative impact on Black people (Huntington 2004; 2011).

More currently, the absolute failure of the former US president Donald Trump to affirm a scientifically valid approach to the Covid pandemic led to a section of society volunteering to embrace the risk of death, a form of politically sanctioned suicide resulting in the USA having the highest rate of deaths in the world. This bad leadership has emboldened a dangerous skepticism against science and a loss of confidence in public health, putting everyone in danger. What future does this lead us to?

The mass media, too, is full of negative visions of dystopian futures. A good example is the television series started in 2010 called *The Walking Dead* (created by Frank Darabont). It is a post-apocalyptic horror television series that pits zombies against humans in general, but also pits humans against each other frequently. The series makes killing to stay alive a moral necessity for everyone. This starkly good-versus-evil narrative creates a cultural mindset in its viewers that there are dangerous others to be faced and killed if one is to survive, which includes not being infected and becoming a zombie oneself. There is no cure, no hope, only life versus 'the walking dead'. The series has been a big success, and here is how Wikipedia sums up its popularity:

> *The Walking Dead* has the highest total viewership of any series in cable television history, including its third through sixth seasons, during which it averaged the most 18- to 49-year-old viewers of all cable or broadcast television series. Total viewership for its fifth-season premiere was 17.3 million, the most-watched series episode in cable history. In 2016, a *New York Times* study of the 50 television series with

> the most Facebook Likes found that like most other zombie series, *The Walking Dead* "is most popular in rural areas, particularly southern Texas and eastern Kentucky."
>
> (Wikipedia 2020c)

This fiction is leaping into our reality via the drugs approved by the US Food and Drug Administration and prescribed by medical professionals to stem the pain and despair many people feel. Prozac and Simulac psychotropic drugs have even been implicated in suicides and homicides. In contrast to these dystopias, this book asserts that the future is possible.

The current fiction version is a direct exposure of the evil machinations of the capitalist system, *Squid Game*. This is a South Korean show that began in 2021 and pulls people who are in deep debt into a game that gives them a chance to become a billionaire. The hitch is that, of the 456 people who start the game, everyone will be killed until there is one winner. The horrid process was constructed as a critique of capitalism, but for its viewers the massive death exhibited drags you into the capitalist cauldron of evil. The television show was written by Hwang Dong-hyuk.

> Hwang wrote *Squid Game* based on his own personal experiences and observations of capitalism and economic class struggle within South Korea. Hwang also considered that his script was targeted towards global issues regarding capitalism, stating, "I wanted to create something that would resonate not just for Korean people but globally. This was my dream." and "I do believe that the overall global economic order is unequal and that around 90% of the people believe that it's unfair. During the pandemic, poorer countries can't get their people vaccinated. They're contracting viruses on the streets and even dying. So I did try to convey a message about modern capitalism. As I said, it's not profound."
>
> ("*Squid Game*" 2022)

The future we need is the opposite of dystopia. We need a positive future. To understand the struggles of Black people, and how Black people have been able to celebrate life even under harsh conditions, we have to seek and evaluate the positive influence of Black Studies. Specifically, Black Studies prepares a diagnosis of the present-past, while seeking a perspective and policies to improve the quality of life in the present-future. This is a recognition that the past and the future are intimately connected to the present—all the dynamics of a dialectical process.

Imagining a society in which all people can lead the good life is to create a utopia, a desired alternative to what exists in a society. Thomas More coined this word in 1516, using a Greek word meaning nowhere (More 1900). It was the design for a society better than what was being experienced in the Europe of his time. So, the use of the word "utopia" means a criticism of society by way of imagining a better one. Oppressed people have this at the heart of their most cherished forms of historical consciousness—religious, political, and social. They seek to answer the question: can't we imagine something better, some realization of freedom?

Black Studies is an educational context for such imagination, both about society and about Black Studies itself. People in Black Studies do not separate the two. The future of the academic discipline is inseparable from the future of society and the institutions of education that house Black Studies. This is what this volume seeks to explore: the future of Black Studies in the context of the future of society. It proceeds by looking at three exciting advances: Afrofuturism, the African Diaspora, and eBlack Studies.

Part I will rethink the theoretical focus on what is being called Afrofuturism. This has mainly been a concept tied to the speculative artistic and technological innovators in music, film, and science fiction. This volume will take a different approach, anchoring thinking about the future in Black intellectual political history. We have always marched toward the future we want.

A tension in Afrofuturism is the philosophical dialectic of idealism versus materialism. Idealism holds that ideas are primary, while materialism holds that material forces are primary in our understanding of reality (Cornforth 1975). To some extent, in Western philosophy, this is the difference between Plato as an idealist and Aristotle as a materialist. This distinction should not be misinterpreted, however, to mean that ideas are not essential, because they are critical and must be developed as a vital part of all human activity, both in science and in art.

Ideas are hypothetical until demonstrated to accurately reflect the nature of material reality. In social life, our morality, our sense of social justice, helps us to imagine a future better than the one we are living in, even though we have the dilemma that there are many conflicting ideas of this future. In any case, the test of any idea about social life is its application in social practice. This book makes the case for enriching

Afrofuturism with the ways various Black people and communities have looked at the future.

Critical rethinking of Afrofuturism is the content of Chapter 1. With this as the basis, the next three chapters will focus on the three main ways that Black people have dealt with the future. Chapter 2, "Imagining the Future," is about how Black intellectuals and artists have projected images of society into the future with speculative thinking, including fantasy in cultural production. This is about positing an imaginary future with a critique of the present. Chapter 3, "Back to the Future," focuses on how the future has been thought about based on the past. This is the *Sankofa Principle*: going back to the past to get a perspective on what future is most desirable. Chapter 4 discusses the main ways that Black people have struggled for their future. They have fought against their oppressors to create a future free from oppression and in this process have connected their future to reforms and even revolution.

Part II will discuss the globalization of Black Studies as it has transformed into African Diaspora studies. Beginning with the historical origin of African Americans before and as a result of the European slave trade dispersal, the African Diaspora is the site of historical similarities and differences that present an opportunity to place the Black experience more firmly in world history. Chapter 5 will discuss the emergence of the African Diaspora as a framework for ideology as well as scholarship. Chapter 6 will focus on how the African Diaspora is increasingly guiding the research and curriculum development of Black Studies. Some departments are changing their names to embrace this new focus. Chapter 7 looks to the African Diaspora itself to examine how Black Studies is being developed on a worldwide scale.

Part III will discuss the development of eBlack Studies, and how the use of information technology is transforming Black Studies. Chapter 8 will survey the importance of science and technology in Black history and Black consciousness. Chapter 9 will review the theoretical literature that clarifies four different theses about the impact of information technology on the Black experience. We will use the Toledo model to identify programmatic innovations in Chapter 10. We will also discuss a new methodological framework for Black Studies based on the use of digital tools.

The basic argument here is that the future of Black Studies will include at least three key developments: (1) the study of how Black people think about and prepare for the future; (2) the study of all Black people in the world by focusing on the African Diaspora; and (3) the study of how information technology is changing the production and distribution of knowledge about the Black experience. Each of these three developments is part of general processes of change. Globalization and information technology is forcing everyone to rethink their understanding of society, and that includes the future. Black Studies will be moving with the times.

In general, these future conceptions have emerged as expressions of two alternative forms of political agency, reform, and revolution, the first improving the system in incremental quantitative ways, versus the second transforming the system in fundamental qualitative ways. Actually, almost all change represents the dialectic of reform and revolution, the relationship between a strategy for freedom (long-range transformative goals, qualitative) and tactics of the ongoing struggle (immediate plans of action, quantitative).

One salient crisis in this process is the individualism that many times captures students and faculty. When Black Studies is delinked from the needs of the community in favor of the idiosyncratic concerns of one or more individuals, it is possible that the original mission of Black Studies has been betrayed. Of course, the future can only exist if there are degrees of freedom for the intellectuals, scholars, and artists, but it is equally important that Black Studies contributes to the historical strategic goal of freedom that involves the entire Black community and the society in general.

With all of these concerns, we will explore the future of Black Studies by reflecting on Afrofuturism, the African Diaspora, and the rise of eBlack Studies, through which information technology is opening new possibilities.

PART I

Black Studies as Afrofuturism

1
Rethinking Afrofuturism

This chapter presents a rethinking of the concept of Afrofuturism. In other words, how African Americans have thought about and studied the future will increasingly be part of the future of Black Studies. This is an intrinsically human experience, especially since all life forms seek to live and that means a concern for the future. Indeed, this is doubly so for humans, as our existential reality is that we know we will die, and that puts a limit on any future we might have.

This chapter will break down Afrofuturism by contrasting utopian thinking with dialectical and historical materialism, contrasting what we can dream up as a most desired future versus what we can actually achieve as we march through the history we live. Following this chapter will be chapters discussing three types of Afrofuturism: imagination as the basis for the future; the historical past as the basis for the future; and creating the future through the struggle for social change, both reform and revolution.

Afrofuturism was coined by Mark Dery in 1993 to cover a wide variety of activities envisioning futures (R. Anderson and Jones 2017). It is important to make a distinction between utopian thinking and a more scientific approach to the future, to distinguish fantasy from fact, speculative guesswork from hypotheses that can be investigated based on evidence. Afrofuturism in Black Studies will include both, but the most important focus has to be the agency of Black people on the march to freedom in all varieties of Afrofuturism. We have to include scholarship, cultural performance, and agency for social change.

One of the scholars responsible for the rise of the current manifestation of Afrofuturism as the name for forms of cultural activism is Alondra Nelson, who edited a special issue of the journal *Social Text* on Afrofuturism. In her introduction, she identified a polarity that had to be addressed: "Forecasts of a utopian (to some) race-free future and pronouncements of the dystopian digital divide are the predominant discourses of blackness and technology in the public sphere" (Nelson 2002, 1).

Nelson had created an online community called Afrofuturism in 1998, which was mainly based in the humanities and the arts. She clarifies further by focusing on technology.

> The Afrofuturism list emerged at a time when it was difficult to find discussions of technology and African American diasporic communities that went beyond the notion of the digital divide. From the beginning, it was clear that there was much theoretical territory to be explored. Early discussions included the concept of digital double consciousness; African diasporic cultural retentions in modern technoculture; digital activism and issues of access; dreams of designing technology based on African mathematical principles; the futuristic visions of black film, video, and music; the implications of the then burgeoning MP3 revolution; and the relationship between feminism and Afrofuturism.
>
> (Nelson 2002, 9)

Her pointing to a positive future leads us to the concept of utopia. Alex Zamalin, in his book *Black Utopia: The History of an Idea from Black Nationalism to Afrofuturism*, presents eight case studies of utopian and anti-utopian Black intellectuals (Zamalin 2019). Placing utopian thinking in a historical context, his first case is Martin Delaney (1812–1885). After racist faculty and students expelled him from Harvard Medical School and a subsequent career in the Union Army, Delaney rejects the racist colonial negation of Black people by turning to the African Diaspora for a new affirmation and vision of a new future. Zamalin summarizes Delaney's basic ideas:

> Delaney found equality, dignity, and freedom in black lives. He said no to white supremacy, exposed the drama of political contingency, and told of power's vulnerability. This was the vision Delaney modeled to inspire resistance to reach black utopia abroad. But it wasn't extended to a defense of gender equality, popular rule, and economic freedom.
>
> (Zamalin 2019, 33)

Utopian projections of new gender relations were discussed in the fiction of Francis Harper (1825–1911) and Pauline Hopkins (1859–1930). The writings of Samuel Delany (1942–) extended a utopian vision to LGBTQ rights. This is an essential correction to the error of silencing the voices of women and gay intellectuals about their own reality.

Zamalin treats W.E.B. Du Bois (1868–1963) as a utopian in his work on the freedom struggles of Black people, especially his work *Black Reconstruction* (1935). This focuses on the concept of democracy:

> For DuBois, democracy illuminated something of the dialectic between beginnings and ends, struggles and reversals, progress and reaction, change and uncertainty, the unknown and the unknown unknown. For all these contradictions, it was the aspiration to live in a democracy that, Du Bois believed, could rebuild the world in which all Americans would want to live.
>
> (Zamalin 2019, 61–62)

Du Bois, a materialist, anchored his work on Reconstruction in historical research. He helped us to see a future of democracy not via pure speculation, but as the result of class struggle led by Black workers.

On a global scale, Zamalin treats Richard Wright as a reality check on pan-African utopian thinking. Wright went to Ghana in 1953 and wrote a book, *Black Power*, detailing his experience and thoughts about the African freedom struggle:

> Without question, *Black Power*'s rhetorical structure as a blend of memoir, political critique, and travelogue obscured Wright's view of freedom. But this careful meditation on what freedom meant to Africans suggested that, for him, it was something more expressive and expansive than was developed by the NAACP political strategy of litigation for political enfranchisement. Wright saw freedom as a lived experience dependent upon but irreducible to certain political rights. It was about shaping one's destiny without another's say, a new beginning in which one would identify what counted as meaningful.
>
> (Zamalin 2019, 89)

The anti-utopian thinkers have pointed out that utopia can lead to an authoritarianism that would negate the vision of freedom associated with utopian thinking. Zamalin uses the work of George Schuyler (1895–1977) as an example of this kind of analysis. Many would argue that this reversal of democracy developed in the socialist countries and in the newly independent African former colonies. There continues to be a debate about to what extent Nkrumah was a mix of a revolutionary emancipator and an authoritarian leader in leading the transformation of Ghana.

Zamalin argues that it is possible to embrace the dialectic of utopian and anti-utopian elements to remain relevant to the freedom struggle:

> Energizing contemporary freedom struggles and imagining the impossible require combining the most productive elements of black utopian imagination and antiutopian critique, rather than accepting the false choice between them. It means reclaiming the sense of freedom without dehumanization and accepting the idea of perfectibility without fundamentalism. It means embracing radical equality and resisting gender and sexual domination. And it means taking seriously radical hope in the face of the unknown without messianic deliverance.
>
> Zamalin (2019, 139–40)

While some Afrofuturist scholars suggest their focus covers a big inclusive category based on technological advances, for our purpose, it is important to focus the concept on historical time. Historical time of the past, present, and future is fundamental to humans. Our consciousness is based on memory and perception, and our ability to imagine a future based on reason, morality, and whatever cultural mix of what we know and believe makes sense to us.

All thoughts about the future, especially broad inclusive thoughts about a new future, are speculative. In fact, they are guesses, even if educated guesses based on scientific research and/or growing out of artistically creativity. We experience them in the present and they can make us feel good or bad, be hopeful or discouraged, be expectant or fearful. No matter, because our being in the world makes thinking about the future a necessity, as well as preparing for it. This is especially true during periods of social and economic change, when old patterns of life are no longer workable and, whether we like it or not, new developments are taking place and life will not be the same. The challenge is to grasp the fundamental logic of the historical process, prepare a plan for the future, and then to practice an intervention to participate in and influence the direction of change. Marx urges us to do just this in his *Thesis on Feuerbach*, number eleven: "The philosophers have only *interpreted* the world, in various ways; the point, however is to *change* it" (Marx and Engels 1969, 15).

A critical study of historical experience is illustrative of this point. Frederick Engels discusses utopian thinking at the time when industrial capitalism was being born and replacing the existing feudal social formation. He makes a biting critique of utopian thinkers about the future in *Socialism Utopian and Scientific*:

> To the crude conditions of capitalistic production and the crude class conditions corresponded crude theories. The solution of the social problems, which as yet lay hidden in undeveloped economic conditions, the Utopians attempted to evolve out of the human brain. Society presented nothing but wrongs; to remove these was the task of reason. It was necessary, then, to discover a new and more perfect system of social order and to impose this upon society from without by propaganda, and wherever it was possible, by the example of model experiments. These new social systems were foredoomed as Utopian; the more completely they were worked out in detail, the more they could not avoid drifting off into pure phantasies.
>
> (Marx and Engels 1973, 119)

Engels discusses three such thinkers: Henri de Saint-Simon (1760–1825), Charles Fourier (1772–1837), and Robert Owen (1771–1858). His focus is their attempt to think up a solution, relying on reason, but not through a study of actual experience and the past practice encoded in political culture. As a consequence of this idealism, the model utopian communities founded on their ideas were not sustainable and did not prove to be clear models for society, although they demonstrated the power of a moral vision. In fact, some positive reforms came out of these efforts including the eight-hour workday and the cooperative movement. These innovative changes live on today. So, while utopian thinking does usually end up as fantasy, the desire for a better life can at times translate such a vision into practical reforms.

Other important examples are the utopian models advocated as part of the decolonization process. In Africa, a key challenge was to imagine a future to replace the disruptive rule by European colonizers. One such experiment was the Ujamaa village scheme under the leadership of President Julius Nyerere (1922–1999) in Tanzania. This scheme was to anchor development in the hands of the African masses who could rebuild the society on the basis of traditional culture. Many scholar activists challenged this view and examined class struggle as a more accurate reflection of the historical process (Campbell 1975; Shivji 1979).

A.M. Babu (1924–1996), former minister of economic development in Tanzania, in the spirit of Engels, rejects the utopian model.

> A glaring example is that of Tanzanian President Nyerere's *Ujamaa* experiment. While it is true that his ideas were motivated by the highest moral convictions on his part, theoretically and in practice they have proved to be limited and unworkable. His conception of development is very close to that of the Narodniks, and Lenin's critique of the latter is applicable to this instance. *Ujamaa*'s declared target is to improve the material conditions of the peasant, "at his own risk and responsibility for the market," by methods firmly rooted in the old system, at the same time resuscitating social values corresponding to a pre-feudal mode of production. The policy does not in the least envisage the need to *transform* him into a new person belonging to a new class—a need created by the development of the productive forces and new relations of production—with corresponding new social values.
>
> (Babu 1981, xv)

The Narodnik tendency that developed in mid-nineteenth-century Russia held the view that the peasantry was capable of creating a post-capitalist society. This view romanticized the rural folk, and failed to take into consideration their actual existence and inability to lead the industrialization of society. This is a fundamental negation of a future by defining it in terms of the past, without realizing that the future will have to be something new based on existing historical developments (Lenin 1914).

There are many instances of African-American utopian thinking. They are instructive for how this kind of speculative thinking leads to practices that fall short of the goal of sustainable progress in securing the well-being of the community. During Reconstruction, Black people founded their own towns. For example, the so-called "exodusters" migrated to Kansas and founded towns such as Nicodemus (Painter 1992). These proved to be transitional movements away from places maintaining the legacy of slavery, but did not develop into models for a permanent solution to the oppression of Black people. This did not end in that period, however, reemerging during the high tide of Black resistance in the 1960s. One case is the utopian community called Soul City, founded by Floyd McKissick (1922–1991) (McKissick 1969; Strain 2004; Minchin 2005).

McKissick, born and educated in North Carolina, became a lawyer in his home state. He rose to a high-ranking national position in the civil rights organization, the Congress of Racial Equality (CORE). Following the lead of James Farmer in CORE, Roy Innes and Floyd McKissick took CORE in the new direction of Black Power, especially Black economic empowerment. Soul City was a utopian retreat from the battlefield of the Civil Rights/Black Liberation Movement, under the assumption that a planned community could achieve the goals of freedom within the capitalist system. It was not to be exclusively a Black town: "Soul City will be an attempt to move into the future, a future where Black people welcome white people as equals" (Strain 2004, 57). The plan was to secure land, organize a planning process, recruit people as residents and a labor force, and then recruit capital investment to create jobs and economic viability:

> Developed by Floyd B. McKissick Enterprises, Incorporated, Soul City would be located on a 5,180-acre site, fifty miles north of the Raleigh/Durham/Chapel Hill area, in a rural, economically depressed part of the piedmont. ... The city was intended not only to stem the migration of rural Blacks to the city, but also to entice urban residents back to the countryside from the slums of U.S. cities. It offered an alternative to urban social miseries.
>
> (Strain 2004, 58–59)

Soul City was located in Warren County, one of the poorest counties in the state. From 1967 to 1977, the first billboard that drivers entering the county (and the state) saw welcomed people to Klan country. Funding for Soul City came from loans and support from the federal government. McKissick, a self-defined political pragmatist, supported Nixon and got his favor, but failed to get the support of Senator Helms even after supporting him. Helms, the arch-segregationist, told McKissick that his first move after being re-elected was to fight against any funding for Soul City, and that proved decisive.

Soul City lasted ten years, 1969–1979, but after that all residential addresses were reverted back to a rural county level system. Although the population dwindled down from its height of a few hundred, some people continued to live there and celebrate its memory. Its biggest obstacle was economic, in that they could not recruit enough business investment to create jobs. They were isolated without sufficient infrastructure and skilled labor. However, they did accomplish some important developments that improved the quality of life of a three-county area, mainly water and sewage systems. They established a health clinic that also provided dental care.

This utopian experiment started with mainstream bank loans and government grants, and was dependent on corporate investment. The people who relocated to Soul City were believers in the utopian ideal and were prepared to put their bodies on the line to help it come alive. Some good things happened, but it was doomed from the very beginning, based on how it got started in the first place.

We are also living in the midst of challenging times. Just as the birth of capitalism led to utopian thinking, so too in this period of transformative change based on the new technologies and class polarization do we have the same result—new utopian thinking. Of course, as has been pointed out, the mainstream is feeding the public images of a dystopian future. To counter this, utopian thinking has re-emerged.

Another important utopian scheme has been the movement to transform the Black Belt south, particularly in the state of Mississippi, into the Republic of New Afrika (RNA) (Obadele 1984; 1974; 1975; Sonebeyatta and Brooks 1971):

> In the late 1960s, a convention of Black delegates met in Detroit, Michigan and proclaimed that Black People in the United States were in fact a Nation of People separate from the American people. This convention of delegates, including Imari Obadele (who was later elected president of the Black Nation) gave that Nation of People a name, the Republic of New Afrika. The Republic of New Afrika took the concept of Black Nationalism to its ultimate stage when, in 1968, it declared Black People to be free and independent of the United States government.
>
> (Black History in America n.d.)

A national leadership was elected and became a force within Black nationalism. People began to relocate to Mississippi from northern cities, but conflict developed as the RNA members were not working within the historical political culture of Black people in Mississippi. Of course, the racist forces used every resource of the state and white supremacists to block their program. The RNA developed an activist militant youth wing that called itself the Malcolm X Grassroots Movement (MXGM). The greatest accomplishment of the MXGM was holding people's assemblies after the Hurricane Katrina disaster that led to the election of one of their members, Chokwe Lumumba (1947–2014), as the mayor of Jackson, Mississippi. Following his early death, the election of his son to work within the city government did not keep revolutionary movement building as the top priority. MXGM forces made a move to reconnect with the utopian vision and build an autonomous process to achieve self-determination.

An example of this is the turn to cooperatives, in the spirit of Robert Owen, as a path to escape the terror of racism and capitalist exploitation. Activists in Jackson, Mississippi, represent such a trend. They make explicit their association with the experience of the Mondragón cooperative movement in the Basque Country, Spain. Here is how they explain their goal of social transformation as one of their key principles:

> Social Transformation: Cooperation in the Cooperation Jackson system is an instrument for social transformation. As Jose Maria Arizmendiarrieta, a founder of the Mondragón system wrote "Cooperation is the authentic integration of people in the economic and social process that shapes the new social order; the cooperators must make the objective extend to all those that hunger and thirst for justice in the working world." The cooperatives of Cooperation Jackson will reinvest the major portion of their surpluses in Jackson and Kush District (the contiguously Afrikan counties of western Mississippi). Following the Mondragón model, a significant portion of our surplus will go toward new job development, to community development (through the use of social funds), to a social security system based on mutual solidarity and responsibility, to cooperation with other institutions advancing the cause of workers in Mississippi, and to collaborative efforts to developing a transformative culture in Mississippi.
>
> (Cooperation Jackson 2020)

This project developed out of "The Jackson–Kush Plan: The Struggle for Self-Determination and Economic Democracy," written by Kali Akuno and adopted by the New Afrikan People's Organization and the Malcolm X Grassroots Movement (Akuno 2012). This is a well-reasoned plan that has attracted a great deal of attention and support. So one might ask, why is this utopian thinking being presented in the same way that Engels presented his argument; after all, Akuno refers to the working class in general terms. The challenge is to base a program on both the quantitative study of the actual social conditions facing the Black community and the subjective consciousness that enables the people to understand their condition and have a desire to fight to change these very conditions (Akuno 2012).

Three issues of the *Negro Digest* several decades earlier had engaged a diverse set of scholars on these very questions about a better future for Black people in higher education. This dialogue was very rich, in that the voices of veteran administrators were contrasted with the visionary voices of young scholars and activists. While all sought a future that improved on what was currently in place, the different viewpoints juxtaposed reform with revolutionary change (McWorter 1968; 1969; 1970).

Darwin Turner (1932–1991), then dean of the graduate school at the Agricultural and Technical State University of North Carolina at Greensboro, argued that the fight for the future was to take place as reforms within the existing institutions:

> Most reform ends in revolution. Perhaps that will be the inevitable result in any effort to reform higher education for Negroes in the United States. Nevertheless, before proposing the revolutionary step of establishing a new institution—a black university—I wish to suggest ways of achieving the desired improvement within the present structure of higher education. … Let us dream of the ideal institution—one which will give growth to Negro teachers and students alike. It is, I repeat, one which can be developed within the current framework of higher education—if it is to be developed at all.
>
> (Turner, cited in McWorter 1968, 15 and 17)

Chuck Hopkins, a student from the protests at Duke University, put forward an activist projection of a new future. He recounted and characterized the launch of Malcolm X Liberation University outside of the current framework of higher education:

> In October 1969, in Durham, North Carolina, the Black community saw its dream of a relevant Black educational institution become a reality with the opening of Malcolm X Liberation University in an old warehouse which had been cleaned out and renovated. On the 25th of October, over 3,000 Black people from Durham and communities around the country gathered in front of the building site to listen to the dedication message of Sister Betty Shabazz, widow of Brother Malcolm X. Sister Betty charged the participants in the ceremonies and Black people around the world with the task of organizing for Black unity and building for the Black nation.
>
> (Hopkins, cited in McWorter 1970, 39)

These two approaches to change—the one working within the system and the other forging new ground outside of the established system—work dialectically together in creating a future. The main point here is that our concern with Afrofuturism has to mainly look to Black people's agency in fighting to create a new future for themselves.

We will continue to face the contradiction of idealism versus materialism in efforts to think about the future as well as in efforts to create the future. People who are idealists have positive intentions based on their ideas, values, and moral standards. However, without a materialist analysis of the actual contradictions in society, and on that basis finding the social forces able to resist and create change, the social transformation toward freedom will not take place. Projects like Cooperation Jackson are necessary but are not sufficient: people need to survive, but they also need to solve their problems once and for all.

There is an Afrofuturism crisis in Black Studies as discussed. There is an urgency to the condition of Black people. This requires clarity in understanding their actual experience. Our task in this volume is to rethink Afrofuturism as a way of understanding how Black people have actually dealt with the future. We will explore answers to three key questions: How have Black people imagined a future of freedom? How have Black people used the past to think about their future? How have Black people dealt with the future in their actual struggles for freedom?

2
Imagining the Future

Afrofuturism is usually associated with a leap into the unknown, especially in science fiction, that includes reflections on space travel and the evolution of new species. There are versions of this that are escapist fantasy, but some fantasy helps us reflect on historical reality. Some of this is creative and targets getting its audience to find new ways to think and feel about reality as a first step into the future. Two very important and often-cited people in this realm are the musician Sun Ra and the writer Octavia Butler.

Travel out of this world, into space, has been a recurrent theme of Black cultural history.

> African Americans have always talked cosmology with a premodern ease, a discourse distantly rooted in African conceptions of the cosmos, but yet also shaped by modern science and tempered by a wariness of how science had sometimes been used against them. … The black cosmic vision is easily seen as part of the theme of travel, of journey, of exodus, of escape which dominates African-American narratives: of people who could fly back to Africa, travel in the spirit, visit or be visited by the dead; of chariots and trains to heaven, the Underground Railroad, Marcus Garvey's steamship line, Rosa Parks on the Mobile bus, freedom riders. It was also a vision which lurked distantly but stubbornly behind blues songs which praised the technology of motion and travel, where trains, cars, airplanes, buses—even transmission systems ("Dynaflow")—were celebrated as part of African-American postagricultural mobility within a Booker T. Washington/*Popular Science* optimism about the future.
>
> (Szwed 2012, 133–35)

Musicians have carried forward the message of planetary travel. Out of the be-bop period King Pleasure developed a philosophy he called "planetism." Here are some of his core ideas:

> Space is perfect (one, same, complete, throughout, etc.).
> Space is everywhere (omnipresent).
> Space is nucleus around which all "matter" gathers.
> All things come from "nothing" (space). It is the medium of differentiation and distinction between all things. Space comprehends and opposes all things. It is reflection (mind, wisdom, etc.).
> ALL things exist, live and react in relation to space.
>
> (King Pleasure, cited in Szwed 2012, 137)

George Clinton, in his alter ego of Dr. Funkenstein, led his bands, Parliament and Funkadelic, into a special scenario He brought space travel into his concert performances.

> During the 1970s and early 1980s, George Clinton—the flamboyant singer, songwriter and mastermind behind the funk, soul and rock collective Parliament-Funkadelic—launched dozens of chart-topping songs, including "Flash Light," "One Nation Under a Groove" and "Atomic Dog." However, his greatest hit was perhaps the P-Funk Mothership, an alien spacecraft stage prop that whizzed over screaming crowds at his stadium concerts and played a central role in cementing Clinton's legacy as one of music's most eccentric—and trailblazing—artists.
>
> The Mothership landed at the Smithsonian's National Museum of African American History and Culture in 2011 after Kevin Strait, project historian for the museum, acquired it to anchor the museum's inaugural "Musical Crossroads" exhibition. Under the direction of Bernie Walden, a former stage and lighting designer for Parliament-Funkadelic, the Mothership was recently reassembled and videotaped in all of its galactic glory.
>
> (Fawcett 2014)

Black music as an exemplar of Afrofuturism, in most accounts, points to the unique life and artistry of Sun Ra (1914–1993). His actual birthplace was Birmingham, Alabama, and his given name at birth was Herman Poole Blount (Szwed 2012, 4). While Sun Ra claimed to have been from outer space, his sister tells a different story: "He was born at my mother's aunt's house over there by the train station. … I know, 'cause I got on my knees and peeped through the keyhole. He's not from no Mars" (Szwed 2012, 6).

Sun Ra was a self-defined born-again, a person free from the racist limitations of his birth in the segregated US South, declaring his preference to be recognized as a being from outer space, a realm of freedom.

The most basic aspect of Sun Ra is that he was a musical genius, from the time his great-aunt Ida gave him a piano on his eleventh birthday; she made sure she took him to hear all of the great musicians who came through Birmingham as well as exposing him to plenty of church music. He studied classical piano compositions and learned how to transcribe music from records. Everyone who came into contact with his work regarded him as a phenomenon.

Sun Ra was a prolific composer, especially able to communicate his theoretical ideas, with much of it performed by members of his band. His categorical summation of his futuristic orientation is the slogan "Space is the Place." He named his band the Arkestra, dressed every person in costumes that suggested otherworldly beings and space travel, and created performances of total theater—music, dance, and voices speaking and singing—with environments that included stage sets and film. He wanted his work to impact people and get them to act like the future they needed:

> The Arkestra's performances were structured into what Sun Ra called the "cosmo drama," or the "myth-ritual," a program which expressed his beliefs and which he sought to offer as a model for changing the people of earth. … Astro-Black mythology was a way of expressing the unity of Egypt and outer space, of bringing a black reading of the Bible together with elements of ancient history and science to update the black sacred cosmos.
>
> (Szwed 2012, 256)

Sun Ra was a controversial figure, but his complex ideas and his focus on outer space and Egypt rooted in his understanding of world religion and mystical traditions brought him a dedicated following. His performances and recordings were the foundation for his cult like following. But, more than just this, Sun Ra was taken seriously by some Black Studies professors.

In the late 1960s and early 1970s, Sun Ra was appointed as a lecturer in the University of California at Berkeley through the Regents' Program and the Department of Afro-American Studies. Every week during the spring quarter of 1971, he met his class, Afro-American Studies 198: "The Black

Man in the Cosmos," in a large room in the music department building. ... The classes ran like rehearsals: first came the lecture, followed by a half hour of solo keyboard or Arkestra performance. But it was a proper course—Sun Ra had after all trained to be a teacher in college—with class handouts, assignments, and a reading list which made even the most *au courant* 1960s professors' courses pale (Szwed 2012, 294).

Sun Ra was certainly far-out, a personality who shocked people because of how he sustained a futuristic vision that connected ancient Egypt with space travel to planets in the universe. What made it work was his ability to connect it to his criticism of how people on the planet were living and his majestic musical performances. He ranks with Count Basie, Duke Ellington, and Fletcher Henderson as a bandleader who kept a large ensemble going for many years playing his countless original compositions. Szwed sums this up:

> To him poetry, dance, and music were linked together as arts of the highest order, and music—especially instrumental music—was the most immediate means for engaging the emotions with a higher reality. Music could provide a metaphysical experience through which one could enter the sublime, and come to know the cosmos. He understood music to be a universal language, and something akin to religion. Music could convey more than feelings about phenomena, it could express its essence, and this could disclose secrets of nature not available to reason, secrets which reveal the true nature of the world. Sun Ra saw that music symbolized the unity in diversity that is the cosmos, and the big band was his space vehicle, African-American aesthetics his culture-synthesizing principle. He was the bandleader as prophetic leader, the music arranger as arranger of the world.
>
> Szwed (2012, 383)

His cultural base in music was the foundation on which he maintained a critical posture toward society historically rooted in his early experiences in the racist environment of Birmingham, Alabama. He tried to get people to think out of their experience, and did so by combining a look backward to ancient Egypt and forward into outer space. He accepted the stance of being a man of/from the future, always in conflict with the present.

Octavia Butler (1947–2006) fits well after this discussion of Sun Ra, as they both sought to fulfill their imaginary destiny out in space. She was a science fiction author who wrote about the future as a way of helping us think about the present; the quality of her work is well recognized, as she won all of the major science fiction literary awards. She was against the kind of oppression we experience in society, on the macro level and the personal level as well. She makes her ethical position clear with this comment on bullying:

> Granted, I speak from my own experience, but it's a familiar experience to anyone who remembers the schoolyard. Of course, not everyone has been a bully or the victim of bullies, but everyone has seen bullying, and seeing it, has responded to it by joining in or objecting, by laughing or keeping silent, by feeling disgusted or feeling interested. …
>
> Simple peck-order bullying is only the beginning of the kind of hierarchical behavior that can lead to racism, sexism, ethnocentrism, classism, and all the other "isms" that cause so much suffering in the world.
>
> Several years ago I wrote a novel called *Dawn* in which extra-solar aliens arrive, look us over, and inform us that we have a pair of characteristics that together constitute a fatal flaw. We are, they admit, intelligent, and that's fine. But we are also hierarchical, and our hierarchical tendencies are older and all too often, they drive our intelligence—that is, they drive us to use our intelligence to try to dominate one another.
>
> (Ball 2006)

Two of her most important novels are *Parable of the Sower* (1993) and *Parable of the Talents* (1998). She takes the name from biblical references: for example, Jesus presented the parable of a sower to his followers.

> "Listen! Behold, a sower went out to sow. And as he sowed, some seed fell along the path, and the birds came and devoured it. Other seed fell on rocky ground, where it did not have much soil, and immediately it sprang up, since it had no depth of soil. And when the sun rose, it was scorched, and since it had no root, it withered away. Other seed fell among thorns, and the thorns grew up and choked it, and it yielded no grain. And other seeds fell into good soil and produced grain, growing up and increasing and yielding thirtyfold and sixtyfold and a hundredfold." And he said, "He who has ears to hear, let him hear."
>
> (American Bible Society 2010, Mark 4:39)

Butler builds her story on this basis. Phillips gives a vivid summation of the environment described by Butler for her sower:

> *Parable of the Sower* is set in California in the year 2024. Butler depicts the golden state in the imagined near future as representative of all the sickness of our present world. In 2024, Los Angeles has become an "oozing sore," a "carcass covered with too many maggots"; "there are fewer and fewer jobs"—children are "growing up with nothing to look forward to"; "debt slavery" is rampant—in general "workers are more throwaways than slaves"; "there are too many poor people"—"living skeletons" are everywhere visible; "thieves, rapists and cannibals" haunt the streets and freeways; "crazies" have banded together with no other purpose in mind than to "burn-the-rich"; "private armies of security guards" protect "estates, enclaves, and businesses"; "there are at least two guns in every household"—gunfire is so common people no longer attend to it. Those who have eyes to see are sharply conscious of the fact that "things are unraveling, disintegrating, bit by bit," that, fundamentally, "the world is falling apart."
>
> (J. Phillips 2002, 300)

She writes these books as the diary of an African-American woman, Lauren Oya Olamina, written from the age of fifteen to eighty-one. Lauren develops the philosophical system of *earthseed*, a guide to the future of humanity. There are many possible ways to interpret these ideas: some see it as a religion, but there is another way. Her father was a minister and, while included in his rituals, she rejected his religion and his god. She invented a way of interpreting her experience. What she would say is that she simply observed nature and society and served up the truth of what she saw. Octavia Butler reveals this as poetic stanzas in her two parable books. It is possible to read Olamina's *Book of the Living*, the summation of *earthseed* from both of her novels, as a work of dialectical and historical materialism. She riffs on her father's word "God," but at the very start says she does not believe in her father's God, and is using the word in her own meaning. It is possible to read this by substituting the word "history" for the word "God."

She states an affirmation of dialectical motion:

> 1. God is change.
>
> (Butler 2012, 3)

She elaborates on her philosophy of history:

> 46. Do not worship God. … Learn from God, with forethought and intelligence, imagination and industry, shape God. When you must, yield to God. Adapt and endure. For you are Earthseed, and God is change.
>
> (Butler 2019, 73)

> 64. To survive, Let the past Teach you—Past customs, struggles, Leaders and thinkers, let these help you. Let them inspire you, warn you, give you strength. But beware: God is change. Past is past. What was cannot come again. To survive, know the past. Let it touch you. Then let the past go.
>
> (Butler 2019, 373)

Butler has a materialist theory of knowledge (epistemology):

> 32. Your teachers are all around you. All that you perceive, all that you experience, all that is given to you, or taken from you, all that you love or hate, need or fear, will teach you—if you will learn. God is your first and your last teacher. God is your harshest teacher: subtle, demanding. Learn or die.
>
> (Butler 2007, 279)

> 33. Respect God: Pray working, pray learning, planning, doing. Pray creating, teaching, reaching. Pray working. Pray to focus your thoughts, still your fears, strengthen your purpose. Respect God. Shape God. Pray working.
>
> (Butler 2007, 294)

She focuses on human agency as a motive force of history, in general and in terms of leadership:

> 15. All struggles are essentially power struggles. Who will rule, who will lead, who will define, refine, confine, design, who will dominate. All struggles are essentially power struggles, and most are no more intellectual than two rams knocking their heads together.
>
> (Butler 2007, 94)

> 54. Choose your leaders with wisdom and forethought. To be led by a coward is to be controlled by all that the coward fears. To be led by a

> fool is to be led by the opportunists who control the fool. To be led by a thief is to offer up your most precious treasures to be stolen. To be led by a liar is to ask to be told lies. To be led by a tyrant is to sell yourself and those you love into slavery.
>
> (Butler 2019, 181)

In sum, we can read these novels as criticisms of society and speculation on what trends are moving us forward. She lays waste to the possibility of constructing a utopian enclave inside a society in crisis with her example of the Acorn community created by Lauren and her colleagues. It was an ideal space that could not withstand the aggression of hostile forces. Her opposite example, with which she ends the novel, is a social movement led by a charismatic leader, Lauren, who maintains her leadership as the chief exponent of *Earthseed.*

Her final and ultimate message, something that she had been advocating from almost the beginning, is futuristic speculation. Much like Sun Ra, she has her version of "Space is the Place".

> The Destiny of Earthseed
> Is to take root among the stars.
> It is to live and to thrive
> On new earths.
> It is to become new beings
> And to consider new questions.
> It is to leap into the heavens
> Again and again.
> It is to explore the vastness
> Of heaven.
> It is to explore the vastness
> Of ourselves.
>
> (Butler 2020)

Imagining a future never happens without an origin, just as a speech never happens without a language. Stuff exists in our consciousness that enables us to take what we know and rethink it in new ways, even fantastical ways. What needs to be understood is how what we come up with compares to the actual lives we lead. This is the main subtext to all science fiction. However, in the end, the future is what we can make of our lives in the context of the historical structure and process of society. It is a struggle.

3

Back to the Future

Another approach to Afrofuturism begins in the historical past. A major approach to the past for African Americans involves their African origin, the time before slavery and their centuries of exploitation. We call this the *Sankofa Principle*. This is represented by one of the Adinkra symbols of the Twi people of Ghana, a bird turning its head backwards. The meaning is "Go back and get it."

The mass relocation of productive African labor for the West was the goal of the slave trade carried out by European governments and commercial enterprises. African people were torn from their homelands, aggregated as multilingual ship cargo, and forced to travel to places unknown to them. However, their captors and oppressors could only control them as an external force. They could not completely force amnesia on them, could not delink them from their history and culture of origin.

Africa remained an issue in three fundamental ways: some African descendants returned to Africa; for others, African was alive in their memory; and for still others who never had experienced Africa, the African past was an object of their imagination. In each case, the past as African origin was a desired future, and thus going back to Africa was advancing to a future of their own.

RETURNING TO AFRICA

We often think of the Atlantic slave trade as only the process of removal, and that requires a certain approach to return. The historical process was more complicated than that. The Atlantic was a dynamic terrain of seafaring that included state-sponsored ships and commercial ships, both legal and illegal. Often overlooked were the illegal ones, the pirates. These pirates were in and out of both the Americas and Africa, not only trafficking in slavery but having African seafaring workers as crew members. Marcus Rediker has done the best historical research on this:

> Numerous men joined the slavers from along the African littoral, and many, such as the Fante and the Kru, had maritime backgrounds. Some were "grumettoes" who worked for short periods aboard the slave ships on the coast. Others made transatlantic voyages. The wage book of the Hawk, sailed by Captain John Smale and crew from Liverpool to the Gold Coast to the Cameroons River, to St. Lucia in 1780–81, listed Ackway, Lancelots, Abey, Cudjoe, Quashey, Liverpool and Joe Dick, all "fantymen" who earned wages for the voyage. Four of them had been given wage advances in gold while on the African coast. Free sailors of African descent also joined the ships as their voyages began in European and American ports, not least because they had relatively few employment opportunities and seafaring was one of the most open and available.
>
> (Rediker 2008, 229)

Rediker and Womack make the point about Blacks being part of the rebellious pirate tendency on the seas.

> A gang of pirates settled in West Africa in the early 1720s, joining and intermixing with the Kru, who were known for their skill in things maritime (and, when enslaved, for their leadership of revolts in the New World). And, of course, for many years pirates had mixed with the native population of Madagascar, helping to produce "a dark Mulatto Race there." Cultural exchanges among European and African sailors and pirates were extensive, resulting, for example, in the well-known similarities of form between African songs and sea shanties. In 1743 some seamen were court-martialed for singing a "negro song" in defiance of discipline. Mutineers also engaged in the same rites performed by slaves before a revolt. In 1731 a band of mutineers drank rum and gunpowder, and on another occasion a sailor signaled his rebellious intentions by "Drinking Water out of a Musket barrel." Piracy clearly did not operate according to the black codes enacted and enforced in Atlantic slave societies. Some slaves and free blacks found freedom aboard the pirate ship, which apart from the maroon communities, was no easy thing to find in the pirates main theater of operations, the Caribbean and the American South. Indeed, pirate ships themselves might be considered multiracial maroon communities, in which rebels used the high seas as others used the mountains

> and the jungles. The ship of pirate captain Thomas Cocklyn was named the *Maroon*, and pirates frequently called themselves "marooners."
> (Rediker and Womack 2005, 55–56)

Africans on the seas were transcontinental migrants linking Africa to the West, returning time and again. A good instance of the desire to return happened after the successful slave revolt on the *Amistad* in 1839. After winning the court case and gaining the right to return, the African survivors, with the help of abolitionists, returned to their families in Africa.

However, the majority of Africans on the seas were transported for permanent relocation. This demographic shift required a process of geographical return back to the African continent. Two African countries were created out of this process of return, Sierra Leone and Liberia. The war against British colonialism was called an American revolution, but the American forces were upholding slavery while the British promised freedom for Black people who joined their forces (Horne 2012).

Abolitionists in England aided 400 freed Africans in London to resettle in Africa in what is now Sierra Leone. Granville Sharp initiated this process under the leadership of his organization, the Committee for the Relief of the Black Poor. The settlement that was founded was named Granville Town. William Wilberforce, after whom Wilberforce University was named, helped with this. The Methodist Church established Wilberforce University in 1856, but closed it in 1862. The African Methodist Episcopal Church took possession of it and reopened the university in 1863. In Liberia, the freedmen established the "Province of Freedom" and the settlement of Granville Town on land purchased from the local Koya Temne subchief King Tom and the regent Naimbana. However, a war resulted from a dispute over the control of the land and the settlers were wiped out in 1789 by the Temne. However, more displaced settlers arrived from Nova Scotia and Jamaica. On the same land as Granville Town, a new town was built named Freetown (Webster, Boahen, and Idowu 1973, 131–46).

The British passed the Slave Trade Act in 1807, outlawing the slave trade, and in 1833, they abolished all of slavery in England.

> When the British navy decided to patrol the West African coast to stop the slave trade, the colonists' new settlement of Freetown became its headquarters. The captured slavers were brought to Sierra Leone and their cargoes of slaves when freed became known as liberated Africans

> or "recaptives." The little colony began to receive an annual influx of hundreds and occasionally thousands of recaptives. Altogether 40,000 were settled in Sierra Leone and the population grew rapidly from 2,000 in 1807 to 11,000 in 1825, and to 40,000 in 1850. Sierra Leone became one of the great cultural "melting pots" of the world, its population being a blend of peoples with different customs, religions, and languages originating from every people and state in West Africa from Senegal to Angola.
>
> (Webster, Boahen, and Idowu 1973, 134)

The British created the basis for Sierra Leone, and the Americans created the basis for Liberia. The Society for the Colonization of Free People of Color of America, usually called the American Colonization Society, was formed in 1816 by a strange collaboration of abolitionists and owners of slaves. They shared the goal of removing free African Americans from the USA. The abolitionists were concerned about what was best for Black people, and the slave owners were concerned with what was best for the slave system. Together they influenced the US government:

> The Society's members pressured Congress and the President for support. In 1819, they received $100,000 from Congress, and on February 6, 1820, the first ship, the *Elizabeth*, sailed from New York for West Africa with three white ACS agents and 88 African-American emigrants aboard.
>
> (Wikipedia 2020g)

The 1810 census found that there were over 10 million people in the USA with fully one-third being slaves and freed men and women. The European Americans found this to be a potential threat and wanted to either remove the Free Black people to protect them (abolitionists) or to protect the slave system (owners of slaves):

> The return of American Negroes to Africa was expected to lead the continent to Christianity, begin the expansion of American trade along the West Coast, and rid the United States of the free Negroes, who were considered undesirable citizens. … About 12,000 emigrated to Liberia, many more than the 3,000 who pioneered Sierra Leone, and, while the British navy freed 40,000 in Freetown, the American navy freed only 2,000 in Monrovia [capital of Liberia].
>
> (Webster, Boahen, and Idowu 1973, 147–48)

Again, much like the resettlement effort in Sierra Leone, the new residents, known as Americo-Liberians, were in conflict with the local indigenous people. It is clear that some who returned moved back seamlessly into their former homelands, but the history of the country has been driven by the basic conflict between those who never left and those who returned with an altered identity based on their experience during slavery (Liebenow 1969; Wilson 1971).

The Liberian country motto was adopted as "The love of Liberty brought us here." But this liberty was not autonomous from their former slave-owning country, as the capital was named after the US President James Monroe, a Harvard professor wrote their founding constitution, and the USA has historically dominated this country as a virtual colony run by their allies the Americo-Liberians. A good test of this is the experience of Marcus Garvey, W.E.B. Du Bois, and the Firestone Natural Rubber Company.

In the early twentieth century, the Liberian government was heavily in debt and its viability as a country was in question. Marcus Garvey had formed his UNIA in 1914, and then established his Black Star Line of ships in 1919. The very next year, he set up the Liberian Construction Loan program to raise money for the Liberian government. The UNIA established its global headquarters in Monrovia with the support of the Liberian government, which included the recruitment of Liberian officials as international officials in the UNIA. W.E.B. Du Bois opposed this development and sided with the US government and corporate interests on the assumption that this would provide a more secure future for Liberia. This came to a head when a plan to lease land to the UNIA at one dollar per acre was replaced with an agreement with Firestone Natural Rubber Company:

> In 1926, the Liberian government granted Firestone a 99-year lease for a million acres (to be chosen by the company wherever in Liberia) at a price of 6 cents per acre, Firestone then set about establishing rubber tree plantations of the non-native South American rubber tree, Hevea brasiliensis, in the country, eventually creating the world's largest rubber plantation. Firestone also provided a $5 million loan at a 7% interest rate to the government to pay the foreign debts it had and to build a harbour needed by Firestone. The loan was given in exchange for complete authority over the government's revenues until the loan was paid.
>
> (Wikipedia 2020d)

George Padmore offers a critical analysis of the Liberian experience from a left perspective, critiquing Garvey because of his alliance with the Americo-Liberians and the inevitable capitalist outcome that would be based on the exploitation of indigenous local labor:

> The situation in Liberia gives us one of the most striking examples of the fallacy in Garvey's utopian scheme of "Black Racialism." It shows that Negro capitalists will oppress and exploit other Negroes, just as whites do, when they are in the economic position to do so. Therefore, the Negro workers must realize that their class interests take precedence over race, which is only being utilized by the black bourgeoisie in order to promote their own economic interests.
>
> (Padmore 1931, 134)

Padmore sums up the Liberian experience in class terms: "True to their historic role, the Negro bourgeoisie of America and Liberia have sold out to Yankee Imperialism" (1931, 146).

There was one positive development even in this context. A few people who returned to Liberia worked to free family members who remained enslaved.

> The idea of financial assistance coming from Africa was not completely unheard of. One well-known case concerns Ibrahima abd-al Rahman, a son of the former *Almamy* (Muslim ruler) of Futa Djalon in Guinea, who had been enslaved in Mississippi for thirty-nine years before sailing for Liberia in 1829. Once in Monrovia, he had informed his family in Futa that he needed money to free his children still enslaved in Natchez. They sent a caravan with $6,000 to $7,000 in gold.
>
> (Diouf 2009, 147)

There is a genre within Afro-American creative literature that uses the past to look to the future. It is especially focused on immediately before and after the Civil War, the movement from slavery to freedom.

A good example of this is the novel *47* by Walter Mosley, which is a science fiction novel set in the context of 1832 slave plantation life. The title is the number of a fourteen-year-old enslaved African teenager on a plantation, where every slave is known by a number that is branded on their shoulder. The story revolves around his relationship with a stranger who comes to his plantation from another planet who uses the name Tall

John, but whose name on his home planet is N'Clect. This story improvises on the folk tale of High John the Conqueror. When Tall John meets the wise man of the Plantation, Mud Albert, they have an exchange:

> "You evah hear tell of the one dey call High John the Conqueror?" Albert asked.
>
> "You mean the trickster from Africa who makes fun'a the mastah an' who means to free alla the slaves an' bring 'em back home?" John answered and asked.
>
> "That's the one. They say that High John was sent by ancient African gods to bring us slaves back home to where our mothers' is still waitin' for us," Albert said. "If'n I put high in yo name instead'a tall dat might jes' be you."
>
> (Mosley 2018, 62–63)

John's reply that it is not him, but rather 47 who might fit that role is revealed in the narrative's development. There are two main contradictions that anchor the novel, that between slave and master in plantation society, and that in the science fiction world of two warring species, the evil Calash and their demon Wall versus the people of Tall John/N'Clect, the Talam.

47 learns that he can choose to control his consciousness and take some control of his life even under slavery. Tall John/N'Clect constantly teaches this lesson:

> Neither master nor nigger be, Tall John had said from the first moments we met. There in the worst aspect of my slavery I came to understand those words' meaning.
>
> I felt the thrill of freedom in my heart.
>
> "John," I said. "John, I understand. I know what you been sayin'. I ain't got no mastuh 'cause I ain't no slave."
>
> (Mosley 2018, 146)

The second contradiction is the desire of Calash to destroy planets and to destroy earth they need to get the technology of the Talam. The destiny of 47 is to confront and defeat Wall, the demon of the Calash. Wall takes on the persona of a slave owner, but is defeated, so 47 and several other slaves are able to get to Canada and gain their freedom. However, 47 is destined to meet up again with Wall for a final battle sometime in the future.

This example of science fiction captures the epic battle of good versus evil in the context of slavery and the use of futuristic technology with reference to an African past of origin. The protagonist, 47, guides the reader to experience the consciousness of a slave regarding freedom and the crisis of using advanced technology for good or evil. This is an important example of using fiction to reflect on historical experience.

So far we have discussed return after the slave trade removal process, but now we have generations of migration out of the continent after slavery, continuing into the twenty-first century. African Americans, without direct known family ties, with or without family oral history or DNA mapping, make symbolic pilgrimages back to Africa, mostly to West Africa. Black travel agents work with Black Studies programs to facilitate this kind of pan-African identity tourism.

> Return is also the result of agency by Africans from the continent. Ghana, in the tradition of the Pan-African orientation of the country's founder Kwame Nkrumah, passed a law allowing dual citizenship for African Americans beginning in 2019. This was in the context of making 2019 the year of return: "In Washington, D.C., in September 2018, Ghana's President Nana Akufo-Addo declared and formally launched the "Year of Return, Ghana 2019" for Africans in the Diaspora, giving fresh impetus to the quest to unite Africans on the continent with their brothers and sisters in the diaspora."
>
> (Tetteh 2018)

Another important case of return is the agency of African families who have emigrated to the USA, leaving family and friends back on the African continent. The government of Ghana has established a Bureau of African Diaspora Affairs to provide services to their people living abroad. One aspect of this is that in the US children with parents from Ghana grow up as African Americans. In order for them to maintain their traditional identity and the language proficiency of their extended family, they have to return and live on the continent. The African Diaspora is a two-way flow of people leaving and returning, whether they do so physically or virtually.

REMEMBERING AFRICA

Even when enslaved Africans did not return to their homeland, Africa was remembered, and what was remembered established goals for the future, values to live by, and models for a good life. The memory of Africa was a blessing compared to the strange and harsh ways of their enslavement, with the comfort of the past becoming an aspiration for the future. The concept of Africa is an abstraction, so that is not what people remembered. People remembered specific experiences from their personal lives, their families, and their village life.

One of the main sources that document remembering are the narratives of the Africans born in Africa who remember being taken and what they were taken from. They were the ones who actually experienced the holocaust against Africa. These include Ukawsaw Gronniosaw (1705–1775), Olaudah Equiano (*c.*1745–31 March 1797), Boyrereau Brinch (1742–1827), and John Jea (1773–18??). These recollections help us understand how the Atlantic "Middle Passage" was experienced by the enslaved Africans.

Equiano shared these memories of being on the slave ship that carried him to Virginia:

> I now saw myself deprived of all chance of returning to my native country, or even the least glimpse of hope of gaining the shore, which I now considered as friendly; and I even wished for my former slavery in preference to my present situation, which was filled with horrors of every kind, still heightened by my ignorance of what I was to undergo. I was not long suffered to indulge my grief; I was soon put down under the decks, and there I received such a salutation in my nostrils as I had never experienced in my life: so that, with the loathsomeness of the stench, and crying together, I became so sick and low that I was not able to eat, nor had I the least desire to taste any thing. I now wished for the last friend, death, to relieve me; but soon, to my grief, two of the white men offered me eatables; and, on my refusing to eat, one of them held me fast by the hands, and laid me across I think the windlass, and tied my feet, while the other flogged me severely. I had never experienced any thing of this kind before; and although, not being used to the water, I naturally feared that element the first time I saw it, yet nevertheless, could I have got over the nettings, I would have jumped over the side, but I could not; and, besides, the crew used to watch us very closely who were not chained down to the decks, lest we should leap into the water: and I have seen some of these poor African prisoners most severely cut for attempting to do so, and hourly whipped for not eating. This indeed was often the case with myself.
>
> (Equiano 2012, Chapter 2)

Equiano introduces us to the terrible time of the slave ships, and that was merely the beginning. Anne C. Bailey introduces us to a new way of investigating memory as her research asks the question of how do the Africans who never left remember the Atlantic slave trade. She makes a comparison to survivors of wars, like Vietnam veterans who didn't want to discuss the horror of wars that were still impacting them on a psychological level.

> I imagine this was somewhat akin to what has happened in Ghana and West and Central African in general, which experienced the bulk of the Atlantic slave trade. More than three centuries of slave trading meant numerous small and big conflicts and skirmishes as well as wars and raiding—all of which have taken their collective toll. Those who remained on the continent—that is, those who were not taken—were like veterans in a war-torn land, in some ways seeking to make peace with their trauma, and in some ways seeking simply to put it behind them. This is one way of explaining why, according to the director of education at Cape Coast Castle (the former slave-trade dungeon), the people of the area are not interested in coming into the castle. In spite of the fact that the Smithsonian and other international donors have invested heavily in its refurbishment to attract visitors from all over the world and to preserve Ghana's historical heritage, many Cape Coast residents feel "they have nothing there. They have heard what happened there from their elders" and want little to do with the place. Even elders who live closer than a hundred meters from the site have not set foot in the castle and show little desire to. These stories all add to the sense of fragmentation of historical memory and identity that is a direct result of the Atlantic slave trade.
>
> (Bailey 2007, 161–62)

A remarkable act of remembering was recorded by Zora Neale Hurston. Hurston recorded the story of Oluale Kossola, known later as Cudjo Lewis, in 1927. He was a survivor of the *Clotilda*, known to be the last slave ship to enter the USA in 1859, doing so illegally. Kossola sums up his experience as a slave, focusing on the harsh conditions he faced:

> De work very hard for us to do' cause we ain' used to workee lak dat. But we doan grieve 'bout dat. We cry 'cause we slave. In night time we cry, we say we born and raised to be free people and now we slave. We

> doan know why we be bring 'way from our country to work lak dis. It strange to us. Everybody lookeee at us strange. We want to tak wid de udder colored folkses but dey doan know whut we say. Some make de fun at us.
>
> (Hurston 2019, 59–60)

After emancipation, Kossola demonstrates how he and others sought to remember Africa in a community they created near Mobile, Alabama:

> We call our village Affican Town. We say dat 'cause we want to go back in de Affica soil and we see we cain go. Derefo' we make de Affica where dey fetch us. Gumpa say, "My folks sell me and yo folks (Americans) buy me." We here and we got to stay.
>
> (Hurston 2019, 68)

Kossola was a living history book. Most family researchers are not so fortunate to have someone who remembers, although many families keep their oral history alive from generation to generation. Using family oral history, and field research, Alex Haley reconstructs his family narrative as a seminal act of remembering. The story in his book *Roots: The Saga of an American Family* is a controversial historical account, because of allegations of plagiarism and the use of questionable oral history, but it remains a popular model for remembering through genealogical research.

His story was about the resistance of seeking freedom by running away but being caught, of fighting to maintain one's African name, of practicing culture even during the forced assimilation of the slave experience. This story was about the past, but it was a model for the present moving into the future, above all else, for people to be freedom seekers.

Finally, Black people remembered Africa without knowing they were doing so. In other words, they were carrying Africa forward in their cultural practices, which were called African survivals (African American Research Center 2019). One of the first scholars who documented this was Lorenzo Turner. His research on the language of the Gullah people of the Sea Islands demonstrated extensive African language retentions in opposition to the racist interpretation that Black people were too intellectually weak to learn proper English (Turner 1949). Robert Farris Thompson has demonstrated that in material culture, like in quilt making, and in religious practices that African Americans maintained an improvisational relationship with their original African cultures (R.F. Thompson 1984).

Black Studies research will continue to document and interpret the African retentions in the African Diaspora, as well as the ways in which these patterns have impacted the cultures of the world. This is a recurring theme in the interpretation of how African Americans have been a solid basis for the uniqueness of American culture in general.

SUMMATION

We have demonstrated that the past is always a living part of the present. People find meaning for their lives in the historical background out of which they and their families have developed. Black Studies will always have a focus on how Black people identify themselves and find meaning in their lives. This will always involve the origin of the Black experience in Africa.

It is important to mention that the Southern experience during slave plantations and afterward tenancy sharecropping is also the historical backdrop for the search for family history and the context for much of family oral history. This is linked by the migration experiences that most Black families share. This is why family reunions and genealogical research are so popular. People seek to maintain transgenerational knowledge that can go back as far as possible.

But with regard to Africa, most people will not have hard evidence of family connection and will likely continue to rely on historical imagination. This includes the DNA testing that only provides statistical probabilities without giving a definitive connection to any geographic place of ancestry.

IMAGINING AFRICA

As the generations marched through time, direct knowledge of Africa before the slave trade was lost, but Africa remained a point of reference in the imagination of African descendant people. This has continued up to this present time. Of course, this realm of imagination has been driven by a battle of ideas, racist distortions that demeaned Africa, mythical idealization of the African past, and the search for historically documented reality. The mass media and formal educational institutions legitimated the fantasy of Tarzan films during which a white European becomes the king of the jungle controlling animals and being feared by demonic

African natives. There was an attempt to separate Egypt from Africa and represent Egyptians in the movies as white people.

However, reflecting the agency of Black intellectuals and activists, there have been two different points of departure for imagining Africa, ideas that make up a positive story and ideas that begin with some forms of material evidence. This is the distinction between idealism and materialism.

Idealism is a philosophical orientation that develops a romantic vision of the African past, a static conception of Africa based on asserting positive values without taking into full account the fundamental historical processes of class conflict and state power. This position often holds that African leaders were benevolent and equality was the universal norm. What is often missing from the research literature is what the African scholars have been publishing at the many important African universities. Excellent sources are the Council for the Development of Social Science Research in Africa and the African Historians Association (Council for the Development of Social Science Research in Africa 2020; Humanities and Social Sciences Online 2018).

Chancellor Williams (1893–1992), formerly a historian based at Howard University, wrote a book that captured the imagination of many about the African past, *The Destruction of Black Civilization: Great Issues of a Race Between 4500 B.C. and 2000 A.D* (1971; C. Williams 1987). One of his major arguments was that all of Africa had one fundamental political system. He alleges that there was a fundamental unity of all African political systems. His concern was that African Americans should have a positive view of Africa, and with that be able to withstand the negative impact of racist distortions of history. His book is regarded as a classic by many nationalists and Afrocentrists.

Based on this kind of idealist summation of African politics, Maulana Karenga made an idealist summation of African culture by formulating a system of ethics and a holiday ritual (Kwanzaa) celebrating and reproducing that system (C. Williams 1987; Karenga 2008).

Karenga's philosophy is based on what he calls the seven principles of Kawaida, stated in Kiswahili and English, called the Nguzo Saba:

Umoja (Unity)
Kujichaguia (Self-Determination)
Ujima (Collective Work and Responsibility)
Ujamaa (Cooperative Economics)

Nia (Purpose)
Kuumba (Creativity)
Imani (Faith)

This idealized vision of African cultural values offers a prescriptive vision of the way people ought to be, to act, and to believe, but the diversity of how people actually live is another question. It is a secular system with great similarity to the ethical (axiological) tenets of a religion. Some people were married based on this framework and a license from the state (Karenga 1980; Baraka and Jones 1969). Holding people to a standard of what ought to be is an ideological dogma, it is not a summation of the people's cultural norms. The critical question is how to define the future: Will it replicate an ideological vision? Or, will it be a result of practical struggles waged by the masses of people?

The Kwanzaa holiday ritual is based on the Nguzo Saba. Molefi Asante helps us to understand this phenomenon:

> Kwanzaa is the most representative creation of the Kawaida tradition in terms of African conception, cultural objectives, and ethical purpose. Initiated by Karenga in 1966, Kwanzaa is a unique intellectual and cultural creation which is now celebrated by over 30 million Africans throughout the world. Karenga states that he founded Kwanzaa for several basic reasons: 1) "to reaffirm and restore our rootedness in African culture"; 2) "to reaffirm and reinforce the bonds between us as a people in both the national and pan-African sense"; 3) "to introduce and reinforce the *Nguzo Saba* (The Seven Principles) and place "at the same time emphasis on the importance of African communitarian values in general"; and finally, 4) "as an act of self-determination … an important way we as African people speak our special cultural truth (in the world)."
>
> (Molefi Asante 2009, 164)

This is an excellent example of how idealism can produce something that resonates with a need felt by the people, embraced by them, and sustained by them. Of course, Kwanzaa has been embraced by the capitalist system as well, as an extension of the Christmas marketplace, and by the US state in the form of an official stamp issued by the US postal service. On its own terms, however, Kwanzaa has been a positive force.

The example of the Marvel comic book film *Black Panther* is a different case of how idealism produces fantasy with little sustainable value. This film about the kingdom of Wakanda and its warrior king, the Black Panther, provides glamorous and romantic images of Black people, voluptuous women warriors, and a kingdom without economic or social contradictions other than rituals of leadership succession (Madhubuti and Boyd 2019).

The film links the notion of the comic book Black Panther with the real Black Panthers of Oakland, California. However, to be a Panther in this film one had to be of royal blood, not a brother or sister from the most exploited part of the community who was forced to fight against racist oppression. Also, the CIA was an ally of the Black Panther and the people of Wakanda. Finally, the people of Wakanda were the beneficiaries of magical technology, the ultimate fantasy.

> So, other than an injection of a feel-good mental virus, this film has little if any sustainable value. However, Black people keep buying it, as their situation is so desperate they seem to need to entertain the impossible to feel good. It became a big hit: "*Black Panther* was the most-tweeted about film of 2018 with more than 5 million tweets globally, and in mid-March it became the most-tweeted about film ever with 35 million. … *Black Panther* is the highest-grossing film of 2018 and became the third-highest-grossing film of all time."
>
> (Wikipedia 2020i)

Of course, this is not without institutional backing. For example, during a trip to the Smithsonian Museum of African American History in 2019, there was more information sold in their retail store about Wakanda than the Africa that really exists. This is a reversal of the mandate of the museum curators that artifacts must be authentic and not imaginative representations. Apparently, a Hollywood film is as important as the actually lived Black experience in the view of the country's national museum.

There is another intellectual trend based on more of a materialist approach to the past as a gateway to imagining Africa—archaeological research. Each new find stimulates historical imagination, from a small amount of evidence to pictures of the people and their social lives. Sometimes a discovery produces new imaginative images. The main point is that every instance of material evidence of past experience helps one to imagine the past and learn from it in order to engage in the speculative projection of a possible future.

From this scientific approach, one of the leading African scholars on Africa's past is Cheikh Anta Diop (1923–1986). Diop was a scientist using the disciplines of physics, historical linguistics, and anthropology to study the history of Africa. He founded and directed the radiocarbon laboratory at the Institut Fondamental de l'Afrique Noire (IFAN). Diop was a renaissance man with a comprehensive approach to attacking key research questions: What is African experience? Is there general unity of culture? Of origin? And, what methodology should scholarship rely on? He provides answers to these in key books, originally in French and then translated into English.

In *The Cultural Unity of Negro Africa: The Domains of Patriarchy and of Matriarchy in Classical Antiquity*, he argues that matriarchy was the basis for cultural unity in Black Africa (Diop 1962). He argues that this is part of the story of how African people migrated from the south to the north bringing cultural patterns with them. His analysis involves a comprehensive use of literary and historical texts, linguistic analysis, and a critical review of relevant scholarship.

In *The African Origin of Civilization: Myth or Reality*, Diop argues the historical importance of Egypt for understanding the history of Africa:

> Ancient Egypt was a Negro civilization. The history of Black Africa will remain suspended in air and cannot be written correctly until African historians dare to connect it with the history of Egypt. In particular the study of languages, institutions, and so forth, cannot be treated properly; in a word, it will be impossible to build African humanities, a body of African human sciences, so long as that relationship does not appear legitimate. The African historian who evades the problem of Egypt is neither modest nor objective, nor unruffled; he is ignorant, cowardly, and neurotic. Imagine, if you can, the uncomfortable position of a western historian who was to write the history of Europe without referring to Greco-Latin Antiquity and try to pass that off as a scientific approach.
>
> (Diop 1997, xiv)

His magnum opus is *Civilization or Barbarism: An Authentic Anthropology*, which summarizes his research on Egypt (Diop 1991). This includes his linking of the language of ancient Egypt with the West

African language of Wolof, in general and specifically in the discussion of mathematics. He sums up his work on the past in terms of what it means for the future:

> Far from being a reveling in the past, a look toward Egypt of antiquity is the best way to conceive and build our cultural future. In reconceived and renewed African culture, Egypt will play the same role that Greco-Latin antiquity plays in Western culture.
>
> (Diop, Salemson, and De Jager 1991, 3)

The historical process includes changing generational experiences, but each generation, one way or another, has had the experience of leaving Africa and contemplating the possibility of return in each of the three ways explored here: to go back, to remember, to imagine. We will confront the reality of the current situation in Part II on the African Diaspora.

4
Struggle for the Future

Whether looking to the past or dreaming up a new reality, one always comes back to the necessary facts of life, to face the reality of the historical conditions one is living in, and how to change those conditions as a matter of fact. This is stated quite clearly in a poem, *Dream to Change the World*, by Martin Carter:

> I have learnt
> from books dear friend
> of men dreaming and living
> and hungering in a room without a light
> who could not die since death was far too poor
> who did not sleep to dream, but dreamed to change
> the world.
>
> (Carter 1997)

Using fiction to direct people to fight for their future is contained in a novel that opened up the twentieth century of struggle. Sutton E. Griggs has a group of Black men pass this resolution in his 1899 novel *Imperium In Imperio*:

> WHEREAS, the history of our treatment by the Anglo-Saxon race is but the history of oppression, and whereas, our patient endurance of evil has not served to decrease this cruelty, but seems rather to increase it; and whereas, the ballot box, the means of peaceful revolution is denied us, therefore;
>
> *Be it Resolved*: That the hour for wreaking vengeance for our multiplied wrongs has come.
>
> *Resolved* secondly: That we at once proceed to war for the purpose of accomplishing the end just named, and for the further purpose of obtaining all our rights due us as men.

> *Resolved* thirdly: That no soldier of the Imperium leave the field of battle until the ends for which this war was inaugurated are fully achieved.
>
> (Griggs 1899, Chapter 18)

A comparable contemporary example in fiction is the fantasy novel *The Black Commandos* by Joseph Jackson (J.D. Jackson 2013). This is a self-published novel that portrays a Black elite acting as an army to defend Black people against racist terror. Wealthy Black people sponsor a process of transforming violent murderers in the Black community into freedom fighters who defeat the Los Angeles police department in battle, who take over the state of Mississippi, and who force the US government into a truce. This fantasy portrays the Black capitalist class as a force for anti-racist transformation by leading a Black mass organization in a violent confrontation with state power and the Ku Klux Klan.

There are many such fictional accounts of the need to struggle for the future, the most serious basis for Afrofuturism as a tendency in intellectual thought. The important task is to reflect on the debates that took place in the context of how people actually did struggle.

But first, a comment on how this fits into Black history in general: the major point that must always be made is that all politics and culture is based on the material conditions that shape the social and economic life of the community. Modes of social cohesion are when several generations experience more or less a similar situation, but, during times of social disruption, a change in the material conditions forces a change in the thinking of people. They face a new situation and need a new analysis

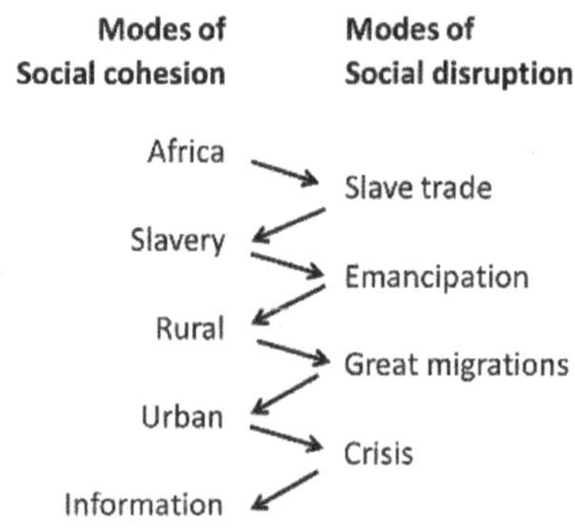

Figure 1 Modes of Social Cohesion and Social Disruption

and new plans for struggle. The arrows of this chart indicate the logic of change between social cohesion and social disruption.

In general terms, we can identify three great debates that took place in the context of great systemic changes of social disruption in the life experiences of Black people: the Emancipation Debate, the Self-Determination Debate of the Great Migrations, and the Black Liberation Debate of the 1960s. In each of these debates, there were three basic positions on methods of struggle: to persuade with negotiation based on moral argument; to emigrate to some other place to establish a new nation; or to fight using physical force against slavery and in the free states gaining and using the vote to force change.

THE EMANCIPATION DEBATE

The Emancipation Debate was about a future of ending slavery and achieving equality for Black people who were free. This debate was concentrated in national and state conventions of free Black people from 1830 to 1864. Bell makes this summary:

> Whether it was in the conventions of the 1830s or in that of 1864, there was a compelling similarity in motivation and an equally compelling similarity in outcome. The desire to lift the entire Black population—slave and nominally free—to a position of equality under constitutional government was motivation enough. But beyond this the men of the convention movement were idealists, and they sought constantly to make the Black man, as well as the white, more worthy of the blessings of liberty and equality in a land in which they deemed mankind to be so capable of being elevated to a position akin almost to that of the gods.
>
> (Bell 1969b, iv)

The basic political options facing Black people emerged during these debates, and for each option we can actually trace the actions attempting to implement such paths to freedom: to emigrate, to negotiate, or to fight.

The first convention in 1830 was held in Philadelphia. Richard Allen, the historic minister of Mother Bethel AME Church, called for this event to take place. The main focus was on emigration to assist people who had been forced to leave Cincinnati and needed help in getting to Canada. Some freedmen had already created a settlement there.

> That emergency grew out of the increasing friction between Negro and white laborers in Cincinnati. Newly emancipated slaves, often highly trained as coopers or blacksmiths; free Negroes seeking to avoid the restrictions of the South; runaway slaves—all sought the same jobs as did native whites or newly arrived immigrants from Europe. When strife developed the city fathers decided to wash their hands of the whole affair by calling up an old law which required people of Negro blood immigrating to the state to post bond in guarantee of good behavior and of self-support. This was tantamount to an order for expatriation, for the bond was so high that it was beyond the reach not only of the average Negro laborer, but of the average laborer of any race. Accepting what appeared to be the inevitable, Cincinnati Negroes began looking for a home elsewhere.
>
> (Bell 1969a, 12–13)

This motion continued emigration efforts taken up by a curious alliance of abolitionists and slave owners, who founded the American Colonization Society in 1818. The abolitionists wanted Blacks to find a place where they could prosper and be safe, while the slave owners wanted free Blacks to get as far away from their slaves as possible. As mentioned above, they made their first major move by shipping almost one hundred Black people off to Liberia in 1820. While that country became a virtual neocolony, the conditions there did not validate emigration as the future for Black people.

The abolitionist William Lloyd Garrison (1805–1879) influenced Black leadership to use moral suasion as the method to win support for ending slavery. This was focused on the slave system. But Black leadership were freedmen who were also concerned about their plight as well. They wanted equality, the vote, and first-class citizenship. Garrison was not in favor of adding the goal of equality to his program of abolition. Along with Garrison, many whites attended the early conventions.

Activists in New York brought forth new militancy demanding improvement in the conditions of the freedmen. Black people had to pay a $250 property tax in order to vote—whites didn't have to pay anything. A state convention was called for August 25, 1841 in Troy, New York:

> It was the first convention held with the chief emphasis upon the suffrage. It was probably the first state colored convention to send an appeal to the state legislature. And, finally, it stands as the first of

> the Negro conventions on record to declare its independence of white meddling. In this respect it is the harbinger of a new age in Negro thought and action. After that date they might incur Garrisonian criticism, but they were never again bothered with a swarm of whites to influence action from the convention floor.
>
> (Bell 1969a, 66)

It is important to contextualize these Black leaders. They were not only part of the national US discourse, but also part of the global discourse of revolutionary change. In the same year that Marx and Engels published *The Communist Manifesto*, 1848, Frederick Douglass linked the fight to end slavery in the USA with the democratic revolutions of Europe:

> The world is in commotion—subjects are shaking down kingdoms, and asserting their rights as citizens—the right of self-government. Serfs are, with manly bearing, repelling the daring tyranny of their assumptive lordlings; and bondmen—yea slaves … have risen up in the majesty of manhood, [and] dashed into fragments … [the] scourge and curse of the human family—slavery.
>
> (Bell 1969a, 100–101)

There were militant voices calling for slave revolts. The two most important militants were Henry Highland Garnet (1815–1882) and David Walker (1796–1830).

> The Ohio convention of 1849 went so far as to recommend the purchase and distribution of five hundred copies of David Walker's *Appeal* and Garnet's *Address to the Slaves*. In this step they were officially promoting the distribution of two of the most radical calls to violence which Negroes had published in the twenty years preceding. Walker's *Appeal*, printed first in the late 'twenties, had been rather successfully buried through the disapproval of the Garrisonian press and other believers in moral suasion. Garnet's *Address* had been presented in the two national conventions of the middle 'forties. The publication of these two addresses under one cover in 1848 met a far more favorable reception than had been accorded to either when first presented to the public, the one in 1829, the other in 1843.
>
> (Bell 1969a, 115)

Of course, the masses of Black people had been fighting the slave system off and on since the first slave ship. It is notable that the first convention was held in 1830, and the great Nat Turner anti-slavery armed rebellion in Virginia took place in 1831.

The politics of the Negro convention movement changed based on the social conditions facing Black people, especially in the two states that sent the most delegates: New York and Pennsylvania. Key participants changed their views as they responded to the possibilities for a future of freedom, including Frederick Douglass and Martin Delaney. Part of this was the tension between focusing on those Black people who were in slavery and the conditions of the freedmen. The conventions were always faced with both realities, as both had to be dealt with in creating a new future of freedom for Black people.

SELF-DETERMINATION DEBATE

After the formal end of slavery, the development of a Black national identity was still anchored in the mass labor of picking cotton, now as sharecroppers rather than as slaves. They worked with the same productive forces (tools), but were now not legally owned; nevertheless, most were chained to the land in a system of debt peonage. Those who were living in the Northern cities lived crowded spatially into tightly defined ghettoes. But with higher education becoming more available, a new intellectual leadership stratum emerged as part of the Black middle class. This intelligentsia was focused as much on a future of freedom in their time as the National Negro Conventions held before the Civil War were in their time.

Much like in physics, in the sense that each action leads to a reaction, historical dialectics of social forces often acts in this same way. Sometimes it is immediate and sometimes it plays out over years, even decades, depending on one's framework of analysis. Hughes, in an important article on a less well-known united front effort, set the stage for the 1920s:

> The idea of creating a mass movement among Black organizations had been discussed for several decades after the end of the Civil War. It took the events of the Red Summer, between June and December 1919, to bring that idea to fruition. During the last six months of 1919 seventy-six Blacks were lynched and there were twenty-five race riots. … Eleven Blacks were burned alive. … In Chicago alone thirty-eight

> persons died, 537 were injured, and around one thousand were left homeless from a four-day reign of terror. The United States in 1919 was not a safe place for Afro-Americans, and public sensitivity on racial issues was at a new low.
>
> (Hughes 1984, 1–3)

A call for a national meeting was issued by Kelly Miller, a dean at Howard University, in order to unite the diverse forces within a common front:

> Given the complexity of the "Negro Problem" and the numerous political persuasions of different Black groups, it is difficult to conceive that any one organization could ever establish a broad enough base to satisfy all parties concerned. However, Miller believed that even if the various factions in the Black community could not agree on specific programs and methods, they could and must agree on certain common and basic principles and goals to achieve.
>
> (Hughes 1984, 3)

He named this conference the Negro Sanhedrin, after the Jewish Sanhedrin that was a council of seventy-one wise elders during the Roman period. Miller joined A. Philip Randolph and William Monroe Trotter in recruiting six organizations to issue the call: The NAACP, the International Uplift League, the Friends of Negro Freedom, African Blood Brotherhood (ABB), the National Equal Rights League, and the National Race Congress (Greenidge 2019, 327–34). At a planning meeting, the ABB was a major player. Their program was clearly the most militant, as it involved the following:

> Armed resistance against lynching, self-determination for the Negro in states where he constituted a majority, enfranchisement, end of Jim Crowism, equal rights, trade unionism, cooperation between Black and white workers, and the eradication of imperialism in Africa and in the West Indies.
>
> (Hughes 1984, 5)

Cyril Briggs of the ABB was the keynote speaker at the main planning meeting, during which he stated: "If we are slaves in Africa we cannot expect to be accepted as freemen in the United States, certainly our status in the United States will affect our status in other parts of the world" (Hughes 1984, 6).

Miller, on the other hand, focused his remarks on the American identity of Black people and the need for the struggle to focus on realizing political rights as citizens. The Sanhedrin met in Chicago in January 1924, from Monday morning until late Friday. Over sixty organizations sent over three hundred delegates. However, after the meeting, little was done directly and hence it raised expectations but did not follow through with organization or political accomplishments. It was a watershed experience, however. Ralph Bunche summed it up this way almost twenty years later: "The Sanhedrin is significant chiefly because of the broadness of its perspective, its nationalism and its intent to build Negro unity. In all three of those qualities it was a modern forerunner of the National Negro Congress" (Hughes 1984, 11).

The first National Negro Congress (NNC) mass meeting was held in Chicago in February 1936. Again, the Great Depression was the crisis that precipitated this gathering of forces into a broad debate to chart a path toward unity and a program for the freedom struggle. Two Harvard graduate students, John Davis and Robert Weaver, initiated the NNC. They were joined by a committee of radical faculty at Howard University that constituted itself as the Joint Committee on National Recovery. The founding took place after a conference was held at Howard in May 1935. It was mainly composed of Howard faculty, but included many workers and trade unionists, representatives of the Socialist and Communist Parties, the National Urban League, church officials, school administrators, government officials, and others.

Jonathan Holloway (currently president of Rutgers University) describes the beginning of the National Negro Congress:

> Inspired by the numerous calls to arms at the Howard University conference, an enthusiastic group gathered at Bunche's campus house after the three day meeting adjourned and sketched out a specific plan that they believed would finally provide a means for a unified workers' movement to develop in the United States. At this meeting the National Negro Congress (NNC) was born.
>
> (J.S. Holloway 2002, 75)

Even though the first meeting of the NNC convened in Chicago a full nine months after the Howard conference, the congress got off to a rousing start with over 800 delegates in attendance and as many as 8,000 people appearing for the open evening sessions. The Communist Party had changed its organizing strategy to build what it called a Popular Front. George Dimitrov, executive secretary of the Communist International, declared the new political line as a "People's Front Against Fascism and War." Given the danger of fascism, the plan was to build broad united fronts that would reach deep into the middle classes in unity with the working class. This was a framework for the NNC, and at its launch was quite a success. Erik Gellman recounts the event:

> On a bitterly cold February weekend, 750 delegates from twenty-eight states traveled to Chicago's South Side Bronzeville neighborhood to register their names at the Eight Regiment Armory for the first conclave of the NNC. Inside the armory, banners read "Jobs and Adequate Relief for a Million Negro Destitute Families" and "Black America Demands an End to Lynching, Mob Violence." Outside, thousands huddled around loudspeakers to hear the speeches of what the Chicago Defender termed "IKN's"—"Internationally Known Negroes." Top Black intellectuals, churchmen, labor leaders, and artists—including Ralph Bunche of Howard University, the Reverend Adam Clayton Powell Jr., James Ford of the Communist Party, Lester Granger of the National Urban League, Roy Wilkens of the NAACP, Langston Hughes, Richard Wright, and Arna Bontemps—debated during sessions on unions, youth, churches, business, war and fascism, the role of women, and interracial relations. ... The NNC convention in Chicago proved unique because its participants not only talked about working-class Blacks but also looked to them for leadership.
>
> (Gellman 2012, 25)

The industrial base of the USA heading into World War II was recovering from the Great Depression, based on the New Deal policies of President Roosevelt and the economist John Maynard Keynes. But Black workers were still getting shafted by the norm of racist discrimination and marginalization. Conditions led people to a new level of militancy and, in response, the leaders of the different social forces of the Black community were coming together into a common front. The NNC was active in trade union organizing, lending at least one of their paid organizers to the Steel Workers Organizers Committee. The NNC also made an impact by supporting the development of the South Side Community Art Center in Chicago as a WPA Project. This became one of the main meeting places for Black artists and facilitated their interaction with political radicals.

The third national meeting of the NNC, held in Washington, DC, in 1940, was attended by over 1,200 delegates, including 370 white delegates. There was increased red baiting from the US Congress and some people began to follow this lead in their criticism of the NNC. The key figure in this was A. Philip Randolph (1889–1979) of the Sleeping Car Porters Union. He had been elected NNC president at the Chicago meeting, but declined to run again at the third meeting. In his speech, he criticized the increased role of whites, the increased role of the CIO, and the increased role of the Communist Party. On the other hand, Randolph continued his fight for fair labor practices by the federal government. This led him to his call for the first great mass March on Washington in 1941, which pushed President Roosevelt to create the Fair Employment Practice Commission. So the strategic unity of the NNC was broken, but the fight kept going, and the debate kept going as well.

Again, there were three basic positions of how Black leaders were charting paths to the future. These positions are summed up in the following quotes. Booker T. Washington (1856–1915) advocated accommodationism:

> The wisest among my race understand that the agitation of questions of social equality is the extremist folly, and that progress in the enjoyment of all the privileges that will come to us must be the result of severe and constant struggle rather than of artificial forcing. No race that has anything to contribute to the markets of the world is long in any degree ostracized. It is important and right that all privileges of the law be ours, but it is vastly more important that we be prepared for the exercise of these privileges. The opportunity to earn a dollar in a factory just now is worth infinitely more than the opportunity to spend a dollar in an opera-house.
>
> (Marable and Mullings 2000, 177)

W.E.B. Du Bois argued a position for social transformation:

> Suppose, now, that the Negro turns to the promise of socialism whither I have long looked for salvation. I was once a member of the celebrated Local No. 1 in New York. I am convinced of the essential truth of the

> Marxian philosophy and believe that eventually land, machines, and materials must belong to the state; that private profit must be abolished; that the system of exploiting labor must disappear; that people who work must have essentially equal income; and that in their hands the political rulership of the state must eventually rest.
>
> (J.S. Holloway and Keppel 2007, 310)

Marcus Garvey (1887–1940) argued for his version of reconnecting with Africa, and, contrary to many interpretations, he was militant and understood that returning and reclaiming Africa meant going to war with the colonial powers:

> And I want you men of Africa, you men of the Negro race, to prepare for the day when Africa will call for a judgment. Africa is preparing to call for a judgment, and that judgment we must have, and it will be a judgment in favor of four hundred million of oppressed people. And the marshal who will carry out the authority of the court will be the new Toussaint L'Overture with the sword and banner of the new African Republic … Cries of: "African must be free!" Now, if Africa is to be free, it means … [i]t is now for the judge to give his finding. The judge will give his findings after all the jurors of the Negro race, four hundred million, will have given their verdict. And then after the judge gives his finding he will have to find a marshal to serve the writ, who will require the New Negro to help him to serve the writ, because the man to whom this writ is to be served is of a desperate character, because he prefers to shed blood and take lives before he will give up what is not his. You have to spill blood in Africa before you get what is belonging to you.
>
> (R.A. Hill, Garvey, and Tolbert 1983, 93–94)

That was the 1930s. These issues continue to be the subject of Black historical reflection in Black Studies.

THE BLACK LIBERATION DEBATE

The dialectic that pushed us forward to the next great debate was the repression of the fascistic period led by Senator Joseph McCarthy from Wisconsin in the 1950s on the one hand, and the 1954 Supreme Court decision (*Brown* v. *Board of Education of Topeka, Kansas*) about integrating public schools. McCarthy had built a repressive culture of fear and retreat by leading an anti-communist crusade in the USA during the first phase of the Cold War with the Soviet Union led by Joseph Stalin. Countering this, the Civil Rights Movement broke through and liberated people to speak and act against racism and related forms of repression. The Brown decision hit Black consciousness like it was a second emancipation proclamation—it energized the people to rebuild the fight for social equality and justice. On the global scale, Black people were energized by the 1957 liberation of Ghana, followed by the Cuban Revolution take-off in 1959. Africa and the African Diaspora were awakened. Black youth grabbed this spirit of change and with their sit-in tactics in 1959 and 1960 sparked a massive movement against Jim Crow practices that had chained Black people down.

The fight against Jim Crow, especially the *de jure* legal forms of segregation that were so pervasive in the Southern states and the de facto form of segregation in the North, was a necessary fight for democracy. But, this enabled the mainstream to help turn the movement from the strategic goal of freedom to one of civil rights, from revolution to reform within the system. This reflected class differences within the Black community, with the middle class fighting for reform compared to the masses of Black people who were gravitating toward the revolutionary path of the freedom struggle to end their oppression in all forms once and for all time.

The base of the Black struggle was the proletarian force formed in the heart of the major industries of steel, auto, and other forms of manufacturing. This was reflected in the Black working-class organizing in places like Detroit, Cleveland, and Chicago.

As the struggle intensified, even within the Civil Rights Movement, a contradiction began to emerge between reformism and linking the fight for reform to a revolutionary strategic vision for societal transformation. A key figure in this tension was Rev. Dr. Martin Luther King (1929–1968). He was born into a church leadership network and reared in the deep theological and rhetorical tradition of Black ministerial leadership. While a student at Morehouse College (1944–1948), he was mentored by Benjamin Mays, just missing Du Bois as he left Atlanta University, the very year King entered.

King became the iconic voice of the Civil Rights Movement, keeping it linked to the Black church, its social justice gospel tradition of theology and an evolving consciousness that increasingly went beyond reform to considering the necessity of fighting for a completely different new system:

> There are 40 million poor people here. And one day we must ask the question, "Why are there 40 million poor people in America?" And when you begin to ask that question, you are raising questions about the economic system, about a broader distribution of wealth. When you ask that question, you begin to question the capitalist economy. And I'm simply saying that more and more, we've got to begin to ask questions about the whole society.
>
> (Cone 1984, 189–90)

He was an intellectual trained by the mainstream, attaining a PhD degree at Boston University. On his journey, he was vilified as a radical who had to be ostracized; he was both embraced and rejected by the militants of SNCC inside the Civil Rights Movement, as well as Malcolm X outside of that movement. He wrote books and laced his speeches with references to great thinkers from Black intellectual history and great minds from all over the world.

One of his most important speeches, one that links him to the rationale and program of research in Black Studies, is a 1967 speech he gave to the American Psychological Association titled "The Role of the Behavioral Scientist in the Civil Rights Movement." He stated,

> Negroes want the social scientist to address the white community and "tell it like it is." White America has an appalling lack of knowledge concerning the reality of Negro life. One reason some advances were made in the South during the past decade was the discovery by northern whites of the brutal facts of southern segregated life. It was the Negro who educated the nation by dramatizing the evils through non-violent protest. The social scientist played little or no role in disclosing truth. The Negro action movement with raw courage did it virtually alone. When the majority of the country could not live with the extremes of brutality they witnessed, political remedies were enacted and customs were altered.
>
> (King, Jr. 1968)

He goes beyond this by pointing out how Black people were not only acting, but were also becoming conscious of the bigger social context for their struggle. King explained the origin of Black Studies and focused on the role of the social sciences:

> Ten years of struggle have sensitized and opened the Negro's eyes to reaching. For the first time in their history Negroes have become aware of the deeper causes for the crudity and cruelty that governed white society's responses to their needs. They discovered that their plight was not a consequence of superficial prejudice but was systemic.
>
> The slashing blows of backlash and front lash have hurt the Negro, but they have also awakened him and revealed the nature of the oppressor. To lose illusion is to gain truth. Negroes have grown wiser and more mature and they are hearing more clearly those who are raising fundamental questions about our society whether the critics be Negro or white. When this process of awareness and independence crystallizes, every rebuke, every evasion, become hammer blows on the wedge that splits the Negro from the larger society.
>
> Social science is needed to explain where this development is going to take us. Are we moving away, not from integration, but from the society which made it a problem in the first place? How deep and at what rate of speed is this process occurring? These are some vital questions to be answered if we are to have a clear sense of our direction.
>
> (King, Jr. 1968)

King was speaking to the white academic mainstream, who had no inclination nor capacity to respond. This task was to be taken up by Black Studies. He somehow knew this:

> On March 19, 1968, the Rev. Dr. Martin Luther King, Jr. proclaimed: "We're going to let our children know that the only philosophers that lived were not Plato and Aristotle, but W.E.B. Du Bois and Alain Locke came through the universe."
>
> (Wikipedia 2020a)

The Black radical tradition was being reborn in an alternative social motion to the Civil Rights Movement, the legacy of Black Nationalism as embodied in the life and work of Malcolm X (1925–1965). Malcolm, like King, was born into his future role. His parents were active members of Garvey's UNIA, and his class orientation linked him to the working class, both in occupation and in being "schooled" not so much in formal institutions, but in apprenticeship relationships in the streets and prisons. Malcolm was recruited into the Nation of Islam (NOI) and became a protégé of Elijah Muhammad, its supreme leader. His consciousness evolved with the social motion of Black resistance, especially in the ideological cauldron of the centers of Black radicalism—Harlem, Detroit, Chicago, and Los Angeles, among other places. Beginning with the dogma of the NOI, Malcolm was plunged into debate with all strands of Black radicalism and was transformed. His personal transformation led a movement transformation from being sectarian to being a force in the dialectical development of the overall Black Liberation Movement.

Malcolm was a revolutionary who thought "out of the box." Being keenly aware of the need for study, he directed people not only to African-American history, but to world history as well:

> Of all our studies, history is best qualified to reward our research. And when you see that you've got problems, all you have to do is examine the historic method used all over the world by others who have problems similar to yours. Once you see how they got theirs straight, then you know how you can get yours straight.
>
> (X and Breitman 1989, 8)

> One of the first things I think young people, especially nowadays, should learn is how to see for yourself and listen for yourself and think for yourself. Then you can come to an intelligent decision for yourself. If you form the habit of going by what you hear others say about someone, or going by what others think about someone, instead of searching that thing out for yourself and seeing for yourself, you will be walking west when you think you are going east, and you will be walking east when you think you are walking west. This generation especially of our people has a burden, more so than any other time in history. The most important thing that we can learn to do today is think for ourselves.
>
> It's good to keep wide open ears and listen to what everybody else has to say, but when you come to make a decision, you have to weigh all of what you've heard on its own, and place it where it belongs, and come to a decision for yourself, you'll never regret it. But if you form the habit of taking what somebody else says about a thing without checking it out for yourself, you'll find that other people will have you hating your friends and loving your enemies. This is one of the things

> that our people are beginning to learn today that it is very important to think out a situation or yourself. If you don't you'll always be maneuvered into a situation where you are never fighting your actual enemies, where you will find yourself fighting your own self.
>
> (X 1965, 4–5)

In actual fact, the main national civil rights leaders made a pact to not debate Malcolm X, as they were aware that the national mood was not trending in their favor and he was too skilled to risk being defeated in a public forum. However, Malcolm did debate, as de facto proxies for King and the rest, James Farmer, Bayard Rustin, Louis Lomax, and James Baldwin (Ogbar 2004, 53–54).

So, for the impact of Malcolm X, and this was indicative of many diverse aspects of the movement, Malcolm sent people into the libraries to dig into the Black intellectual and radical tradition to get clarity and direction for the struggle as it was developing. He was a master teacher in the community, in the mosque, and via speeches on many campuses.

The Black Liberation debate swung into high gear, and it was this high tide of study and struggle that created Black Studies on campus. So at the beginning of the current institutional phase of Black Studies, activists became professors and yet continued to be activists. The turning point was the great Black Power conference in Newark in 1967 followed by the founding conference of the African Heritage Studies Association in 1970 at Howard University. Major conferences carried the debate into electoral politics, into a consensus about a pan-African consciousness. There were also Black Panther gatherings that led us to rethink the US Constitution, notably one in Philadelphia in 1970 attended by 7,000 people.

Perhaps the highpoint of the Marxist Nationalist Debate in the movement was the 1974 African Liberation Support Committee (ALSC) national conference at Howard University. As a movement, ALSC was based in the community and on campus. ALSC's forty-two chapters as of 1974 reflected quite a regional spread: there were fourteen in the South, thirteen in the Northeast, ten in the Midwest, and five in the West.

The critically important aspect of ALSC was its history of combining mass activism with intense ideological struggle. The year of activity leading up to the debate at Howard University in 1974 makes this point.

This combined spirited speeches and a massive unity protest march. In addition to workshops, there were two panels giving three speakers forty-five minutes each to make a full and complete statement of their ideological and political position. The speakers on the panels were the following:

PANEL 1
Muhammad Ahmad, African People's Party
Kwame Ture, All-African People's Revolutionary Party
Abdul Alkalimat, People's College

PANEL 2
Kwadjo Akpan, Pan-African Congress USA
Imamu Baraka, Congress of African People
Owusu Sadaukai, Malcolm X Liberation University

The full speeches were reprinted in the USA (*The African World* newspaper) and in London (the *Race Today* journal). This led to a national moment of study, especially connecting the study of scientific socialism in the African liberation movements with what was happening in the US Black Liberation Movement.

The high point of the Marxist-Nationalist Debate in Black Studies was at the 1977 African Heritage Studies Association conference held in Detroit at Wayne State University under the chair of Professor Geneva Smitherman. This was perhaps the only time that a national conference cancelled twelve break-out sessions because the participants demanded the debate that started at 9am go forward all day! The platform speakers and the positions they advocated were Kwame Ture (pan-Africanism), Haki Madhubuti (Nationalism), and Abdul Alkalimat (Marxism). Everyone learned and most were sent back to the library to do more reading to learn more and to affirm the need for Black Studies as it connected to the struggle (People's College presentation given by Abdul Alkalimat; People's College 1977).

Two decades later, activists in the Black Liberation Movement reunited and continued the debate in the Black Radical Congress (BRC). Of the five people who started the BRC, four were Black Studies faculty (Barbara Ransby, Leith Mullings, Manning Marable, and Abdul Alkalimat) and one a trade union official (Bill Fletcher). This was a reboot of the National Negro Congress. Every part of the freedom movement came to be counted in the debate; the desire to unite was a powerful imperative that kept the debate going.

After describing the origin of the BRC, and locating it in the history of united front efforts by the Black Freedom Movement, Sundiata Cha-Jua placed a challenge before the BRC activists to create what he termed a radical education project:

> What should be the criterion for a "radical education project" for Marxist activists in the BRC? First, and foremost, an educational project must increase its participants knowledge of the core Marxist concepts and theories. Second, it ought to heighten our concrete knowledge of the current phase of capitalism and racial oppression. It should answer such questions as how globalization and new technologies are effecting job creation, location, and organization of the labor process and their impact on people of African descent. Third, because we believe in the unity of theory and practice, our capacity to engage the capitalist structures of racial domination and ideologies of degradation and accommodation. Fourth, the Black Freedom Movement is not only national, but also has international and local dimensions, thus a radical education project must reflect all three dimensions.
>
> (Cha-Jua 1998, 18)

These are the key questions for Black Studies activists to reignite the debate and recommit activists to building a unity of our freedom forces in search of the future. This can only be driven by both the Black academics on campus and the activists in the community working in dialogue with each other.

WHY IS THIS NECESSARY? WHY WAS UNITY LOST?

1. The material class basis got hit with transformative technology—workers faced unstable families and weak institutions, decline of trade unions, the attack against anything "public," and turning our communities into drug-infested war zones, forbidden zones where nobody wants to live.

2. The global developments in Africa were reversed and Afro-Pessimism—Soske (2004), and not to be confused with Wilderson (2020)—took hold. The organizations we fought for turned into their opposites: for example, the ANC in South Africa or ZANU in Zimbabwe.

3. In Black Studies, we had an extreme polarity tear our unity apart—right politics took over, the postmodernism of those who were raised up into the mainstream, Afrocentrism for those few inside to reign

> over the masses, who were more marginalized. The context of the masses of people—the structural exploitation and genocidal racism—was delinked. The postmodernists focused on the texts, but out of context, and the Afrocentrists looked more backward to past highs, but failed to project a path for future highs.

The fight for the future in Black Studies has two polar opposites in play. Some of the leading public intellectuals have been co-opted into mainstream structures of power like the Council on Foreign Affairs, while other maintain radical connections to the Black Liberation Movement. These two paths are dialectically related, taking them at face value as legitimate attempts to advance the interests of Black people. One argues that the system can be reformed, while the other calls for more fundamental radical transformation informed by the radical Black tradition. The leading path at the origin of the current phase of Black Studies has been the radical Black tradition, but this has been superseded by the path of working within the mainstream for reforms.

The neoliberal university is increasingly making it hard to maintain an autonomous radical Black posture within Black Studies. This is a reflection of fundamental changes in the society toward a less democratic, socially oppressive, and economically polarized society. The fundamental crisis is a deep contradiction in the current stage of capitalism. If the capitalist system is building a system for the production and distribution of goods and services without the need for human labor, and therefore without wages being paid out, then the system can only exist if consumption is not based on money.

This means that it will be study circles in the community, the exploited and oppressed becoming conscious of what is going down in order for Black people to have the future they want. No ignorant people have ever been able to throw off the shackles of their oppression. This points to the need to reinvent Black Studies and anchor it in the community. The dystopia of today will continue unless we develop a new type of Black Studies.

PART II

Black Studies as Diaspora Studies

The main focus of our history of Black Studies has been on the African American (US) experience. However, it is important to include in this history how Black Studies focused also on Africa and the African Diaspora from the very beginning and is embracing it as a new paradigm for its future. The two main theoretical approaches both embrace the African Diaspora. The Afrocentric position begins with ancient Africa, and over historical time connects to the Black experience throughout the African Diaspora. The Black Experientialists begin with the more recent African-American experience and then reach out in all directions of time and space to study the continuities and discontinuities of it with the global African experience (Alkalimat 2021). In this context, we will survey how these manifestations of Black Studies have impacted the intellectual activity of Black people in the USA and throughout the African Diaspora itself in higher education. Our first concern is to reflect on and clarify the concept of the African Diaspora.

The African Diaspora is an emergent concept in Black Studies, because the African Diaspora is becoming a transformative aspect of world society and culture. There is a push and pull of people making African migration more accelerated than ever before. The crisis of neocolonial domination by Europe and state corruption with comprador ruling classes are driving African masses to leave their countries of origin. Some are migrating to other locations on the African continent and others are leaving Africa for Europe or the USA. This has involved the African middle class as well as the impoverished, some moving out via visas and plane tickets and others moving through illegal channels.

The global economy is also bringing all parts of the world together, with capitalist corporations becoming more global than national in their basic interests. Forms of oppression take on global patterns so increasingly African peoples have to be understood on a global level. This creates the need for global tabulation of demographic data, comparative studies of legal forms of racial discrimination, and all other aspects of societal experience.

5

History, Ideology, and Culture

What is the African Diaspora? The origin of the African Diaspora begins with the dispersal of African peoples out of the African continent. There have been four major dispersals of people out of Africa: the spread of humanity from its origin in Africa; the spread of civilization from the Nile Valley and other African empires; the spread of traditional African culture because of the European slave trade; and migration out of modern Africa.

Spread of humanity: Our species, *Homo sapiens*, first developed in Africa. All humans originated in the migration of these first humans out of the African continent:

> The common ancestor who gave rise to our tight mitochondrial DNA lineage must have lived about 200,000 years ago. This date, of course, perfectly accords with the idea of a separate recent evolution of *Homo sapiens* shortly before it began its African exodus about 100,000 years ago. In other words, one small group of *Homo sapiens* living 200 millennia ago must have been the source of all our present, only slightly mutated mitochondrial DNA samples—and therefore be the fount of all humanity.
>
> (Stringer and McKie 1998, 117)

This is a biological description of how humanity originated and then spread throughout the world. Thus began different patterns and rates of social development.

Spread of civilization: Egypt is one of the great seedbeds of civilization in all areas of life, including art, science, religion, politics, and warfare. Egypt spread its advances into the world, especially impacting Greece and Rome as the basis for European development. There is also evidence that people from the African empires of Mali and Songhay were global explorers. The world-famous Sankore University, established at Timbuktu, attracted people from many other countries, creating an influential flow of information (Clarke 1977).

Spread of traditional African culture: The European slave trade captured and spread African people and their traditional culture all over the world, especially to the Americas (Manning 2010).

Spread of modern Africans: Over the last century, especially since the 1960s, there has been a post-colonial migration out of Africa. This migration has been a process of upward social mobility and has consisted mostly of students, professionals, and business people.

Each dispersal has been debated over whether and how to affirm what Africa contributed to world history. Scholarly reactions to the third dispersal led to a major debate that directly impacts our understanding of the African Diaspora. One position is that Africans brought culture and civilization as a value-added process throughout their dispersal. The opposite position is that Black people lacked their own cultural and civilizational assets, so they needed value, and therefore benefited from contact with Europeans, even if under the conditions of slavery or some other form of colonial domination. Melville Herskovits and Lorenzo Turner argued the value-added position, while the value-needed position was argued by Robert Park and E. Franklin Frazier. One position posits continuity of Africa's connection with the African Diaspora, while the other posits discontinuity.

Robert Park (1864–1944) was a leading sociologist at the University of Chicago. He studied Black people and served in many social reform positions, working to defend the human rights of Black people, including serving as an associate of Booker T. Washington and the first president of the Chicago Urban League. However, he exhibited a benign form of paternalistic racism in his notion that Black people were different, "the lady of the races." He held out hope for African Americans, in that they were considered a blank slate for the assimilationist imperative of Eurocentric America. He stated the following in 1919:

> My own impression is that the amount of African tradition which the Negro brought to the United States was very small. In fact, there is every reason to believe, it seems to me, that the Negro, when he landed in the United States, left behind him almost everything but his dark complexion and his tropical temperament. It is very difficult to find in the South today anything that can be traced directly back to Africa. (Herskovits 2017, 3)

E. Franklin Frazier (1894–1962), a PhD in sociology from the University of Chicago, was a student of Park. Frazier reflected the view of the Black middle class that the survival and well-being of Black people in the USA was based on their capacity to assimilate into the normative structure of Eurocentric America. He was motivated to counter the racist attack that Black people were inferior and incapable of that accomplishment based on their African heritage. Frazier focused on the future and not the past. He stated his view in 1940:

> Probably never before in history has a people been so nearly completely stripped of its social heritage as the Negroes who were brought to America. Other conquered races have continued to worship their household gods within the intimate circle of their kinsmen. But American slavery destroyed household gods and dissolved the bonds of sympathy and affection between the men of the same blood and household. Old men and women might have brooded over memories of their African homeland, but they could not change the world about them. Through force of circumstance, they had to acquire a new language, adopt new habits of labor, and take over, however imperfectly, the folkways of the American environment. Their children, who knew only the American environment, soon forgot the few memories that had been passed on to them and developed motivations and modes of behavior in harmony with the New World. Their children's children have often recalled with skepticism the fragments of stories concerning Africa which have been preserved in their families. But, of the habits and customs as well as the hopes and fears that characterized the life of their forebearers in Africa, nothing remains.
>
> (Herskovits 2017, 3–4)

Both of these positions by Park and Frazier used arguments to combat racism, but in doing so liquidated the historical identity fundamental to being children of Africa. In their views, African Americans had been delinked from Africa. However, there is an opposite position held by Melville Herskovits (1895–1963) and Lorenzo Turner (1890–1972). Herskovits was a white anthropologist who did fieldwork in Africa as well as in many countries of the African Diaspora: Surinam, Haiti, Benin, Brazil, Ghana, and Nigeria. His research for the *American Dilemma* project led by Gunnar Myrdal was a critical summation of his views published as a book, *The Myth of the Negro Past* (1941; Herskovits 2017).

He made this general point in 1948:

> A substantial number of retentions of African custom without reinterpretation—that is, in immediately recognizable form—have carried over to Afroamerican cultures. In most instances, the African character of these retentions is at once apparent because of their similarity to African cultural elements that have been observed and recorded in Africa. But an increasing number of non-European cultural elements, recorded in Africa or merely noted in passing, have been coming to light in the cultures of New World Negroes. These elements, when studied in Africa in the light of their New World incidence and setting, have either pointed the way to investigations that have revealed African counterparts in an autochthonous setting, where they had been overlooked, or have stimulated inquiries which have shown the corresponding elements in Africa to possess a different, sometimes a deeper significance that had previously been assigned to them.
>
> (Herskovits and Herskovits 1969, 19–20)

His African-American counterpart was Lorenzo Turner, a linguist who took the time to learn both English and African languages. Turner stated his general position:

> A study of the influences of African culture upon the Western Hemisphere reveals that the slaves on reaching the New World did not wholly abandon their native culture, but retained much of it with surprising little change. Much of it also has been considerably modified by contact with Western Civilization, and a good deal of it, as would be expected, has been lost entirely. Those aspects of African culture which have been most tenacious throughout the New World are survivals in languages, folk literature, religion, art, the dance, and music; but some survivals from the economic and social life of the African can also be found in the New World.
>
> (Davis 1958, 102–103)

Turner did empirical fieldwork among the Gullah people. He stated,

> Up to the present time I have found in the vocabulary of the Negroes in coastal South Carolina and Georgia approximately four thousand West African words, besides many survivals in syntax, inflection, sounds,

> and intonation. ... I have recorded in Georgia a few songs the words of which are entirely African. In some songs both African and English words appear. This is true also of many folk-tales. There are many compound words one part of which is African and the other English. Sometimes whole African phrases appear in Gullah without change either of meaning or of pronunciation. Frequently African phrases have been translated into English. African given names are numerous.
> (Herskovits 2017, 276)

He makes an important methodological point:

> The Gullah Negro when talking to strangers is likely to use speech that is for the most part English in vocabulary, but when he talks to his associates and to members of his family, his speech is different. My first phonograph recordings of the speech of the Gullah Negroes contain fewer African words by far than those made when I was no longer a stranger to them. One has to live among them to know their speech well.
> (Herskovits 2017, 279)

One of the greatest goals of the colonial oppressors of Africa has been to delink African people from their history and each other. This is as true on the African continent as it is for the global African Diaspora, and nowhere has this been more impactful than in the USA. Over the many generations since the European slave trade, US exceptionalism has been force-fed into the consciousness of African Americans with the goal of negating any connection to Africa and the African Diaspora. The demeaning campaign to deny that Africa has made any significant contribution to global culture, art, or science is part of this process. The Eurocentric lie is that Africa needed to be colonized by the Europeans to save them from their primitive savage existence. On the other hand, African peoples found meaning and solidarity in maintaining connections, through interaction and the reconstruction of memory. Being in the world for Black people always has required a link back to Africa.

This reveals a contradiction in the concept of an African Diaspora, the opposite agency of the European and the African, the interaction of forced assimilation into a colonizing empire versus the autonomous self-determining survival of African culture. A diaspora is a dispersal of people from a common origin who maintain similarities, a linked identity, and often some form of historical memory and contemporary interaction.

Everywhere in the world, African people struggle with the contradiction of their organic cultural origin and the imposition of a European colonial domination. When we say that Black people are an African people, we have to contrast the objectivity of their being, their experience, with their subjective consciousness, who they think they are, or historically who they remember they are.

In the everyday lives of Black people, traces of Africa live through language and speech patterns; food; styles of performing religion, clothing, and hair aesthetics; and certainly musical forms and content, beginning with the syncopation of the drums. Some rituals and cultural practices continued in the Americas. However, colonization, especially the negation of humanity forced on Black people during slavery, both defined a universal experience of Africans as oppressed people, but also demonically negated African identity by its representation of Africa in the most negative way as a continent with no enduring contribution to human civilization and culture.

For these reasons, most African Americans in the African Diaspora were African but didn't know it, or certainly didn't want to admit it. Of course, this was not universally true, even from the very beginning, as we learn from *Roots* by Alex Haley, by the church naming itself the African Methodist Episcopal Church in 1816, and in so many other ways (Haley 2016; Wesley and Allen 1969).

The African Diaspora is the context that leads people to return to Africa, mainly in memory and cultural identification, but sometimes in actual migration. Within the concept of return, there is the contradiction between replication versus imagination, trying to recreate something versus thinking up something new.

There is a great diversity to the African experience, making what is universally African quite an abstraction. When making a conscious choice to connect with Africa, a common choice is with personal names. For example, we have the day names of the Akan people of Ghana. For example, for males, the day names are Monday—Kojo, Wednesday—Kwaku, Friday—Kofi, and Saturday—Kwame. And, for females, the corresponding names are Ajoba, Akuba, Afua, and Ama. Many African Americans have chosen this particularity, while many Africans in Ghana have chosen Western names for their children, usually along with an African name. Of course, this pattern is also in hairstyles, as African stylists who have migrated to the United States from the African continent offer traditional hairstyles from diverse cultures. Meanwhile, on the outside of hair care establishments in cities on the African continent, you often see paintings of hairstyles worn by African Americans like James Brown or Michael Jackson. In other words, replication takes place interchangeably throughout the African Diaspora.

On the other hand, there is an imagined all-African culture created alongside replication of traditional cultures throughout the African Diaspora. A good example of this is Kwanzaa. It posits itself as the embodiment of African tradition, but is an imagined cultural practice from the Diaspora rather than a replication of something from any particular traditional African context. Indeed, Kwanzaa is also being practiced on the African continent, and in other parts of the African Diaspora (Karenga 2008).

Finally, we have the contradiction of intervention versus reinvention, traveling back to the African continent versus affirming the space of the African Diaspora as African space. Making the trip to the African continent for an African American is symbolically similar to a Muslim making the Hajj to Mecca. It is the simultaneous affirmation of a particular and a universal, the experience of societies, at least on the surface, run by Black people, giving freedom and self-determination concrete examples, while at the same time forcing the realization that African Americans are both a part of the African Diaspora and a unique particularity unto themselves as well. There is a long history of Black geographically based communities taking on names that connect with Africa, for example, renaming the Black Belt South the Republic of New Afrika, naming neighborhoods Africatown in Mobile, Alabama, or Seattle, Washington, or the renaming of East Palo Alto, California, as Nairobi, and in such places fashioning programs to implement self-determination for a journey to freedom.

So, in sum, we have unpacked the concept of return for people in the African Diaspora. There has been the objectivity of retaining Africanness, while subjectively not remembering that one is doing so, of replicating and imagining Africa, as well as intervening on the African continent and reinventing Africa elsewhere in the space of the African Diaspora. The return to the past has to be linked to a future that is being created anew.

We still need a working definition of the African Diaspora. Michael Gomez presents this useful summary:

> Why continue to speak of the African Diaspora as a unified experience? There is no easy answer or scholarly consensus, but there are a number of factors that together suggest a related condition. These are

> (1) African as the land of origin; (2) an experience of enslavement, (3) the struggle of adapting to a new environment while preserving as much of the African cultural background as possible; (4) the reification of color and race; (5) a continuing struggle against discrimination; and (6) the ongoing significance of Africa to African-descended population. With these factors in mind, one can state that the African Diaspora consists of the connections of people of African descent around the world, who are linked as much by their common experience as their genetic makeup, if not more so.
>
> (Gomez 2008, 2)

PAN-AFRICANISM AS AFRICAN DIASPORA IDEOLOGY

Keeping in mind these theoretical reflections on what constitutes the African Diaspora, we will now turn to the ideological development of a focus on the African Diaspora in the context of the history of Black Studies.

Pan-Africanism is an ideological position that represents positive agency toward Africa, both positive identification with African descendent peoples and advocacy for their well-being. It is the political culture of unification, based on the positive dynamic for freedom in Africa and the African Diaspora. The historical scholarship of Hakim Adi and Marika Sherwood is a treasure trove of information on individuals and organizations that represent pan-Africanism (Adi 2018; Adi and Sherwood 2007; Adi, Sherwood, and Padmore 1995; Sherwood 2011b). So there have been many pan-African initiatives throughout the African Diaspora from the late nineteenth century till contemporary times. Key early figures include Alexander Crummell (1818–1898), Edward Wilmot Blyden (1832–1912), and Henry McNeal Turner (1834–1915). Key early organizations include Thomas T. Fortune's Afro-American League (1890); the American Negro Academy, founded by Alexander Crummell (1897); and others formed in the banner year of 1912: the International Conference on the Negro, convened by Booker T. Washington in Tuskegee; the Negro Society for Historical Research, formed by John Bruce and Arturo Schomburg in New York; and the London-based *African Times and Orient Review*, published by Duse Mohammed Ali (Adi 2018, 25–28).

> These prophetic Pan-Africanists were activists who embraced the strategic necessity for educating the masses of African peoples. One

> important case is Joseph Ephraim Casey Hayford (1866–1930): "He strongly favoured the creation of a university in West Africa that might become a centre of excellence for students from the region and throughout the African diaspora. Like (Wilmot) Blyden, he argued that such a university must provide an Africanised curriculum so as to promote African culture and overcome the Eurocentrism that accompanied the European partition of Africa and colonial rule. Casey Hayford attempted to implement some of his ideas on the promotion of African culture and self-respect, when in 1915 he established the Gold Coast National Research Association."
>
> (Adi and Sherwood 2007, 83)

There have been two major networks organizing efforts that have shaped pan-Africanism in the twentieth century: one is represented by Marcus Garvey and the other by W.E.B. Du Bois. Garvey created a mass-based movement building from the grassroots level, while Du Bois organized with political, cultural, and intellectual leaders from Africa and the African Diaspora. These two actions created a new stage of pan-African activism coordinated on a global level.

Garvey, born in Jamaica, led the development of the largest mass movement of Black people in the twentieth century in all parts of the African Diaspora (Adi 2018, 25–41). He was assisted by each of his wives in turn, Amy Ashwood Garvey (1897–1969) and Amy Jacques Garvey (1895–1973) (Taylor 2002; Martin 2008). Garvey's grassroots movement sparked a fundamental resistance to racist colonization by proclaiming Black identity as a proud and heroic feature of being human in the world. His most famous slogan was "Africa for the Africans," a clarion call for Black people everywhere to reclaim ownership of their ancestral homeland. At every level of literacy, in every part of the world, Garvey sent his message.

He formed an organization that built a pan-African movement throughout the African Diaspora, The Universal Negro Improvement Association and African Communities' League (UNIA 1914). His organizers, armed with the UNIA newspaper, *The Negro World*, succeeded in building the largest mass movement. The headquarters moved from Jamaica to New York in the USA, but the largest base in that country was in Chicago. This was a grassroots effort (Rolinson 2008; Tolbert 1980).

Adi documents how the UNIA socially defined the African Diaspora with the spread of its organizational base (2018, 34–38). There were many branches in Africa, including in Sierra Leone, Liberia, Gold Coast (Ghana), Nigeria, South Africa, Southwest Africa, and Mozambique. Furthermore,

> Marcus Garvey and the UNIA also exerted a significant influence on Africans in the diaspora. According to one historian, in addition to those in the United States, UNIA branches were established in Cuba, Panama, Costa Rica, Canada, Columbia, Mexico, Australia, Brazil, Ecuador, Venezuela, as well as throughout the Caribbean. Cuba contained the largest number with over fifty branches, followed by Panama with forty-seven.
>
> (Adi 2018, 38–39)

Garvey and the UNIA initiated educational programs to train up a cadre of organizers. This effort launched Booker T. Washington University in New York, Liberty University in Claremont, Virginia, and the School of African Philosophy in Toronto, Canada (Garvey, Hill, and Bair 1987, xlvii–xlix). Hill describes the beginning of the Toronto School:

> The first session of the school was held in September 1937, following the second regional conference of the American and Canadian branches of the UNIA in August. Garvey served as principal of the school and led the classes, which met daily, in day and evening sessions, from 1 to 23 September. Entrance was restricted to individuals with a high school education. Eleven students enrolled in the session, including four women and seven men, all from the northern or eastern United States or Canada. Ten of them passed the final examination and received appointments as UNIA regional commissioners.
>
> (Garvey, Hill, and Bair 1987, xliv)

The legacy of Garvey is firmly planted in Black consciousness throughout the African Diaspora. A small, dedicated activists network is keeping the UNIA alive (see UNIA n.d.), and the memory of Garvey and his activities are regular topics in Black Studies curricula, especially because of the work of Robert Hill (Hill, Garvey, and Universal Negro Improvement Association 2006), Tony Martin (1986), and Rupert Lewis (1988).

W.E.B. Du Bois is an interesting contrast to Garvey, in that he led a movement that organized the Black elites of the African Diaspora, intellectuals who gathered in the capitals of the so-called "colonial mother countries." After growing up and being educated in New England and the South, he did graduate study at the height of higher education at Harvard University in the USA and at the University of Berlin in Germany. His dissertation on the European slave trade of Africans became a defining work of scholarship on the African Diaspora, as it was the first volume in the Harvard Historical Series (Du Bois 2010). Du Bois became an icon of pan-Africanism (Adi 2018, 43–59).

His status is reflected in this comment by Jomo Kenyatta, Prime Minister of Kenya conveyed to Du Bois's wife, the writer Shirley Graham Du Bois:

> News of the death of your husband and my old friend has brought great sorrow to me and my people in Kenya. The world will always remember his long years of dedication to the cause of complete Freedom of Africa and his voice of Pan-Africanism. Our loss in this great statesman can never be replaced.
>
> (Secretariat for an Encyclopedia Africana 1963)

Du Bois placed Africa in a central position as the major forces marched toward world war in his article in the *Atlantic Monthly*, "The African Roots of War" (1915). This article laid out the same basic analysis that Lenin later developed in his analysis of imperialism. Du Bois was consistent in his studies of Africa and the African Diaspora (Du Bois 2001 [1915]; 1972).

Du Bois was a central activist in what are considered the five pan-African congresses (1919, Paris; 1921, London, Brussels, and Paris; 1923, London and Lisbon; 1927, New York City; and 1945, Manchester), and a sixth important gathering that had convened earlier, in 1900 (London). He mobilized the National Association for the Advancement of Colored People (NAACP) in his capacity as editor of *The Crisis* magazine to be actively involved in the development of the consciousness of the African Diaspora.

The delegates for the Fifth Congress in Manchester came from the following places: South Africa, Gold Coast (Ghana), India, Togoland, Nigeria, Jamaica, Nyasaland (Malawi), Sierra Leone, UK (England), British Honduras (Belize), Scotland, the USA, Gambia, Trinidad, British Guiana (Guyana), Kenya, Barbados, Bermuda, Ceylon (Sri Lanka), and Uganda. Activists from Africa and the African Diaspora were coming together as agents of freedom (Adi, Sherwood, and Padmore 1995, 125–61).

This meeting led to the great tide of struggle to liberate Africa from colonization. It was a great advance from the other meetings:

> For the first time there was a strong worker and student participation, and most of the over two hundred delegates who attended came from Africa. They represented re-awakening African political consciousness, and it was no surprise when the Congress adopted socialism as its political philosophy.
>
> (Nkrumah 1980, 42)

In his remarks summing up the Fifth Pan-African Congress, Du Bois anchors the pan-African concept in the consciousness of African peoples in the African Diaspora:

> The idea of one Africa uniting the thought and ideals of all native peoples of the dark continent belongs to the twentieth century, and stems naturally from the West Indies and the United States. Here various groups of Africans, quite separate in origin, became so united in experience, and so exposed to the impact of a new culture, that they began to think of Africa as one idea and one land. Thus, late in the eighteenth century, when a separate Negro Church was formed in Philadelphia, it called itself "African," and there were various "African" societies in many parts of the United States.
>
> (Adi, Sherwood, and Padmore 1995, 62)

After the 1945 Manchester Pan-African Congress, Nkrumah and Du Bois continued their historic collaboration. Nkrumah led Ghana to its independence in 1957 and became its first prime minister and president. This was the first African country south of the Sahara to gain its independence. The very next year he convened the 1958 All-African Peoples' Conference, which sparked so many movements that 1960, which saw seventeen countries gain their independence, was proclaimed Africa Year by the UN:

> This Conference represented freedom fighter movements, nationalist parties, as well as trade unions, co-operative and youth movements from all over Africa. Some three hundred delegates attended. It was

> the first time members of freedom movements from British, French, Portuguese Spanish and the racist minority regimes had met together to discuss common problems and to formulate plans. … One of the national movements invited to the conference was the FLN of Algeria. Frantz Fanon was a member of the five-man delegation. … Present at the 1958 All-African Peoples' Conference in Accra were Patrice Lumumba, Julius Nyerere, Kenneth Kaunda, Kanyama Chiume, Oginga Odinga, Joshua Nkomo, and many others who were to become notable political leaders.
>
> (Milne 2000, 86–87)

Having set this political program in motion to free Africa from European colonization, Nkrumah invited Du Bois to come to Ghana to complete his project of compiling comprehensive scholarship in an *Encyclopedia Africana*. While this has not yet been completed, its goal became the most important and ambitious project in Black Studies as Diaspora Studies.

Finally, it is important to acknowledge that the realization of an African Diaspora has been a pan-African orientation gained from cultural initiatives. Before the 1960s, to link Blacks in the USA with the African Diaspora we need only mention Katherine Dunham in dance, the drum masters of Chano Pozo from Cuba and Olatunji from Nigeria, and Aaron Douglass, Lois Mailou Jones, and James A. Porter in art. The Black Diaspora was performed in the cultural life of African Americans.

DIASPORA STUDIES IN BLACK INTELLECTUAL HISTORY

Black scholars were aware of the need to study the African Diaspora from the earliest times. Fisk University established the first African Studies Program in the USA in 1943 under the leadership of Mark Hanna Watkins and E.W. Smith. (Wikipedia 2020e). Howard University set up an African Studies graduate degree program in 1953 and an undergraduate degree program in 1991 (Logan 1969, 436).

Horace Mann Bond, in his inaugural address as president of Lincoln University, stated that the university had been set up for "the redemption of Africa by American Negroes":

> Bond was able to enlarge the stature of his university in African educational circles as well as his own circles. For example, he was able to establish the African Studies Institute at Lincoln University in the

> early 1950s and to increase the number of African students studying at Lincoln and elsewhere in the United States. He also helped his brother, J. Max Bond, to become president of the College of Liberia.
>
> (Urban 1992, 148–49)

But well before this, students from Africa and the African Diaspora migrated to the USA to attend HBCUs. A good example is the Afro-Cubans who came to study at Tuskegee under the leadership of Booker T. Washington. The great Afro-Cuban leader Juan Gualberto Gómez sent his son there in 1901; the son roomed with Booker T. Washington's son at Tuskegee and then both went off to Phillips Exeter, a private school in New England, in 1906 (Alkalimat 2016, 41).

Carter Woodson, another great innovator for Black Studies history, supported studies that focused on the African Diaspora. His organization, The Association for the Study of Negro Life and History (ASALH), built a foundation for Black scholarship on the Diaspora. This is especially true for his two publishing projects: Associated Publishers for books and *The Journal for Negro History* for journal articles. The *Journal for Negro History* published sixty-six articles in its first four years (1916–1919), with one-third (twenty-one) being about Africa and the African Diaspora. Topics for these articles were Haiti, Brazil, Jamaica, Liberia, Canada, the processes of the slave trade, and colonization.

One of the key texts published by Associated Publishers was an English translation from the Portuguese of a book by Arthur Ramos, *The Negro in Brazil* (1939). The importance of this book is stated in the introduction by Richard Pattee, the translator:

> There is no question that Brazil is one of the nations of the new world which has been the most profoundly influenced by the penetration of the Negro. Aside from the United States, no American republic possesses as large a colored population. The present volume indicates how far-reaching and general this influence has been; how no region or section of the vast territory of Brazil has entirely escaped the impact of the Negro. From the beginning of its existence as a prolongation of the Portuguese motherland, Brazil has received and absorbed the Negro. Dr. Ramos has emphasized again and again how the economic structure, social order and political organization have been determined in part by the presence of millions of Negroes and mulattoes in the country.
>
> (Ramos 1980, 2)

This statement includes some colonial-type language, but the book by Ramos is more of a statement without such limitations. Here is how Ramos describes the great Black state of Palmares, a free territory set up by Africans who emancipated themselves and through a courageous act of self-determination created their own country within Brazil that existed from 1630 to 1697:

> The nature and significance of Palmares may be summarized as the case of a Negro state, organized exclusively by Brazilian slaves, in which talent for leadership was displayed on a remarkable high scale, in public administration, military strategy, economic and social cooperation and legislative procedure. Palmares will always remain as a monument to the innate ability of the Brazilian Negro to create for himself without outside aid or encouragement the essential implements of a social order. It is a curious and instructive case of the fusion of African elements and experience with the demands of a new environment to form a miniature state, manifesting all of the attributes of a civilized community.
>
> (Ramos 1980, 65)

Another book about the Diaspora published by Woodson's Associated Publishers was *Distinguished Negroes Abroad* (1946) by Beatrice J. Fleming and Marion J. Pryde. This book was for high school students to learn about thirty-four great Black people from the African Diaspora: four in Asia, twenty in Europe, six in the West Indies, and four in South America. Each chapter is followed by questions and suggestions to aid the students in their study. This demonstrates the importance of making sure that young people develop with an appreciation of their connection to the African Diaspora.

Another institution for Diaspora scholarship has been the Schomburg Center for Research in Black Culture in New York City. The Afro-Puerto Rican bibliophile Arturo Schomburg sold his collection of over 10,000 items to the New York Public Library system as a reference collection on the African Diaspora. It became an anchor for the intellectual life of Harlem and a national resource:

> Founded in 1925 and named a National Historic Landmark in 2017, the Schomburg Center for Research in Black Culture is one of the world's leading cultural institutions devoted to the research, pres-

> ervation, and exhibition of materials focused on African American, African Diaspora, and African experiences. As a research division of The New York Public Library, the Schomburg Center features diverse programming and collections spanning over 11 million items that illuminate the richness of global black history, arts, and culture. Established with the collections of Arturo Alfonso Schomburg 93 years ago, the Schomburg has collected, preserved, and provided access to materials documenting black life in America and worldwide. It has also promoted the study and interpretation of the history and culture of people of African descent.
>
> (New York Public Library n.d.)

Critical contributions to Diaspora consciousness were also based on the intellectual and political activism of the Trinidad three: C.L.R. James (1901–1989), George Padmore (1903–1959), and Claudia Jones (1915–1964). All three were leading Black communists engaged in activism in Trinidad, the United States, and England. James and Jones were cultural activists and Padmore led Comintern initiatives to connect pan-Africanism throughout the African Diaspora to the international working-class struggle for socialism (Dhondy 2001; Baptiste and Lewis 2009; C.B. Davies 2008).

ORGANIZATIONAL BACKGROUND TO DIASPORA STUDIES

At a national level, several organizations help us to understand Black intellectual-elite agency in scholarship and political activism about Africa and the African Diaspora. In the context of post-World War II Cold War tensions between the conflicting systems of capitalism and socialism that dominated the relations of most countries with the USA, different organizational initiatives advanced policy and research projects that created Diaspora-wide relationships.

The leading organization that reflected left politics was the Council on African Affairs (1937–1955):

> Describing itself as a non-profit and non-partisan organization, the Council on African Affairs was established in 1937 under the guidance of Max Yergan and Paul Robeson. Its purpose was threefold: (1) to give concrete help to the struggles of the African masses; (2) to dissem-

> inate accurate information concerning Africa and its peoples; (3) to influence the adoption of governmental policies designed to promote African advancement and freedom and preserve international peace. The Council held public meetings and forums and published a monthly bulletin, *New Africa*, as well as a number of pamphlets. Its motto was "Africa's Problems are Your Problems."
>
> (A.C. Hill and Kilson 1969, 209)

The Council on African Affairs's technique was to organize and support councils at the local level "to Promote the cause of African freedom and progress," to petition governments, and to present to the United Nations a program to implement its charter. Paul Robeson was the Council's first chairman and Max Yergan its first executive director. Members of the board were largely Negroes of liberal and academic interest, and some whites were also included (A.C. Hill and Kilson 1969, 210).

The council was clearly pro-African, pro-labor, and, in the context of the Cold War, pro-USSR. W.E.B. Du Bois and Alphaeus Hunton joined Paul Robeson in the leadership. By 1948, the fascist scare tactics of Senator Joseph McCarthy had branded the Council on African Affairs as a subversive organization, and due to intense government harassment, it was dissolved in 1955.

The US government was aware that this kind of activity was not in its interest, and some leading Black academics were of the same opinion about communism as an ideological force in the Black Liberation Movement. Something had to be done.

The next major development emerged in the mainstream in the 1950s. We can follow it through the activities of Horace Mann Bond, educator and president of Lincoln University:

> The first, the African American Institute, was founded as the Institute for African-American Relations (IAAR) in 1953. Just before the IAAR's inception, Bond corresponded with a white who was interested in Africa about the point of view that the proposed organization might take. The two agreed that blacks in the IAAR might follow a more avowedly pro-African, nationalist line, while whites could be more "objective" and entertain ideas that might not be inimical to colonial influence in Africa. This sort of balance was a characteristic that both men considered to be necessary in order to receive funding from foundations and government agencies. ... In 1958, the name

> of the organization was changed to the African-American Institute (AAI), and the statement of purpose was redrawn in accordance with the wishes of Alan Pifer of the Carnegie Corporation.
>
> (Urban 1992, 158)

The second organization, the American Society of African Culture (AMSAC), was limited to African Americans, and did not allow any direct white participation. A delegation of African-American intellectuals attended a 1956 conference in Paris, sponsored by the Society of African Culture (Société africaine de culture) (SAC) led by Alioune Diop. This included Horace Mann Bond, John Davis, William Fontaine, John Ivy, and Mercer Cook. AMSAC took its lead from the SAC conference in formally organizing the next year. The preamble to their constitution clearly established their mission as part of the historical development of African Diaspora Studies:

> American scholars, artists and writers of African descent join together in the American Society of African Culture to study the effect of African culture on American life, to examine the cultural contributions of African peoples to their societies; and to help the Western World and, more particularly, Americans to sweep away the prejudices that limit an appreciation of the cultural contributions of African peoples. Our purpose is also to study those conditions which effect the development of ethnic, national and universal culture and to acknowledge the ultimate immunity of the great cultural contributions of man to the distortions that result from political, economic and nationalistic bias.
>
> (A.C. Hill and Kilson 1969, 216)

One of AMSAC's continuing contributions was a special anthology edited by John Davis put out by the Paris SAC publishing house Présence Africaine, *Africa Seen by American Negroes* (1958). In his introduction to the volume, Davis takes exception to articles by both E. Franklin Frazier and W.E.B. Du Bois, although they are included with twenty other articles:

> Every American Negro who has written or worked in the African field was asked to contribute to this issue so that all points of view might be represented, even those with which the American Society disagreed. Obviously the Society does not agree with Frazier's thesis that there is nothing that the American Negro can contribute to African develop-

> ment. If this were so, there would be little reason for the existence of the Society. Nor can we agree with Du Bois when he says that there is nothing that western capital can offer Africa.
>
> (Davis 1958, 1)

It must be added that an issue of the AMSAC journal, *African Forum* (1, no. 3, 1966) focused on African socialism and included a diversity of views. The issue included an article arguing scientific socialism by Kwame Nkrumah, a cultural argument by Léopold Sédar Senghor, and a pragmatic argument from Martin Kilson. But their indefensible allegiance was uncovered as coming from CIA funding (Gaines 2008, 253–54).

The complex ties of AMSAC with the CIA have been well documented (Wilford 2009, 197–224). Wilford points out that the danger the CIA focused on was the left leadership of the Council on African Affairs:

> What recent tradition of engagement with Africa there was among black Americans belonged mainly to the left and such organizations as the Council on African Affairs (CAA), which espoused a mixture of socialist economic ideals and a diasporic cultural consciousness known as pan-Africanism.
>
> (Wilford 2009, 199)

Plummer points directly to how the CIA made its move:

> Both SAC and AMSAC in their years had oriented African and diaspora intelligentsia away from that revolutionary ferment. AMSAC shared its New York headquarters with the Council on Race and Caste in World Affairs, which, unbeknownst to most AMSAC members, was a CIA front. The Council on Race and Caste in World Affairs merged with AMSAC in 1957 and channeled CIA funds to it.
>
> (Plummer 2013, 30)

CULTURAL BACKGROUND TO DIASPORA STUDIES

This process of global pan-Africanism took off in cultural terms with a 1956 meeting in Paris. Présence Africaine, a cultural organization based in Paris, with a journal, publishing house, and a bookstore, hosted the meeting. The second conference by the Paris organizers was held in Rome, in 1959. Présence Africaine published the proceedings of both conferences (Freedom Archives 2020). The next major gathering took place in Africa! The best connection that Présence Africaine had in Africa was the motion of anti-colonial African forces fighting for liberation, based on the national liberation policies of the Algerian government. Delegations came from all the national liberation organizations, in some cases alienating their neocolonial regimes. Participants from the USA included members of the Black Panther Party, led by Eldridge Cleaver. Kwame Ture (aka Stokely Carmichael) was also there (Rhodes 2017, 264–66).

The next major international festival was FESTAC in Nigeria in 1977. FESTAC was not in line with the pro-négritude approach of the 1966 Dakar festival, nor was it as political as the 1969 Algiers festival. Nigeria had, and continues to have, the largest population of all African countries. It has oil as the engine of its national economy. Nigerians are also the largest contributor to populating the African Diaspora. It seemed logical that Nigeria would play such a role as host for FESTAC 77 (FESTAC 1977). There were over 16,000 participants. The organizers built a village of new apartments to house them.

The FESTAC plan divided the world into zones, with the coordinators of each zone being part of the international planning process. Two major struggles defined how the festival developed. Within Nigeria, there were many issues around the oil revenue and how it would be utilized. Nigeria has a stark class structure with extremes of the superrich and the destitute poor. In the Diaspora, issues of representation were key, especially the contradiction between the official governments of the African Diaspora, bearing colonial legacies, and the African-descendent artistic communities often connected to progressive political movements.

One critical issue was the refusal of the British government to loan a carved ivory royal mask of Benin representing the Queen Mother, Iyoba of Benin, that had been chosen as the FESTAC symbol. They claimed they feared it would not be returned. The Nigerian government then had a local sculptor craft a replica. Part of the tragic legacy of FESTAC is that this artist was never paid for this (Alkalimat n.d).

Jeff Donaldson and Hoyt Fuller, both veterans of the Chicago Black Arts Movement, led the US delegation. Hoyt was an editor (*Negro Digest/Black World/First World*) and Jeff was head of the art department at Howard University. A massive US delegation of over 500 attended, covering every major cultural form, both artists and historians/critics. Three key intellectuals spoke for African Americans at the international symposium: Ronald Walker, Maulana Karenga, and Abdul Alkalimat (Walters 1993, 82–83).

Another important process was the annual London-based International Book Fair of Radical Black and Third World Books and its festival. These events were held from 1982 to 1995. The main organizers were John La Rose and Sarah White, along with their bookstore, New Beacon. New Beacon was the first Black bookshop in England. They were joined by Jessica and Eric Huntley, of Bogle-L'Ouverture Publications, and Race Today Publications headed by Darcus Howe:

> The Book Fair was initiated and organized by the Caribbean section of the black population in Britain. Its influence and reach extended to India and Pakistan, to West, Central, East and South Africa, to the Caribbean, Central America and the United States, to German, France and Belgium. It was politically a continuation in the tradition of the 1945 Pan African Congress held in Manchester which laid the basis for the post World War II independence movements established by the Caribbean Artists Movement between 1966 and 1972.
>
> (White, Harris, and Beezmohun 2005, 1; Walmsley 1992)

Each book fair was electrically charged with activists and artists from throughout the third world, especially the Africa and the African Diaspora. This is reflected in the people who gave the keynote addresses to open each fair (Table 1).

Table 1 Keynote Speakers at the International Book Fair of Radical Black and Third World Books, London

Year	*Name*	*Country*
1982	C.L.R. James	Trinidad
1983	Kole Omotoso	Nigeria
1984	Edward Kamau Brathwaite	Barbados
1985	Wole Soyinka	Nigeria
1986	Earl McLeod	Trinidad
1987	Ngũgĩ Wa Thiong'o	Kenya
1988	Abdul Alkalimat	USA
1989	Farrukh Dhondy	India
1990	Jayne Cortez	USA
1991	John La Rose	Trinidad
1993	Margaret Busby	Ghana
1995	Pearl Connor-Mogotsi	Trinidad

Source: The London book fair activities have been archived with the George Padmore Institute (International Book Fairs n.d.).

POLITICAL BACKGROUND TO DIASPORA STUDIES

Ever since Du Bois connected the NAACP to the global pan-African Congress movement, Black social justice organizations have engaged in programmatic activities connected to the African Diaspora. Following the rise of Black Power as a widely adopted ideological slogan, key organizations made major advances in this regard. Three such organizations were the Student Nonviolent Coordinating Committee (SNCC), the Black Panther Party (BPP), and the League of Revolutionary Black Workers (LRBW).

SNCC moved from the specifics of fighting for democratic rights in the US South to fighting for a general program for human rights. This involved establishing an international commission headed by James Forman, the long-time executive secretary of SNCC. He clarifies its mission in his autobiography:

> I myself became director of the newly created International Affairs Commission, based in New York, a position that I held until the summer of 1969. Working on international affairs, I felt that I could help inject an anti-imperialist position not only into SNCC but into the black movement as a whole. For all the people and nations with whom we would want to have international associations were against racism, capitalism, and imperialism. In addition, they were striving in the main to build socialist societies. I was never able to get SNCC to declare itself for socialism, but I did not worry about that too much at the time. To have achieved a realization that our fight was against racism, capitalism, and imperialism represented a major victory in itself.
>
> (Forman 1972, 481)

SNCC took a position in favor of the Palestinian struggle in opposition to the aggression of Israel, and that led to Zionist attacks and eventually SNCC's decline (Carson 1995, 265–86).

The BPP's position was similar to SNCC's position as defined by Forman, but the BPP went further by declaring itself for socialism. The Panthers had representatives go to many countries to establish international solidarity relations. One of the most useful connections was made at the 1969 Pan-African Cultural Festival held in Algeria. Eldridge Cleaver had gone underground, but surfaced in Algeria:

> The week of the United Front Against Fascism Conference in Oakland in July 1969, Eldridge Cleaver returned to public view at the Pan-African Cultural Festival in Algiers, Algeria. There the Black Panthers' anti-imperialist politics found fertile ground. The Party posited, as had the venerable W.E.B. DuBois twenty-five years earlier, that blacks in America were subjected and oppressed and denied self-determination much like those in the colonies in Africa.
>
> (Bloom and Martin 2016, 314)

The BPP connected Black radicalism to China, Vietnam, Cuba, and progressive forces in many European countries. Their newspaper, the *Black Panther*, carried many reports on international struggles.

The LRBW linked the Black Liberation Movement to the international situation based on the initiative of Black industrial workers, the first major case of militant activism on the shop floor since the 1930s. They were driven by the dual influences of Black Nationalism and Marxism, being influenced by James Boggs and Malcolm X. They called attention to the film that popularized the struggle in Algeria, *The Battle of Algiers*, and the writings of Frantz Fanon, Che Guevara, Ho Chi Minh, and Mao Tse-Tung.

More explicitly, several organizations developed with a diasporic vision and name: the All-African People's Revolutionary Party (AAPRP), led by Kwame Ture (aka Stokely Carmichael); the African People's Party (APP), led by Muhammad Ahmad (aka Max Stanford); and the African People's Socialist Party (APSP), led by Omali Yeshitela (aka Joseph Waller). All three initiated campaigns that linked the struggle in the USA with struggles throughout the African Diaspora. They were and have remained relatively small, but with a core of committed militants who have been an important influence in Black radical thought, especially in Black Studies.

The key unity movement that pulled all of these radical elements into one framework was the African Liberation Support Committee (ALSC). This organization was the result of an agreement made between the Liberation Front of Mozambique (FRELIMO) and Owusu Sadaukai (Howard Fuller) during a trip he made inside the liberated territory of Mozambique in 1971 (Fuller and Page 2014, 121–46). The first African Liberation Day called by activists in the African Diaspora brought together nearly 60,000 people in 6 demonstrations: Washington, DC (30,000), San Francisco (10,000), Toronto (3,000), Antigua (8,000), Dominica (5,000), and Grenada (2,000). Every militant radical tendency in the Black Liberation

Movement was involved in ALSC, from the most nationalist to the doctrinaire Marxists.

The 1973–1974 national executive committee of ALSC had eleven members, including six who were or became teachers in Black Studies programs at the college level. The armed struggle in the southern African colonies, along with Guinea-Bissau in the west, not only led to militant demonstrations, but also to the ideological growth of the movement based on research and study. The high point was a debate before a packed audience in Cramton Auditorium at Howard University. Documents made public leading up to the debate and the speeches during it were reprinted on college campuses and distributed throughout the African Diaspora, including by the *African World* from the Student Organization for Black Unity (SOBU) and *Race Today* in London (Fuller and Page 2014, 149–59; Bush 2000, 212).

Organized mobilization for support of African liberation was next taken up by TransAfrica, founded in 1977 by Randall Robinson, a Harvard-educated lawyer. He was aided by Willard Johnson, political science faculty at MIT, and Herschelle Challenor, a program officer at the Ford Foundation. The mission of TransAfrica was clear:

> The work of TransAfrica Forum is summarized by the words from a section of the declaration of the 5th Pan-African Congress (1945), which reads in part: "We believe the success of Afro-Americans is bound up with the emancipation of all African peoples and also other dependent peoples and laboring classes everywhere." As such, the organization serves as a major research, educational, and organizing institution for the African-American community offering constructive analyses of issues concerning U.S. policy as it affects Africa and the Diaspora in the Caribbean and Latin America. A center for activism focusing on conditions in the African World, we sponsor seminars, conferences, community awareness projects and training programs. These activities allow us to play a significant role in presenting to the general public alternative perspectives on the economic, political, and moral ramifications of U.S. foreign policy.
>
> (TransAfrica 2005)

Their work included helping to establish the Free South Africa Movement in 1984, which in turn led to Nelson Mandela being released from prison in 1990 and being able to run for and be elected president of South Africa in 1994.

6

African Diaspora Studies in Contemporary Academic Practice

Given this background to the rise of formal academic studies of the African Diaspora, it is clear that Black Studies has always come out of a historical context that has linked the experiences of African descendent peoples in the USA with African peoples all over the world. We will now turn to how Diaspora Studies has taken its place within the formal organization of Black Studies academic programs and departments.

NAMES OF BLACK STUDIES PROGRAMS

We conducted a series of studies in 2006–2007 that located 311 degree-granting programs in Black Studies. Table 2 analyzes the names of the units.

Table 2 Names of Degree Programs in Black Studies

Name	*Number*	*Percentage*
African American or Afro-American	100	32
Africana	63	20
African and African American	45	14
Black	37	12
Pan-African	7	2
African	5	2
Africology	1	0
Total Diasporic Names	258	83
Other names	53	17

Source: Alkalimat 2007.

Each region's Black Studies units have Diaspora names more than 90 percent of the time, except the Western region (57 percent). This is because, in the Western region of the USA, Blacks and Latinos have united in struggle to create multicultural or ethnic studies.

The states with the largest number of Black Studies programs are New York (in the East) and California (in the West). The regional pattern of Diaspora names holds—83 percent of the academic units in New York have Diasporic names and in California 55 percent do. The most popular Diaspora name is Africana Studies, and here the data are even more clear—in New York it is 40 percent and in California 5 percent. On the other hand, there is a reverse trend with regard to the name Ethnic Studies—in New York it is at 9 percent and in California at 32 percent.

We repeated the study in 2013. At this time, we made a distinction between national names (e.g., African American, Afro-American, and Black) and Diaspora names (Africana, African and African American Studies, and Pan-African Studies). Using this categorization, 49 percent of all units had Diaspora names. The regional breakdown directly correlates with migratory patterns from Africa and the Caribbean: 65 percent Northeast, 55 percent South, 40 percent Midwest, and 30 percent West.

Some programs have changed their name to include the concept of Diaspora, as shown in Table 3.

Table 3 Twelve Colleges and Universities with "Diaspora" in their Black Studies Program Name

Institution	*Name of Black Studies Unit*
American University	African American and African Diaspora Studies
Columbia University	African American and African Diaspora Studies
Indiana University	African American and African Diaspora Studies
University of Wyoming	African American and Diaspora Studies
Vanderbilt University	African American and Diaspora Studies
Boston College	African and African Diaspora Studies
Central Michigan University	African and African Diaspora Studies
College of Staten Island	African and African Diaspora Studies
University of Texas-Austin	African and African Diaspora Studies
University of Wisconsin at Milwaukee	African and African Diaspora Studies
Kenyon College	African Diaspora Studies
DePaul University	Africana and Black Diaspora Studies

KEY TEXTS THAT DEFINE DIASPORA STUDIES

The cornerstone for any curricular innovation is relevant scholarship codified into key texts that can anchor the required reading for courses. A set of key texts defines a necessary vocabulary, historical developments, social trends, key events, organizations, and personalities as the content of Diaspora Studies. Because of the take-off of academic Black Studies in the late 1960s and 1970s, and more recently, we can identify key texts in several content areas of Diaspora Studies (Table 4).

At the most general level, key texts open the door to the African Diaspora by documenting the direct historical connection between Africa and Black people in the West. Haley connected his family history back to a Gambian village and stimulated Black people to accept the challenge of pursuing their own family genealogy through space and time. Thompson, following the linguistic work of Lorenzo Turner and the anthropology of Melville Herskovits, traced art and philosophy from specific African cultures through the Caribbean to the USA. Stuckey did something similar by reinterpreting the collective cultural activism of Black people in the "ring shout," in which a counterclockwise dance would direct singing to the ancestors and gods. Gilroy posits a summary of cultural influences in what he terms the "Black Atlantic," an ecological system of interaction linking Africa, the Caribbean, the USA, and Europe (Haley 2016; R.F. Thompson 1984; Stuckey 1987; Gilroy 2007).

In recent times, the work of Gomez, Manning, and Falola present historical syntheses of the African Diaspora. Gomez presents a historical account of the transformation of separation through enslavement to reconnection: "Old World Dimensions" and "New World Realities." Manning, as a student of world history, presents a chronological synthesis: "Connections to 1600," "Survival 1600–1800," "Emancipation 1800–1900," "Citizenship 1900–1960," and "Equality 1960–2000." Falola posits a similar dialectic to Gomez ("The Old Diaspora: Slavery and Identity Politics" versus "The New Diaspora: Transnationalism and Globalization"). Falola adds some specificity with three chapters on "Yoruba Ethnicity in the Diaspora" (Gomez 2008; Manning 2010; Falola 2014).

Africa became a major focus for study based on four path-breaking books in the 1970s and 1980s by Chancellor Williams, Walter Rodney, Cheikh Anta Diop, and St. Clair Drake. Williams, Diop, and Drake focused on the historical origins of ancient African civilizations and their impact on world history, as well as a cultural basis for the unity of African

Table 4 Definitional Texts of African Diaspora Studies

Subject area	*Early Texts*	*Recent Texts*
General	Alex Haley, *Roots: The Saga of an American Family* (1976); Robert Farris Thompson, *Flash of the Spirit: African and Afro-American Art and Philosophy* (1983); Sterling Stuckey, *Slave Culture: Nationalist Theory and the Foundations of Black America* (1987); Paul Gilroy, *The Black Atlantic: Modernity and Double Consciousness* (1993)	Michael Gomez, *Reversing Sail: A History of the African Diaspora* (2005); Patrick Manning, *The African Diaspora: A History Through Culture* (2009); Toyin Falola, *The African Diaspora: Slavery, Modernity, and Globalization* (2013)
Africa	Walter Rodney, *How Europe Underdeveloped Africa* (1972); Cheikh Anta Diop, *The African Origin of Civilization: Myth or Reality?* (1974); St. Clair Drake, *Black Folk Here and There: An Essay in History and Anthropology* (1987)	Kwame Anthony Appiah and Henry Louis Gates, Jr., *Encyclopedia of Africa* (2010)
Pan-Africanism	C.L.R. James, *A History of Pan-African Revolt* (1969); Vincent Bakpetu Thompson, *Africa and Unity: The Evolution of Pan-Africanism* (1977); Ronald Walters, *Pan Africanism in the African Diaspora: An Analysis of Modern Afrocentric Political Movements* (1993)	Hakim Adi, *Pan-Africanism: A History* (2018)
Latin America	Leslie Rout, *The African Experience in Spanish America: 1502 to the Present* (1976); Ivan Van Sertima, *They Came Before Columbus: The African Presence in Ancient America* (1976)	Alejandro de la Fuente and George Reid Andrews, *Afro-Latin American Studies: An Introduction* (2018); Paul Ortiz, *An African American and Latinx History of the United States* (2018)
Anthologies	Joseph Harris, *Global Dimensions of the African Diaspora* (1993); Isidore Okpewho, Carole Boyce Davies, and Ali A. Mazrui, *African Diaspora: African Origins and New World Identities* (1999)	Carole Boyce Davies, *Encyclopedia of the African Diaspora* (2008) Dalene Clark Hine, Trica Danielle Keaton, and Stephen Small, *Black Europe and the African Diaspora* (2009); Tejumola Olaniyan and James H. Sweet, *The African Diaspora and the Disciplines* (2010)

cultures. Rodney targeted European colonialism and imperialism as the source of underdevelopment in Africa, linking its poverty to Europe's extraction of African wealth. Appiah and Gates edited a massive comprehensive compendium on Africa as a more recent useful text (C. Williams 1987; Asante 2007; Drake 1987; Rodney 1981; Appiah and Gates 2005).

Pan-Africanism is ideological advocacy for the liberation of African people. An early 1938 text by C.L.R. James was reprinted in the 1960s, and became a stimulus to pan-African thought. Buhle speaks to this:

> His greatest contribution lay in his comparative studies and their Pan-African synthesis. Unlike most other West Indians, who came to England thinking Africans to be savages, James insists he had been prepared to see them as other oppressed but intelligent, capable peoples. His foremost contribution lay in historical study. *A History of Negro Revolt* (1938) put together the material he had gathered on Toussaint and the Haitian revolution with assorted developments across the Black world.
>
> (Buhle 1989, 57)

Thompson and Walters published contrasting summary surveys of pan-Africanism. Thompson's focuses in on how pan-Africanism promoted unity on the African continent. Walters presents a study of political movements, mainly in relation to the movements in the United States, in Ghana, England, South Africa, Brazil, and the Caribbean. As indicated earlier, the work of Marika Sherwood and Hakim Adi has been the most productive and innovative scholarship in this area. Particularly powerful is the recent book by Adi, a tour de force in which he presents a global chronological analysis covering many organizations and people who are usually not included (Walters 1993; Adi and Sherwood 2007; Adi 2018; V.B. Thompson 1977).

Scholarship about the African Diaspora is so diverse that it frequently appears in an anthology of articles. J.E. Holloway (2005) presents articles that investigate how African culture has survived in the cultural practices of Black peoples in the West. More narrowly, Harris (1993) and Okpewho, Boyce Davies, and Mazrui (2002) present historical and cultural studies that target specific countries (e.g., Brazil, Cuba, and Haiti) and Hine, Keaton, and Small (2009) focus on Black Europe as part of the African Diaspora, with studies on Europe as a whole and specific studies on Italy, Germany, and France. Finally, it is important to mention Olaniyan and

Sweet (2010), as they present articles on how the African Diaspora has impacted academic disciplines within the social sciences and humanities. This review of key texts in Africa Diaspora Studies is merely a glimpse of a fast-growing scholarly literature.

KEY INSTITUTIONS FOR THE STUDY OF THE AFRICAN DIASPORA

The vanguard department for Afro-Latino Studies is at Hunter College CUNY in New York City:

> The Department of Africana and Puerto Rican/Latino Studies is an interdisciplinary program in the School of Arts and Sciences. The curriculum of the department, which offers courses in the humanities and social sciences, is devoted to the exploration and analysis of the history and culture of two heritages: the heritage of African people in the Americas, the Caribbean, and Africa; the heritage of Puerto Ricans; and the broader Latino experience in the United States. The multidisciplinary curriculum and the duality of heritages make the structure of the department unique and its curricular offerings challenging. Where it is applicable, the similarities and experiences of the two societies are emphasized but, generally speaking, the curriculum treats the two sequences as separate entities attempting to offer students of all backgrounds an alternative approach to the prevalent Eurocentric perspective.
>
> (Hunter College 2020)

The Center for Black Studies Research (CBSR) at the University of California at Santa Barbara (UCSB) is the lead unit that focuses on Haiti. "The CBSR houses the Congress of Santa Barbara (KOSANBA), a scholarly association for the study of Haitian Vodou and culture established at an international meeting held at UCSB in 1997" (UCSB 2020b).

Since 1995, Claudine Michel has been the senior editor of the main journal in the field (which is also based at UCSB), the *Journal of Haitian Studies*,

> the flagship journal in the field of Haitian Studies and the official publication of the Haitian Studies Association. It is the only refereed scholarly journal dedicated solely to scholarship on Haiti and Haiti's relations with the international community. It addresses histories of oppression

> and resistance movements as well as the political and cultural contributions that Haiti makes toward larger liberation struggles.
>
> (UCSB 2020a)

The unit at Michigan State University (MSU), by contrast, early on adopted a conceptual and comparative rather than national approach to the Diaspora under the leadership of Ruth Simms Hamilton (1931–2003). Her contribution is memorialized by the MSU Press with their "Ruth Simms Hamilton Diaspora Series":

> Named after the late Dr. Ruth Simms Hamilton, the book series highlights the global experiences and dynamic dimensions of peoples of African descent. It maps their historical and contemporary movements, speaks from their radical (unique) narratives, and explores their critical relationships with one another. By exploring Afrodescendants within their particular and broader sociocultural, historical, political, and economic contexts, it contemplates similarities, difference, continuity, and transformation.
>
> (Blain 2016)

The African and African American Studies program at Michigan State University has transitioned to become a department. Previously, they required their graduate students to have research experience in different parts of the African Diaspora:

> Alternative knowledge production of the experiences of African Americans, Diasporas and continental Africans requires tools of analysis that focus on alternative ways of knowing that will generate broader and richer interpretations of these experiences. That is why through our two required internship courses (AAAS 893a and AAAS 893c), the AAAS core curriculum utilizes a methodology that embraces community and indigenous cultural knowledge attained through visual and oral accounts as well as experiential engagement in the development of African American, African and Afro-Caribbean and Latin communities. This way, in concert with the Black Studies disciplinary tradition of socio-political activism and engagement, AAAS's core curriculum prepares its graduates to impart knowledge while learning. It prepares graduate students to effect social reform, social improvement and economic development for disadvantaged African American, African and Caribbean and Afro-Latin communities (AAAS 832).

> AAAS 893a, Internship in African American and African Studies (must be performed in an African American community). Student is expected to submit a research paper and/or make a research presentation to AAAS before a grade can be submitted.
>
> AAAS 893c, Internship in African American and African Studies (must be performed in a Black community outside of the United States). Student is expected to submit a research paper or make a research presentation to AAAS before a grade can be submitted.
>
> AAAS 832, Multi-Cultural Pedagogy and Methods Seminar in African American and African Studies (Methods, leadership and mentoring for graduate students of undergraduate students of color).
>
> (Michigan State University n.d.)

The University of California at Berkeley's doctoral program in African American Studies, despite the title, focuses broadly on the African Diaspora:

> Since its inception in 1970, African American Studies at Berkeley has continued to alter the very fabric of university life and teaching. The women and men of this field have integrated the study of the African Diaspora into the university in a way all people can participate and feel a part of. Over a span of 40 years, the Department has evolved into an academic unit that is respected as a model among departments nationally. That is, it has become an interdisciplinary, multi-racial intellectual center that hosts, attracts, and produces some of the most diverse, complex thinking, scholars and scholarship in the world.
>
> (R. Williams 2010)

KEY INDIVIDUALS IN AFRICAN DIASPORA STUDIES

More than any other country in the world, the USA has drawn scholars and students from all parts of the African Diaspora to study and work in its institutions of higher learning. This is a "brain drain" from less resourced institutions in the third world. Yet, it has created a global standard for Diaspora Studies that requires both content and people who reflect the African Diaspora. The people mentioned here are only a small sample of people from outside of the USA who have made major contributions to Diaspora Studies in that country.

At Northwestern University, two of the many people who can be mentioned from the faculty history are Jan Carew (1920–2012) and Dennis

Brutus (1924–2009). Carew joined Northwestern in 1973 as a professor of African American and Third World Studies, chairing the department from 1973 to 1976 and retiring in 1987. Darlene Clark Hines states about him that "he helped to extend our understanding of the African diaspora through his illuminating scholarship, teaching and service. … I will always treasure his wisdom, draw inspiration from his lifelong commitment to social justice, and relish his quiet dignity" (Anyaso 2013). Carew wrote several novels based on the history of his home country of Guyana, as well as an insightful collection of essays on the African presence in the Americas. He also wrote an illuminating book on Malcolm X, based on his interactions with the latter and research he did on Malcolm X's mother, who was from Grenada (J. Carew 1961; J.R. Carew and Dawes 2009; J. Carew and X 1994; J.R. Carew 2006).

Brutus was a South African refugee who taught at Northwestern from 1971 to 1986. He was active in the anti-apartheid movement, especially in sports. He was a poet and published many collections of his work. One of his great accomplishments was working with a global network of African writers to share their work in the United States (Karim and Sustar 2006; Brutus 1991; 1973).

There are scholars from the African Diaspora in most programs. Some examples of note have been the following: at the University of Massachusetts Amherst, Chinua Achebe (Nigeria), Abdulrahman Mohamed Babu (Tanzania), and Ekwueme Michael Thelwell (Jamaica); at Yale University, Hazel Carby (UK) and Paul Gilroy (UK); at Syracuse University, Horace Campbell (Jamaica) and Micere Githae Mugo (Kenya); at Cornell University, Locksley Edmondson (Jamaica) and Carole Boyce Davies (Trinidad and Tobago); at the University of Michigan, Lorna Goodison (Jamaica); at City University of New York Graduate Center, Édouard Glissant (Martinique); at Harvard University, Orlando Patterson (Jamaica), Alejandro de la Fuente (Cuba), and Biodun Jeyifo (Nigeria); and at Brown University, Anthony Bogues (Jamaica) and Brian Meeks (Jamaica). Even based on this small sample, it is safe to say that African Diaspora scholars have been firmly based in Black Studies programs in the USA.

DIASPORA STUDIES AS AFRO-LATINO STUDIES

An important consideration for Diaspora Studies is the relationship between people who identify as African Americans and Latinos (Yelvington 2001). There was considerable overlap, because the European slave trade imported more Africans into South and Central America than into the United States. Two contrasting arguments were made in the 1970s by Leslie Rout (1935–1987) and Ivan Van Sertima (1935–2009). Rout (1976) surveys the African experience in Latin America by discussing the slave trade, enslavement, and African resistance, including the fight against colonization for independence. He then discusses the post-independence experience of Black people in twelve countries. Van Sertima (2003) advances the thesis that Africans came to the New World on their own, before Columbus.

An important initiative that demonstrated productive scholarship in Afro-Latino Studies was the launch of the journal *Afro-Hispanic Review* in 1981. There were eighteen consulting editors, of whom six were based in Latin America countries: Colombia (three), Ecuador, Peru, and Puerto Rico.

More recently, Alejandro de la Fuente and George Reid Andrews (as co-authors) and Paul Ortiz have published books that intend to make a formal link between Black Studies and Latino Studies. Fuente and Andrews construct an anthology with fifteen articles in four sections: "Inequalities," "Politics," "Culture," and "Transnational Spaces." They make the argument that they are creating a new field of study, although they fail to refer to previous work:

> The volume seeks to introduce readers to the dynamic and growing field of Afro-Latin American studies. We define the field, first, as the study of the people of African ancestry in Latin America, and second, as the study of the larger societies in which those people live. Under the first heading, scholars study Black histories, cultures, strategies, and struggles in the region. Under the second, they study blackness, and race more generally, as a category of difference, as an engine of stratification and inequality, and as a key variable in processes of national formation.
>
> (Fuente and Andrews 2018, 1)

Ortiz bases his book on personal experience:

> At Duke University, I offered a seminar titled Black/Latino Histories, Cultures, and Politics, as part of a one-year visiting assistant professorship after I finished my history doctorate there in 2000. I had already taught separate courses in African American and Latinx studies as

> a graduate student. However, Duke students involved in labor organizing, human rights, and health advocacy told me that what they desperately needed was a new kind of course that placed the histories of the Black and Latinx diaspora in dialog. Students were searching for a course of study that addressed the upsurge of immigration by people from Central America and Mexico to North Carolina. Lacking in critical discourse were insights into how these demographic shifts would impact the potential for social change in a state where African Americans had historically been oppressed. Even now, students in my African American and Latinx research seminar at the University of Florida are asking questions about the history of the Americas that cannot be answered using historical frameworks that have been rendered obsolete by the forces of globalization.
>
> (Ortiz 2018, x–xi)

Several institutions already make the connection between Black Studies and Latinx Studies, as shown in Table 5. All four institutions are in New York State, two in New York City. As of 2018, the state of New York had the second largest population of Puerto Ricans and the largest population of Dominican Americans in 2017 (Vargas-Ramos 2018; Noe-Bustamante, Flores, and Shah n.d.).

Table 5 Four Black Studies Programs Named to Incorporate Latino Studies

Institution	*Name of Program*
Baruch College CUNY	Black and Latino Studies
Colgate University	Africana and Latin American Studies
Hunter College CUNY	Department of Africana and Puerto Rican/Latino Studies
SUNY Oneonta	Department of Africana and Latino Studies

To gauge the possibility of building a unified study program of Afro-Latino Studies, we included the following question in our 2013 study of 361 Black Studies programs (Alkalimat et al. 2013, 11): How many have Latino Studies programs? We excluded all programs strictly focused on Latin America, in order to have a peer comparison with the Latino nationalities in the United States, mainly Mexican and Puerto Rican, but including people from all countries in the Caribbean and Central and South America. Of all the schools with Black Studies, 53 percent have Latino Studies, with clear regional differences being evident: 91 percent of units in the West do, 61 percent in the Midwest, 42 percent in the Northeast, and 26 percent in the South.

In our 2006 study of Black Studies programs in the state of New York, we documented courses on the Latino experience based on course titles (Table 6).

Table 6 Percentage of Black Studies Course Names that Include Latino Topics in New York

Course title reference	*Number of courses*	*Number of schools*	*Percentage of all schools*
Puerto Rico	29	3	5
Brazil	6	4	7
Dominican Republic	5	3	5
All country names	40	8	14
Latino	15	5	9
Latin America	11	10	17
Hispanic	4	3	5
The Americas	2	2	3
All regional names	32	14	24
Other than country or regional name	6	4	7
TOTAL	78	21	36

However, language remains a key problem to deal with regarding bringing Black Studies and Latino Studies together. In our 2006/2007 data, only a small number of Black Studies programs include the study of Spanish in their curriculum: just 3 percent of California programs and 9 percent of New York. This compares to the study of traditional African languages, which is in the curriculum of 13 percent of programs in California and 17 percent in New York (Alkalimat 2006, 21–22; 2007, 14).

One of the reasons that this Black–Latino collaboration is on the rise is the agency of the African descendent populations in countries like Cuba, Puerto Rico, Peru, Brazil, Venezuela, and Colombia. The ideological basis for this has been championed by such important leaders as Fidel Castro, who proclaimed that all Cubans are Africans, and Hugo Chávez, who embraced his identity as an Afro-Venezuelan and led a campaign to end racism in that country.

KEY ORGANIZATIONS FOR AFRICAN DIASPORA STUDIES

Perhaps the most significant force in academic activity is the organizational impetus that provides a context for collectivizing research developments and building networks for research and teaching. As early as 1969, militant Black Studies activists broke away from the mainstream African Studies Association to create an organization that reflected the ideological agency to build unity across the African Diaspora. John Henrik Clarke, one of the leaders of this movement, stated the mission of the new organization, the African Heritage Studies Association:

> The intent of the African Heritage Studies Association is to use African history to effect a world union of African people. The association of scholars of African descent is committed to the preservation, interpretation, and creative presentation of the historical and cultural heritage of African people, both on the ancestral soil of Africa and in diaspora in the Americas and throughout the world. We interpret African history from a Pan-Africanist perspective that defines all black people as an African people.
>
> (Clarke 1976, 11)

A countermotion was organized by the mainstream Social Science Research Council (SSRC). This was an organization that brought all of the professional social science organizations under a single umbrella. The SSRC took the lead in organizing academics into area studies, international programming that connected with post-World War II designs of the USA to extend its influence in competition with European colonialism. They established a Committee on Afro-American Societies and Cultures (1968–1975), which was in direct opposition to the rise of Black Power thinking among Black academics. This was a move by white academics led by Sidney Mintz of Yale University to dominate, while Black academics would revolt and refuse to fully participate. The same thing had happened in the 1940s, when Melville Herskovits organized the Committee on Negro Studies within the American Council of Learned Societies' Committee on Negro Studies, but Black academics would not join it (Yelvington 2018).

The major current organizational initiative for African Diaspora Studies is the Association for the Study of the Worldwide African Diaspora (ASWAD). They reach out to the African Diaspora by having their website in six languages (English, Spanish, French, Dutch, Portuguese, and Krio). ASWAD has held their international conference every two years since 2001, and half have been outside of the United States:

2001	New York City
2003	Chicago
2005	Rio de Janeiro, Brazil
2007	Barbados
2009	Accra, Ghana
2011	Pittsburgh
2013	Santo Domingo, Dominican Republic
2015	Charleston, South Carolina
2017	Seville, Spain
2019	Williamsburg, Virginia

ASWAD sets forth their aims clearly in their mission statement:

> The Association for the Study of the Worldwide African Diaspora (ASWAD) is a not-for-profit, tax deductible organization of international scholars seeking to further our understanding of the African Diaspora, that is, the dispersal of people of African descent throughout the world. Through the examination of history, dance, anthropology, literature, women's studies, education, geology, political science, sociology, language, art, music, film, theater, biology, photography, etc., we seek to share the most recent research both within and across disciplinary and other conventional boundaries. We seek to do this by way of conferences and symposia held periodically, as well as through publications. In addition, we look for ways to share our work with students and the general community. All who share such interests are welcome to join ASWAD.
>
> (ASWAD 2020)

So far we have discussed African Diaspora Studies within the United States, and how people have migrated to the USA and how institutions and organizations have reached out to the African Diaspora. We now turn to African Diaspora Studies in the African Diaspora outside of the USA.

7

Diaspora Studies in the African Diaspora

At a global level, there have been two kinds of analysis of African peoples: the efforts of the colonial powers to provide the knowledge base for their policies of direct and indirect rule over their subject peoples; and the efforts of these very oppressed peoples to create a knowledge base for their liberation. In each case, the colonial empires covered a large swath of the African Diaspora and therefore Diaspora Studies was taken up in both approaches. Our survey will discuss this by geographical regions.

EUROPE

The European study of the Black experience has been dominated by a colonial point of view, but has been challenged more and more from the critical Black perspective, what is being called by some scholars a movement to "decolonize the mind." From this perspective, Stephen Small offers an indictment of academic literature:

> The mainstream academic literature on Black Europe is highly problematic. In focusing on the past, it is shaped by a relentless propensity to highlight national glory and uplift, while ignoring inveterate racism, brutality and exploitation. In focusing on the present, it operates under the thrall of a colonized mind. It highlights immigration, adaptation (or failed assimilation), tolerance and gratitude. It addresses Black people primarily as sub-categories of other groups—whether immigrants, refugees or asylums seekers, Muslims, criminals or sex workers, or as undifferentiated category of "women." In general, this literature pays scant attention to race/gender intersections, and is overwhelmingly conceptualized and produced via national-specific studies that foreground and emphasize unique national trajectories and contempo-

> rary configurations; while downplaying, marginalizing or denying the underlying commonalities that they all so clearly share.
>
> (Small 2018, 218)

Thus, we are not going to focus on this literature except as a background to each national case we will include. What is important is to clarify the demographic reality of Black Europe. Small provides a clear picture of Black Europe:

> I estimate that over 93% of Black people in Europe (6,717,000) can be found in just twelve nations (which have a total estimated population of more than 380 million people). … The United Kingdom (2 million); France (2 million); Netherlands (323,000); Portugal (150,000); Belgium (250,000); Spain (500,000); Italy (325,000); Germany (800,000); Denmark (46,000); Norway (78,000); Sweden (180,000); Republic of Ireland (65,000). … Within these twelve nations, Black people are concentrated in a limited number of urban areas—mainly because this is where the jobs were to be found when Black people were recruited in significant numbers from the early 1900s, or where they were directed as refugees since the 1990s.
>
> (Small 2018, 76–77)

So out of the forty-six countries in Europe, the Black population is concentrated in twelve, but of that 55 percent of all Black people in Europe are in the UK and France, although this does include Black people in Martinique and Guadeloupe (700,000), as they are "legally" departments of France. Clearly, the main Black presence in Europe is found in the UK, specifically in the cities of London, Birmingham, and Manchester.

McEachrane presents an analysis of what he calls reconceptualizing the African Diasporas in Europe:

> [W]e should distinguish between continental, cultural and racial conceptualisations of African diasporas—not least when studying and understanding these in Europe. Although so-called Old African Diasporas in the New World, that were created out of the Middle Passage, developed overlapping racial and cultural identities, in contemporary Europe the situation is more complicated. Here we largely find so-called New African Diasporas with more immediate backgrounds in Africa.
>
> (McEachrane 2021, 2)

He goes on to sum up three waves of studies that focus on the African Diasporas in Europe.

> The first wave, represented by the works of Stuart Hall and Paul Gilroy, is marked by an anti-nationalist and anti-essentialist expansion of African Diaspora Studies beyond the USA and the New World to also include Black political culture and identity making in the UK, Europe and across the entire "Black Atlantic" as Gilroy famously termed it. A second wave, represented by the works of Michelle Wright, Gloria Wekker, Fatima El-Tayeb, and others, have called for an expanded understanding of African diasporas in Europe—beyond the focus on those that resulted from the Middle Passage—to include New African Diasporas and a greater multiplicity of Black identities ... I make an argument for a (re)conceptualisation of African diasporas in Europe toward a racial and socio-political sense that includes, but goes beyond, matters of identity and culture.
>
> (McEachrane 2021, 2)

While these are important distinctions, what follows is a description of what research and cultural study has been done in several countries.

ENGLAND

Two mainstream institutions in which Africa has been studied to maintain the imperial colonial policy of England are the School of Oriental and African Studies (SOAS) University of London and Rhodes House of Oxford University. In addition, the Institute of Race Relations in London (IRR) was established in 1958 at the time of "race riots" in the UK. The role of these institutions changed with the historical mandates for British imperialism, especially the demands of the Black colonized peoples.

For their part, Africans in the UK exercised their agency in an academic setting by founding the West African Students' Union (WASU) in 1925 in London (Olusanya 1982; Adi 1998). It became the center of discourse about Africa by Africans, housed in a physical building called Africa House.

One of the historical events that symbolized a fundamental change in the Black presence in England was the arrival of the ship *Empire Windrush* in London from Kingston, Jamaica, in 1948. Over five hundred West Indian workers came and brought the agency of the African Diaspora into full view, now inside England and not just as part of the external empire. Stuart Hall defines the moment:

> Postwar black migration, beginning in earnest with the arrival of the *Empire Windrush* in 1948, transformed the face of British society and brought British identity itself into question. It touched a deep reservoir of negative and stereotypical attitudes in Britain and racialized differences—a legacy inherited from Britain's imperial role and brought to the surface by the arrival of significant numbers of black migrants from the Caribbean on the "home territory" of a society which imagined itself to be liberal, tolerant, and racially homogeneous.
>
> (Hall and Morley 2019a, 367)

This event is the mass motion that contextualizes, before and after, the great contributions made by the Trinidad Three: C.L.R. James, George Padmore, and Claudia Jones. These three people made great contributions in culture and politics, creating links throughout the African Diaspora from their base in London. Especially important in cultural terms is the analysis of cricket by James and the creation of Carnival in London by Jones (James 1993; Davies 2008; Sherwood 2015).

An important organization that added great content to cultural awareness of the African Diaspora was the Caribbean Artists Movement (CAM), which existed for seven years (1966–1972). This organization was created by Caribbean artists who had relocated to London: Edward Kamau Brathwaite (1930–2020, Barbados), John La Rose (1927–2006, Trinidad and Tobago), and Andrew Salkey (1928–1995, Jamaica). Their beginning was very similar to that of the Black Arts Movement in the USA. The definitive history of CAM is by Anne Walmsley (1992), who links CAM to Black Studies in the form of Caribbean studies (Walmsley 1992, 315–16).

Alleyne carries forward an analysis of the activities of John La Rose, what he calls the New Beacon Circle, named after the bookshop and publishing company formed by John La Rose and his partner Sarah White. Their work in the International Book Fair of Radical Black and Third World Books brought forth a renaissance of Black cultural and intellectual production (Alleyne 2007).

As mentioned, Stuart Hall led a major movement in cultural studies that connected major theorists to the issues of identity and the cultural production of the African Diasporas. His most famous quote is "Race is the modality in which class is lived." He was an important voice linking the Black struggle to the class struggle (Hall and Morley 2019a; 2019b; Hall, Gilroy, and Gilmore 2021).

During Ken Livingstone's term as the radical mayor of London (2000–2008), there was a heightened stream of government funding for Black cultural work that led to an increase in the number of journals, book publishers, art galleries, and cultural organizations. In 1987, October was chosen as the annual UK Black History Month, following the lead of the USA, where February was designated as Black History Month.

Following the pattern in the USA, several initiatives have developed to build a Black Studies presence in mainstream educational institutions of higher education.

1. Community initiatives inside and outside the educational system
2. Undergraduate degree programs
3. Graduate degree programs
4. Specialized research institutes
5. Archives and museums
6. Individual academic appointments
7. Using a listserv to share information

Gus John identifies the form of the initiative in local areas:

> Schools in some local areas in Britain introduced Black Studies programmes. The rationale, understandably was that black students would have their self-esteem enhanced by learning about achievements of blacks in history, learning that black could indeed be "beautiful" and that we are not intrinsically backward. Characters from history and the particular struggles they waged against all odds were identified and discussed. Many such historical figures became household names.
>
> (John 2006, 109)

Black Parents Movement organized and founded Saturday school to supplement what was going on in their children's formal education. Black Studies survived for a time in the community as acts of self-determination (Andrews 2013).

It is important to point out the contributions that Black women have made to understanding the Black experience, especially in clarifying the role of gender and the struggle against patriarchy. Margaret Busby made important contributions as a publisher and editor. She established a canon of Black women's literature. She edited the anthology *Daughters of Africa* (1992) and its follow-up *New Daughters of Africa* (2019). Another important contributor to Black Women's Studies in the UK is Stella Dadzie. She was a founding member of the Organisation of Women of African and Asian Descent (OWAAD) in the 1970s. She wrote and edited several books that helped advanced anti-racist practices in education and advanced Black Women's Studies (Bryan, Dadzie, and Scafe 1985; Dadzie 2000; 2020).

Another great community-based Black Studies activity was carnival. Groups plan for the Carnival over the course of a year, preparing costumes, studying their theme, and practicing. Each Carnival group is a school. Michael La Rose founded the People's War Carnival Band in London. Michael was elected vice-chairperson of the Carnival Development Committee (CDC) and later founded the Association for a People's Carnival (APC) and Reclaim Our Carnival (ROC). He explains the background of Carnival:

> We are all familiar with images of Notting Hill Carnival in London or the West Indian Parade in New York. They are of masquerade (costumes), music, dancing and happy people. But what is behind the masquerade? There is a rich history, culture, language and a lot of hard work and struggle. The Caribbean Carnival described here is a celebration of the end of slavery as well as an affirmation of survival. Carnival is where Africa and Europe met in the cauldron of the Caribbean slave system to produce a new festival for the world.
>
> The four elements of Carnival are song, music, costume and dance, which translate as calypso/soca, steelpan, mas (masquerade), and "wine" (dance) in the Caribbean Carnival. Trinidad is the island in the Caribbean with the most developed and well-known Carnival. Wherever the Trinidadians go they transplant their Carnival culture. Carnival first came to Trinidad with the French Catholic plantation slave owners during the 1700s. It consisted of indoor masked balls and was an exclusive, high society event.
>
> (La Rose 2015)

An undergraduate degree program in Black Studies has recently been established at Birmingham City University (BCU) under the leadership of Kehinde Andrews (Andrews 2018a; Small 2018, 168; Andrews, cited in Bhambra, Gebrial, and Nişancioğlu 2018, 129–44). He embraces the radicalism of the early development of Black Studies in the United States:

> At the heart of BCU's Black Studies program is a direct critique of the university establishment. We are currently teaching our first cohort of students. I have spent so much time questioning the role of the university in general, and academics in particular, that the students have been wondering why they came. But this critical introduction was necessary to shake them (and us) out of complacency. A degree in Black Studies is nothing to celebrate until we can prove that it is useful in terms of changing the conditions facing Black communities. Black Studies is far more than just learning about Black people, it is the "science of liberation," engaging with the mechanisms to improve conditions for Africa and the Diaspora.
>
> (Andrews 2018b)

The Black Studies program at Birmingham City University has held two major conferences, and in the spirit of the 1960s Black Studies movement in the USA has been community oriented. Andrews makes this point in a *Black Scholar* article:

> Black Studies offers the possibility of transforming the relationship between the university and the community. The ivory tower of the university has often treated Black communities as deviant subcultures to be studied. It is no surprise that during the early days of my doctoral research I was accused by some in my community of being a "spy" because of my role. The transformative potential of Black Studies lies in the wider community being so instrumental in the battle to see it established in the first place. Hopefully, by embedding the community component into the discipline it can serve, rather than exploit or ignore, community needs.
>
> (Andrews 2016)

As I have indicated, the scholarship of Hakim Adi has been a major force in the development of Black Studies in the UK, especially his research work on pan-Africanism with his colleague Marika Sherwood. He has had an appointment at the University of Chichester as professor of the History of Africa and the African Diaspora. He is now leading an online MA program in the History of Africa and the African Diaspora (Adi 2017).

In addition to his formal educational leadership, he is one of the organizers training youth in a Black Studies program called The Young Historians Project:

> We are a non-profit organisation formed by young people encouraging the development of young historians of African and Caribbean heritage in Britain. We're a team of young people aged 16–25 working on dynamic projects, documenting pivotal and often overlooked historical moments.
>
> We hope that through this and future projects more young people of African and Caribbean heritage will rediscover history and develop the skills to become the historians of the future. Each one, Teach one.
>
> (Young Historians 2020)

Marika Sherwood and Hakim Adi led the development of an organization that promoted Black Studies.

> The Black and Asian Studies Association (BASA) was set up in London in 1991. Until October 1997 it was known as the Association for the Study of African, Caribbean and Asian Culture and History In Britain (ASACACHIB). Founder members who attended the inaugural meeting at the Institute of Commonwealth Studies on 5 February 1991 include Stephen Bourne, Jeffrey Green, David Killingray, Marika Sherwood and Hakim Adi. The Association was set up to foster research and to provide information on the history of Black peoples in Britain. This has been done through a triannual Newsletter—first published in September 1991—and an annual conference. They have also worked with local organisations to highlight the Black Presence in British society.
>
> (BASA n.d.)

They published sixty-four issues of their newsletter from 1991 to 2013. A very important video documentation of a conference was made to sum up the twenty-seven-year history of BASA that featured both Marika Sherwood and Hakim Adi (BASA 2018).

Another graduate-level program has been started at Goldsmiths, University of London. They are offering an MA in Black British History, an MA in Black British Literature, and an MA in Race, Media, and Social Justice. A PhD in Black Studies has been started at the University of Nottingham. The University of West London has an MA in Global Black Studies, Decolonization, and Social Justice; and the University of Bristol offers an MA in Black Humanities.

A fourth example of Black Studies development in the UK is in the form of a research center. One recently established is the Sarah Parker Remond Centre for the Study of Racism and Racialisation at the University College London, directed by Paul Gilroy:

> UCL's Sarah Parker Remond Centre for the Study of Racism & Racialisation was established in 2019 in response to student-led demands for the transformation of the curriculum and a reparative reckoning with the powerful, but often unacknowledged, colonial and imperial histories of our university, our city and our nation. ... Alongside its role in coordinating and facilitating existing initiatives, the Centre is committed to the production of new, historically-informed, critical knowledge addressed to some of the most urgent social and political questions of our time. Its affiliates explore the impact of racism, scientific, metaphysical and cultural, on the development of all varieties of academic inquiry. There is particular interest in the complex legacies of race-thinking across the Humanities and Social Sciences as well as the continuing effects of racialised inequality in the workings of government, law, the arts, culture, science, technology and social life.
>
> (Gilroy 2020)

Another academic center is the Institute for Black Atlantic Research (IBAR) at the University of Central Lancashire (UCLan).

> IBAR is a research institute utilizing UCLan's interdisciplinary and internationally renowned research pedigree in African Atlantic studies particularly in the Schools of Humanities and the Social Sciences and Art, Design and Performance (ADP). IBAR fosters partnerships with museums, galleries, broadcasters and community organisations to promote the study of the Black Atlantic in the North West and beyond Partner organisations including the International Slavery Museum, Whitworth Art Gallery, Manchester Art Gallery, Tate Galleries, Front Room Theatre Company, Lancashire Museums, Lancaster Jazz Festival and Preston Black History Group. Its emphasis on art and culture makes it distinctive in comparison to other centres in the field locally,

> nationally and internationally which are typically devoted to historical and/or social science concerns.
>
> (UCLan 2020)

The Ahmed Iqbal Ullah Race Relations Resource Centre and Education Trust is a research agency located on the campus of the University of Manchester. Their activities include "running oral history projects, hosting events and exhibitions, and working with schools, for past, present and future generations." They maintain an extensive library that covers Black Studies and other issues of "race relations" (AIUET 2020).

One key archive is the Black Cultural Archives located in the Brixton area of London.

> Black Cultural Archives grew from a community response to the New Cross Massacre (1981), the Police and Criminal Evidence Act (1984); underachievement of Black children in British schools, the failings of the Race Relations Act 1976, and the negative impacts of racism against, and a lack of popular recognition of, and representation by people of African and Caribbean descent in the UK. Our founders, including the iconic Len Garrison, came to the conclusion that what was needed was a space where members of the community, especially young people, could come and find positive representations of themselves in history and culture. This act of self-help expanded into the creation of what our founders called an "archive museum" that evidenced and painted a more comprehensive picture of Black presence in Britain.
>
> (Black Cultural Archives 2020)

Another mainstream institution is the International Slavery Museum located in the historical slave port of Liverpool.

> The International Slavery Museum opened on 23 August 2007. Not only was this the date of the annual Slavery Remembrance Day, but the year 2007 was particularly significant as it was the bicentenary of the abolition of the British slave trade.
>
> The International Slavery Museum highlights the international importance of slavery, both in a historic and contemporary context. Working in partnership with other museums with a focus on freedom

> and enslavement, the museum provides opportunities for greater awareness and understanding of the legacy of slavery today.
>
> It is located in Liverpool's Albert Dock, at the centre of a World Heritage site and only yards away from the dry docks where 18th century slave trading ships were repaired and fitted out.
>
> (National Museums Liverpool 2020)

Individuals have had various kinds of academic appointments, both full-time and as adjuncts, without the formal title of Black Studies but functionally playing that kind of role. Pat Daley is Professor of the Human Geography of Africa at Oxford University. She was co-founder of the Oxford University Black and Minority Ethnic staff network (University of Oxford 2020). Olivette Otele is currently Professor of History of Slavery and Memory of Enslavement at University of Bristol and Vice-President of the Royal Historical Society (Wikipedia 2020b).

The British Black Studies Listserv is a key vehicle for sharing information in Black Studies. It is a daily list, archiving its content back to its origin in 2014 (British Black Studies n.d.). There is also a section of the British Association for American Studies that includes Black topics in its annual meeting and website (British Association for American Studies 2020). Another organization is the Society for Multi-Ethnic Studies: Europe and the Americas, which was established in 1998 and holds biennial international conferences (MESEA n.d.).

There are local Black initiatives in many UK cities, for example, the Preston Black History Group (2020) and the Northamptonshire Black History Association (2020), as well as special exhibits, such as a recent one on Black Coal Miners (Digging Deep 2020).

FRANCE

Black Studies in France covers several stages. During the 1930s, a small group of Black intellectuals in Paris developed the concept of négritude and proclaimed the autonomy of Black consciousness as their main value orientation in politics and culture. The next important influence comes from African-American expatriate artists, writers, and musicians. In the post-World War I and II years, several initiatives developed through the 1960s that linked Black cultural and intellectual development in France to the global African Diaspora. Finally, Black Studies in higher education begins in a formal way in the 1960s and continues into the twenty-first century.

The entire historical development of Black agency in France was chronicled by Macodou Ndiaye and Florence Alexis in their compilation *Les Noirs en France: Du 18ème siècle a nos jours* (2019). An appreciation of the uniqueness of Black culture and Black people by the French, autonomous from French culture, emerged in the 1920s, as described by Tyler Stovall:

> Blackness became the rage in Paris during the 1920s. The distinguished art collector Paul Guillaume became a champion of primitivism, at one point asserting that "the intelligence of modern man (or woman) must be Negro." The radical group of Parisian writers and artists who took the name surrealists championed black art for its subjectivity and directness of expression. In Paris black was not just beautiful, but creative, mysterious, seductive, and soulful.
>
> (Stovall 2012, 31)

To fully implement their colonialism, the French government set up the Institut Français d'Afrique Noire (French Institute of Black Africa) in 1938, which eventually had eleven offices throughout the colonies. This was the scientific and cultural institution for training colonial and eventually neocolonial administrators to rule more effectively. They set up the University of Dakar in 1957 to prepare indigenous staff to maintain the French colonial administration. After independence, most of these offices remained active, often turning into national archives or cultural museums. Its main center has always been in Dakar, Senegal.

A breakthrough by Black people themselves came in the years following World War I in opposition to the dominant French policy of assimilation. This policy backfired, as students recruited from the colonies revolted in search of their own Black identity. *La Revue du monde noir* (*Review of the Black World*) was founded in 1931 by Paulette Nardal of Martinique and Leo Sajous of Haiti. In 1932, a group of students from Martinique, under the influence of Marxism and Surrealism, organized a journal, *Légitime défense* (*The Right to Self-Defense*). This was a movement somewhat limited to the West Indian students linked to the French Communist Party. Both journals created a new possibility for Black self-expression.

As part of the first wave, a major figure from Senegal, Léopold Sédar Senghor (1906–2001) began his professional career in France in the 1920s. He arrived in France in 1928, and eventually passed his *aggregation*, which qualified him to teach. French culture was based on the purity of the French language, and Senghor specialized in its grammar and rose to the highest level of achievement. He taught in France from 1935 to 1945, and later after returning home was elected president of Senegal from 1960 to 1980.

Aimé Césaire (1913–2008) came to France from Martinique in 1932 to study at the elite Lycée Louis-le-Grand (high school) and the École Normale Supérieure (college). Césaire went beyond the French language and specialized in Latin and Greek, by which he demonstrated his mastery of European culture—but that was not his only goal. He united both Africans and West Indians, based on his view that "The road to West Indian national identity lay through Africa" (Césaire, cited in Tomich 1979, 353). Césaire created a journal, *L'Etudiant Noir* (*The Black Student*), to advocate this view that was markedly different from the two previously mentioned journals, in 1935.

The journal made the double move, away from Eurocentrism and toward the unity of Africa and the African Diaspora. Tomich places this in context:

> Césaire, Damas, Senghor and the group around *L'Etudiant Noir* aligned themselves firmly on the Left, but they tried in their various ways to adapt Marxism to the particularities of the Negro condition. European Marxism alone was not adequate to fit the needs of these young colonial intellectuals and they cast their nets more widely to develop the foundations of their revolt. … The task *L'Etudiant Noir* set for itself was the disalienation of the colonized Black. They no longer desired to integrate themselves into French life, but rather aspired to be the autonomous creators of their own culture. There was a need for new values and new images of the Black man to replace those supplied by the colonial regime.
>
> (Tomich 1979, 371–72)

Another leading figure in the development of négritude was Alioune Diop (1910–1980). He left Senegal for Paris in 1937, and following others before him, became a teacher and an elected politician. He founded an important journal in 1947, *Présence Africaine*. Under the same name, he had expanded this by 1949 to include a book publishing firm and a bookstore located on Rue des Écoles near the Sorbonne. The focus was on Africa, the Caribbean, and African Americans, except for an important 1959 book, *Un Nègre à Paris* (*An African in Paris*), by Bernard Dadie

(1984) on being African in Paris. Présence Africaine's best-selling book of all time is *Discourse on Colonialism* by Césaire, published in 1955.

Diop was instrumental in organizing the formation of the First International Congress of Negro Writers and Artists in 1956, convened at the Sorbonne in Paris.

This meeting exploded with a confrontation over a militant anti-colonialism with a Marxist theoretical bent versus the moderate American delegation and Africans influenced by religious and cultural tendencies. Diop was nevertheless able to produce a final resolution that held together the unity of those assembled there. After following up with the Second Congress of Negro Writers and Artists in Rome in 1959, Senghor, as president of Senegal, took the lead in organizing the First World Festival of Negro Arts in Dakar (1966). Those involved in these international meetings, from all political positions, became the authors and cultural creators of material that has anchored Black Studies curriculum up to today.

Another major development was the influence that African-American expatriates had on the diverse Black population in Paris, both after World War I and then again after World War II. There were so many, as Black intellectuals of all kinds found Paris an escape from the racist pressure in the USA. After World War I, key people were Henry Ossawa Tanner, Anna Julia Cooper, Loïs Mailou Jones, Josephine Baker, and Bricktop (Ada Louise Smith). After World War II, there were three writers who stood out after arriving in Paris: Richard Wright (1946), James Baldwin (1948), and Chester Himes (1953).

Two major tendencies took off and attacked the very foundations of French Eurocentric domination, both in theory and in practice. The thinkers who led the way are Cheikh Anta Diop (1923–1986) and Frantz Fanon (1925–1961). They participated in the abovementioned international conferences but were not yet the major voices that they became later. Both made foundational contributions to the intellectual development of Black Studies in France and throughout the world.

Cheikh Anta Diop, born in Diourbel, Senegal, was educated in traditional Muslim schools and a French colonial college, and then headed to Paris for higher education in 1946 at the age of twenty-three. He presented his first PhD thesis in 1954; it was rejected after a seven-hour debate with his examination committee. Based on his second thesis, he was awarded the PhD in 1960. This controversial history reflects the beginning of his lifelong fight against Eurocentrism in order to establish a foundation thesis for Black Studies on a global level (A.B. Fall, cited in Kaya 2000, 22–25).

Diop is aggressive in arguing that African historical importance rivals Europe, significantly turning Eurocentrism on its head:

> Far from being a reveling in the past, a look toward Egypt and antiquity is the best way to conceive and build our cultural future. In reconceived and renewed African culture, Egypt will play the same role that Greco-Latin antiquity plays in Western culture.
>
> (Diop 1991, 3)

Diop became a master scholar with skills in many disciplines: history, Egyptology, physics, linguistics, anthropology, economics, and sociology. He raised critical questions that situate the African experience in world history, in terms that place the African experience as a quintessential human experience. What is the origin of human culture? Does the origin of Egyptian culture derive from Africa, and does it in turn influence Africa? Has Africa contributed to the development of human cultural advancement in general?

The strength of Diop's argument is that his critical assessment always begins by focusing on the dominant Eurocentric theories that detach Egypt from Africa, and basically turn Egyptian culture white. He then makes historical, linguistic, and psychological arguments supported by evidence from his research.

Fanon was born in Martinique and had Aimé Césaire as a high school teacher. He then studied medicine and psychiatry in France and served in the French military. As a medical student, Fanon helped to organize the Union of Students from Overseas France, in other words the colonies, and edited the union's newspaper, *Tam Tam* (Gendzier 1985, 17). He was close to the editorial collective around *Présence Africaine* and other French intellectuals like Jean-Paul Sartre. His writings have become a key influence in the development of Black Studies, especially in using psychology to expose colonial domination and affirm the agency of the oppressed.

Fanon followed in the French tradition of focusing on culture, but as his intellectual development took place during a heightened period of anti-colonial revolt his trajectory was revolutionary. He first critically took up the lynchpin of French culture and language, in his first book

Black Skin, White Masks (1952). He starts with this definition of a Black person that fits the dual-self thesis of Du Bois:

> The Black man has two dimensions. One with his fellows, the other with the white man. A Negro behaves differently with the white man and with another Negro. That this self-division is a direct result of colonialist subjugation is beyond question.
>
> (Fanon and Markmann 1967, 17)

He clarifies that the function of mastering French is to be with the white man: "Historically, it must be understood that the Negro wants to speak French because it is the key that can open doors which were barred to him fifty years ago" (Fanon and Markmann 1967, 38).

But, of course, he must answer the question of so what, in the end what real differences does this make? "Yes, the black man is supposed to be a good nigger; once this has been laid down, the rest follows of itself" (Fanon and Markmann 1967, 35).

One of Fanon's most important contributions was his analysis of the dialectical development of the Black intellectual in revolt, connecting Black Studies to the Black Liberation Movement:

> If we wanted to trace in the works of native writers the different phases which characterize this evolution we would find spread out before us a panorama on three levels. In the first phase, the native intellectual gives proof that he has assimilated the culture of the occupying power. … In the second phase we find the native is disturbed; he decides to remember who he is. … Finally in the third phase, which is called the fighting phase, the native, after having tried to lose himself in the people and with the people, will on the contrary shake the people. … The native intellectual nevertheless sooner or later will realize that you do not show proof of your nation from its culture but that you substantiate its existence in the fight which the people wage against the forces of oppression.
>
> (Fanon 1965, 178–79)

Michel Fabre (1910–2003) initiated the formal academic study of the African Diaspora in France. His archives, located at Emory University in Atlanta, Georgia, give some biographical information on him:

> Michel Jacques Fabre was educated at the University of London and the Université de Paris and École Normale Supérieure prior to serving in the French Navy from 1959–1962. After leaving the military, he taught as a professor at Wellesley College, Harvard University, the University of Paris (X), the University of Paris (VIII), and was professor of American and Afro-American studies at la Sorbonne Nouvelle of the University of Paris (III) beginning in 1970. Together with his wife, Geneviève Fabre, he founded the Center for Afro-American Studies at the University of Paris.
>
> (Emory University 2007)

Fabre edited and published an *AFRAM Newsletter* (ISSN 0243-7090) twice a year as the major academic source of news in France about the African Diaspora. The newsletter carried information about conferences, book reviews, bibliographies, and short essays. The focus was on Africa, Australia, the Caribbean, and the African-American experience; there was little information about the Black experience in Europe.

Fabre is a leading biographer of Richard Wright, who also wrote broad summations of the African-American experience (Fabre 2009; 1993, 175–94; 1970; Fabre and Oren 1971). He makes a survey of African-American writers who lived in France, especially W.E.B Du Bois, Langston Hughes, Alain Locke, Countee Cullen, Claude McKay, Jessie Fauset, Gwendolyn Bennett, Richard Wright, James Baldwin, Chester Himes, William Gardner Smith, William Melvin Kelley, Melvin Dixon, Ted Joans, and James Emanuel.

A key turning point in the consciousness of Black people in France came in 2005 when two Black teenagers died after being pursued by the police, being electrocuted while hiding in an electricity substation. This ignited a national set of rebellions in the major urban areas with working-class Black ghettoes. Suddenly the Black presence was a new subject in French discourse. At least four initiatives have come out of this that focus on the actual Black experience in France. This is moving toward the formalization of Black Studies in connection to Black community social action.

Black academics began to turn their attention to Black France, from the Diaspora to those who had become part of the French population from birth. Pap Ndiaye is a current leading scholar studying the African Diaspora. Ndiaye (2009) continues the mainstream trend of writing about the Black experience in the USA. However, at the same time, following the militant uprising of Black youth in 2005, he had been in the vanguard of the study of the Black experience in France, while at the Institute of Political Studies in the L'École des Hautes Études en Sciences Sociales in Paris. He engages with the blind spot of research data on the Black experience in France, which was a result of the mainstream view that to collect such statistics would be disruptive. In February 2021, he became director of the Palais de la Porte Dorée's Musée de l'Histoire de l'Immigration (Museum of the History of Immigration).

Ndiaye has joined with others to connect scholarship with activism in the interest of the well-being of the French Black population. This includes the formation of the Conseil Répresentatif des Associations Noires (CRAN, the Representative Council for Black Associations of France) in 2005 (CRAN n.d.). One of its co-founders, Patrick Lozès, clarifies what they discovered about French scholarship:

> In 2003, early in our thinking which led to the creation of CRAN, we asked ourselves if studies concerning the situation of Blacks in France existed in sociology, anthropology, history, or demography. It soon became clear that this type of study had never been realized. Works exist on "African families," "African students," civil servants from the DOM/TOM, "migrants," "immigrants," from sub-Saharan Africa, and "illegal immigrants," but astonishingly no study had been done on French Blacks.
>
> (Lozès 2012, 107)

In a 2016 lecture at the University of Chicago, Ndiaye connects this to the lack of explicit Black struggle in France as compared to the USA:

> In the United States the rise of Black Studies, African American Studies, is clearly related to the Civil Rights Movement. Social and political movements have had a clear impact on social research. Whereas in the French case the marginality of Black Studies can also be attributed to a lack of political mobilization and the series of defeats anti-racism has experienced since the 1980s.
>
> (CSRPC 2016)

Ndiaye has written the major contemporary work of Black Studies in France, *La Condition Noire: Essai sur une minorite francaise* (*The Black Condition: An Essay on a French Minority*; 2011). He challenges the silence of French social science on the issues of Black people, clearly critiquing the blind policy of the French government for not keeping statistics on the Black social experience. Historically, this is reflected in keeping the history of colonization separate from national history. This is especially weak, in that the soldiers from Senegal who settled in France have been denied the legacy of their descendants being Black French.

Sylvain Pattieu, Emmanuelle Sibeud, and Tyler Stovall have been carrying forward the work started by Ndiaye in a seminar at the Paris 8 University on the history of Black populations. Their work has resulted in an important anthology, *The Black Populations of France: Histories from Metropole to Colony* (Pattieu, Sibeud, and Stovall 2022).

Another major development is a program for French secondary students launched by the Ministries of National Education and the Overseas, the Inter-Ministerial Delegation for the Fight against Racism, Antisemitism, and Anti-LGBT Hatred (DILCRAH), and the Foundation for the Memory of Slavery. Primary and secondary teachers are encouraged to get their students to do projects on the colonial experience and its subsequent aftermath for Blacks in France. This is a Black Studies initiative (Trouillard 2020).

Another project is Black Studies as a community program. A Black committee in Bordeaux, France has followed the USA in launching Black History Month as of 2018. Like in the USA, February is the designated month, the entirety of which is devoted to a program of films, art exhibits, panel discussions, lectures, and performances (Black History Month Bordeaux n.d.; 2018).

GERMANY

There is a history of Blacks in Germany that is connected to the six African colonies historically under German control since the nineteenth century: Burundi, Cameroon, Namibia, Rwanda, Tanganyika, and Togo (Aitken 2015). These countries were defined by the international conference in Berlin, 1884–1885. German views about Black people were firmly based in German philosophical thought, such as that of Georg Wilhelm Friedrich Hegel (1770–1831) and Immanuel Kant (1724–1804). This was true even though they were preceded in German academic philosophy by an African, Anthony Wilhelm Amo (1703–1759). Amo taught at the University of Jena years before Hegel earned a position in that same philosophy department. Amo was a clear example of intellectual achievement. However, Hegel advocated the prevailing racism: "The Blacks must be understood as an infantile nation which has not transcended its disinterested or uninterested ingenuousness. They are sold and permit themselves to be sold without thought whether this is right or not" (Hegel, cited in Gilman 1983, 94). Kant had made the same point: "The Blacks of Africa have no sense naturally which exceeds the childish" (Kant, cited in Gilman 1983, 101).

But, like other European colonial powers, Germany set up a research and training program to manage their colonies:

> African Studies have a long tradition in Berlin. In 1887, the Department of Oriental Languages was founded at the Friedrich-Wilhelm-University (which is now the Humboldt-University). Its purpose was the training of German colonial officials as well as the teaching of African languages. In 1925, Diedrich Westermann became the first professor in African Studies at the university. The history of African Studies has always been closely connected with the political history of Germany: with the German Empire, the Weimar Republic, the "Dritte Reich" and the GDR. Following the reunification of the two German states in 1990, the Department of African Studies was re-founded in its current form.
>
> (IAAW 2020)

There have been at least three major stages in the development of the Afro-German population: as a result of World War I immigration; as a result of World War II immigration; and after the 1960s and the global end of direct colonial rule. After World War I, Germany lost direct control of its colonies and was occupied by the French. The crisis resulted from France's decision to use its colonial subjects as the occupying force:

> The employment of some forty odd thousand French-African colonials to occupy the Rhineland was seen by Germans, on both the right and the left, as an affront to the nation. The campaign against the occupation almost immediately took on racial overtones, decrying the placement of these "lowly" Africans in a position of authority over the "superior" white Germans.
>
> (Wipplinger 2013, 108; Blackshire-Belay 2001, 269)

Even given this negative response, Black people were active in Germany. African Americans did study in Germany, but without a Black community to be part of. These included W.E.B. Du Bois in history and sociology (1892–1894), Alain Locke in philosophy (1910–1911), and Ernest Everett Just in biology (1929 and later; Hopkins 1992, 124). Furthermore, because of the strength of the German left, the Comintern was based in Hamburg, founding the International Trade Union Committee of Negro Workers there under the leadership of James Ford (USA) followed by George Padmore (Trinidad; Adi 2013, 123–61).

From 1937 on, the Nazi forces sterilized at least 385 Afro-Germans, but some did survive the Nazi period. One example is Hans Massaquoi, who moved to the USA as an adult and eventually became editor of *Ebony* magazine (Massaquoi 2014). The Nazi experience demeaned Black people, but did not entirely wipe them out.

African-American soldiers stationed in Germany after World War II not only faced German racism, but also living and working in the segregated US armed forces. Some of these soldiers stayed in Germany and took on German wives and girlfriends, which resulted in children who were derisively called "Rhineland Bastards." The main development of an Afro-German population resulted from the post-World War II presence of African-American soldiers and others from the African Diaspora, mainly Black men having children with white German women. The children grew up in their mother's families and did not grow up socialized as Afro-Germans, just a particular sort of being German.

So, in summary,

> there was no Black community in Germany but merely "a diverse group" of Blacks who came "from a wide range of class, ethnic, geographic, and even historical backgrounds," there was no Black German community in the United States, no audible Black German voices who could have told the Black German story as insiders.
>
> (Michelle Wright, cited in Diedrich 2016, 139)

But the 1960s began to change things on a global level. Powerful Black political culture came blasting out that extended the global reach of the African Diaspora through such popular cultural artists as Bob Marley from Jamaica, Fela Kuti from Nigeria, and of course Detroit's Motown. Coupled with the experience of racism in German, this put the Afro-German youth on the path to explore their own Black identity. These were mainly young people in search of their fathers and a Black identity outside of the racist German experience in which they grew up.

The German academic mainstream followed the popular focus on Africa and the African Americans. In 1969 the Association for African Studies in Germany (Vereinigung für Afrikawissenschaften in Deutschland, VAD.e.V.) was formed and became the main professional association of academic work in that area (Association for African Studies in Germany n.d.).

American Studies begins after World War II in Germany, engineered by the US CIA (Saunders 2013, 19–20, 72–83). The major institution became Amerika Haus (America House), established in 1956–1957 in Berlin. This was the center for cultural and academic programs about the USA, often featuring visiting scholars and artists. The John F. Kennedy (JFK) Institute for North American Studies of the Free University of Berlin was then established in 1963. This is a formal German institution that holds classes and grants degrees at the undergraduate and graduate levels. It has the largest American Studies library collection in Germany, and one of the largest collections of African-American materials in Europe.

Two of the leading scholars at the JFK Institute were Ekkehart Krippendorff and Werner Sollors. Krippendorff, a political scientist and literary critic, specialized in American politics. Sollors was similarly a humanities scholar who specialized in African-American literature. He subsequently joined the faculty of Harvard University in the USA. In 1981, the JFK Institute published a two-volume bibliography of their extensive Afro-American Studies holdings (Sollors 1972).

This institute brought two African-American scholars as guest professors, and they played key roles in helping the Afro-Germans to self-organize. Audre Lorde was there in 1984 and Abdul Alkalimat (as Gerald McWorter) followed her in 1985.

Audre Lorde made a great impact on German feminism. She inspired the women's movement, especially the lesbians within it, to embrace the Black German experience and provide community for isolated Afro-German women:

> At the time of her health crisis, an intense chapter in Lorde's life began in Berlin-Germany, when she joined the Free University in Berlin in 1984 as a guest professor. An interesting coincidence is that her arrival in Germany occurred exactly a hundred years after the Berlin Conference on Africa (The Scramble for Africa). Lorde became a central

> symbolic figure for the German feminist movement, especially for a group of young Black lesbian women, who had just begun to organize politically. Audre Lorde became involved in Berlin's feminist scene at a decisive point, when she recognized and grasped the opportunity to help jump-start the movement inspired by Black Feminism. She implemented her powers of articulation as well as her activist and analytical expertise, in order to formulate and structure the internal and external requirements and demands of the Black Feminist movement in Germany. To these efforts she lent her narrative and political force as well as her transnational visions for the future.
>
> (K. Everett 2015)

She became a role model for the young Afro-German women, especially in Berlin. Berlin was a sanctuary city for youth before the wall came down, in that while in Berlin you were exempt from the military and higher education was free. Moreover, when young Afro-Germans came to Berlin from their home locations, they ceased being alone and could find what was developing as an Afro-German community.

Abdul Alkalimat taught four courses at the JFK Institute:

1. Introduction to American Politics and Society, jointly with Krippendorff
2. Introduction to Afro-American Studies
3. Problems of Class and Race
4. Class and Power in Contemporary American Society

Many Afro-Germans and African students attended these courses. There, relationships developed and organizing took off. In 1985, Afro-German youth formed a mass organization, the Initiative of Black People (Initiative Schwarze Menschen in Deutschland Bund, ISD). This became a magnet to aggregate Afro-Germans of all generations to share experience, to educate themselves about their history and current situation, and to advocate for policy changes. One of the critical issues was reparations for atrocities committed in Namibia (formerly Southwest Africa, a colony of Germany). Key people in Berlin at the early stage of organizing for the ISD were students in the JFK Institute courses, the poet May Opitz and the economist David Nii Addy (Ayim, Oguntoye, and Schultz 2018).

Another important initiative was a journal produced by Vusi Mchunu, a poet and cultural activist from South Africa then living in Berlin as a student at the JFK Institute of the Free University. He named the journal *AWA-FINNABA: An African Literary Cultural Journal*. Mchunu states the following in the editorial of the March 1988 issue:

> This issue is yet another milestone in our tireless endeavors to promote and publicize progressive literary and analytical works by Third World people, by people of African descent all over the world and by comrades well disposed towards Third World matters. … AWA-FINNABA is slowly establishing some reputation as the only regular mouthpiece of South African and African Writers, critics, and analysts in Western Germany.
>
> (Mchunu 1988, 3)

African Americans have made contributions to African Diaspora culture in Germany, with the most important recent development being the work of Donald Muldrow Griffith in Berlin, originally born in Chicago. He founded three important cultural institutions: the Fountainhead Tanz Théâtre (1980), the Black Cultural Festival and Black International Cinema Berlin (1986), and the Collegium: Forum and Television Program (1995). In the program of the thirty-second film fair, Griffith explains why he started the event:

> An idea of a Black Cultural Festival arose, as an awareness of the existence of persons from Africa and the African Diaspora became increasing apparent, including knowledge about the military forces of the USA, British, and French personnel stationed in West Berlin. Accompanying our maturation process, was the need to provide ourselves and the public with information regarding the historical contributions of descendants from the African continent.
>
> With the support of our German colleagues and as interest from the above stated groups developed, we established the 1st Black Cultural Festival in Europe in 1986, during 3 weeks of excitement, ideas and toil!
>
> (Griffith 2017, 3)

By 1999, the Afro-German spirit of unity was sweeping the country and a new organization was formed, the Black German Cultural Society. This global effort united Afro-Germans in Germany and the USA:

> [The] Black German Cultural Society (BGCS) founded 1999, established itself as the premiere organization serving as a resource, networking organization as well as a forum to facilitate awareness, discussions, and reflection of important issues that impact Black Germans, Post WWII Afro-Germans (known as Brown Babies and Mischlingskinder), and their descendants.
>
> (BGCS n.d.)

So the Afro-Germans in Germany also link to an Afro-German Diaspora, mainly in Europe, Africa, and the USA. In fact, Afro-Germans in their Diaspora have been active in conducting scholarship and maintaining a political culture of reconstructing memory and healing. A major network works through a website called Black Central Europe. Their purpose is clear:

> Our mission is both to show the historical presence of Black people and to understand how racialized ideas of history, national belonging, and citizenship have been produced and adapted over time. By challenging these and drawing attention to other ways of thinking about who belongs in society, we can undermine the exclusionary ideas that continue to trouble us today.
>
> (Black Central Europe n.d.)

The global system of online networks at Michigan State University, H-Net, includes a major network that frequently includes the Afro-German experience, H-Black-Europe (H-Net n.d.). More generally, there is the German Studies Association (German Studies Association n.d.) with frequently sponsored panels at its meetings.

Many conferences have aggregated researchers and activists to report on the Afro-German experience. As with the general literature, this often focuses on autobiography and the sharing of personal experiences. Especially valuable conferences are those that have brought scholars and individual Afro-Germans together in conversation, among them:

1. 2000 University of Buffalo (Donovan 2000)
2. 2006 University of Massachusetts Amherst (University of Massachusetts Amherst n.d.)
3. 2012 Barnard (Rutgers University–Camden 2012)
4. 2020 Rutgers (Rutgers University–Camden 2020)

USSR/RUSSIA

There are two outstanding facts that differentiate Russia from other European countries: (1) Russia never had any African colonies; and (2) it did not subject Africans to slavery. The broad sweep of the Russian empire did, however, subjugate Asian peoples into the peasantry system that worked like the slave system in the USA. Racism, in the form of national chauvinism, was very much part of the political culture of the empire. Some few Black people at very early stages did gain some prominence:

> Negroes present in tsarist Russia fall into three main categories. The first is the small native Negro population which for at least two centuries was scattered in small settlements in the Caucasus mountains near the Black Sea. … The second category of Negroes in Russia is comprised of the servants and workers who were present in large numbers in the 18th and 19th centuries, owing to the fashion among the wealthy nobility and tsars of maintaining a certain number of black servants. … The third category of Negroes in Russia was comprised of visitors of various types, including artists, athletes, and foreign service officers.
>
> (Blakely 1976, 352, 354, and 356)

The first celebrated person in Black Russian history usually mentioned is Abram Petrovich Gannibal (1696–1781). He was an African slave who rose via the patronage of Tsar Peter the Great to the high status of a free aristocrat and general. He is remembered most often as the maternal great-grandfather of the Russian national literary icon, Alexander Pushkin (1799–1837). Pushkin is the greatest Russian poet, and the founder of modern Russian literature. Both of these highly accomplished men are examples of Black people who became part of the Russian elite, but not examples of a broader pattern of the social experiences of Black people, or a Black community. They were Black, but mainly Russian.

Some African Americans did live and prosper in Russia, one of them being Frederick Bruce Thomas (1872–1928). Thomas, the son of former Mississippi slaves, emigrated to Russia in 1899. He had skills as a high-society waiter and worked his way into a lucrative entrepreneurial career for nineteen years running restaurants and nightclubs. The 1917 revolution saw him as part of the capitalist class and he was forced to leave, finally dying as a poor person in Turkey (Alexandrov 2013).

The history of Black people as a socio-historical community or nationality in Russian thought begins with the Russian Revolution in 1917. This development had three basic mechanisms: the institutions established for the training of revolutionaries from Africa and the African Diaspora; the policies of the revolution as developed by the Communist International (Comintern); and especially the role of African Americans who came to Russia to train and resettle.

There were several initiatives to provide education for people from the European colonies, encompassing the entire African Diaspora. The Soviets recruited activists and advanced students to attend such institutions as the Communist University for the Toilers of the East (founded in 1921). The curriculum in the Anglo-American section covered the following content areas: political economy, history of the Communist International, Leninism, historical materialism, party-building, military science, current politics, and the English language, and

> [t]he fourteen-month course involved ten months plus ten days in classroom work ("theoretical study"), two months of practical work including three days on a collective farm, and fifteen days in party organizational work. Five days were set aside for revolutionary holidays, and assignments came in the fifteenth month.
>
> (McClellan 1993, 375–76)

After the 1961 assassination of Patrice Lumumba, the institution changed its name and orientation to Patrice Lumumba University. R.A. Tuzmukhamedov describes some of the courses offered at Patrice Lumumba University in 1968, when it had over 4,000 students from eighty-five countries:

> Many of the courses read at the University deal with the developing countries, in particular the African countries. These are: The National-Liberation Movement and International Law, The National-Liberation Movement and Working-Class Movement, State Law and Political Ideas in Africa, The History of Africa, History and Regional Geology of Asia, Africa, and Latin America, Neutralism in International Relations, The Historical Forms of Colonialism, The Mineral Deposits of Asia, Africa, and Latin America, Prospecting in Asia, Africa, and Latin American Infectious Diseases (including a course in Tropical Diseases), Tropical Horticulture, etc.
>
> (Tuzmukhamedov, cited in Gavrilov 1969, 175–76)

In the Comintern, set up by the USSR to coordinate world revolution, there was a focus on colonized people under the rubric of the national question. The leaders settled on a theoretical definition of a nation as being "a historically constituted, stable community of people, formed on the basis of a common language, territory, economic life, and psychological make-up manifested in a common culture" (Stalin 1954).

In 1928, during the Sixth Congress of the Comintern, three key resolutions were adopted on the national question that applied to Africa and the African Diaspora, specifically in the USA, Cuba, and South Africa. In each case, the Comintern posited the existence of a Black nation deserving a program of self-determination. In the USA, it was the Black Belt South. In Cuba, it was the province of Oriente, which had the greatest concentration of Afro-Cubans. In South Africa, it was the entire country:

> South Africa is a black country, the majority of its population is black and so is the majority of the workers and peasants. The bulk of the South African population is the black peasantry, whose land has been expropriated by the white minority. Seven-eighths of the land is owned by the whites. Hence the national question in South Africa, which is based upon the agrarian question lies at the foundation of the revolution in South Africa. The black peasantry constitutes the basic moving force of the revolution in alliance with and under the leadership of the working class.
>
> (Marxist Internet Archive n.d.)

The Comintern instructed each of the three communist parties to increase their Black membership. The South African case is exemplary: "The entire Cape branch of the CPSA [South African Communist Party], with one exception, supported the resolution. The party was also making rapid gains. African membership increased from 200 in 1927 to 1600 out of 1750 total members in 1928" (Kelley 2014, 259).

The Cuban party also had major advances:

> Between the 1930s and the 1940s, in fact, the proportion of Black leftists who were union organizers and/or in the leadership of Communist Party organizations (under their various shifting titles) and who ran as Communist in several elections surged in response to the post-revolutionary (1933) prominence of the popular classes and to Communists' emphasis on the issue of racial justice.
>
> (Pappademos 2011, 217)

In the USA, the communist party sent cadre organizers into the South in the late 1920s. Black enrollment began to increase because of the role the party played in the legal defense of a group of young Black men unjustly accused of rape known as the Scottsboro Boys. In their 1928 decision, the Comintern issued a document that argued African Americans were a nation and upheld their right to self-determination. This was advocated by African Americans at the meetings, especially Harry Haywood (1976; 1978, 245–80).

Because of these progressive positions that led to a rise in Black activism on a global level, the image of the USSR as a country free of racial oppression led some Black people to migrate there in search of a better life, some to settle and some to visit. Joy Gleason Carew discusses the historical experience of African Americans going to the Soviet Union. She is a Black woman who mastered the Russian language and visited there many times:

> My first sojourn in the Soviet Union occurred in the spring and early summer of 1967 with my Russian class from Ohio State University. Like Harry Haywood, a political activist of the 1920s, who made his first crossing in the spring of 1926, my classmates and I also experienced the rough Atlantic seas and were relieved to finally land in Leningrad. Still, I was delighted to have made the crossing on the *MS Pushkin*, named after the "father" of Russian literature, a descendant of an African.
>
> (J.G. Carew 2010, x)

Joy Carew's is the definitive survey of the diverse Black experiences in Russia. Among other figures, she discusses Claude McKay, Otto Huiswood, Harry Haywood, W.E.B. Du Bois, Robert Robinson, George Washington Carver, Oliver Golden, Langston Hughes, and Paul Robeson.

Robert Robinson (1906–1994, an industrial specialist) and Oliver Golden (1887–1940, an agricultural specialist) migrated to settle and work in the USSR. Robinson was originally from Jamaica; he worked at a Ford auto plant after becoming a naturalized US citizen. He, along with hundreds of skilled US industrial workers, went to live in the USSR in the 1930s. He excelled at his job; fame came to him when he fought against a racist attack by other US guest workers. This fame got him elected to the Moscow Soviet (city council) in 1934. He stayed for forty-four years, had children, and never joined the communist party as he became alienated from the experience. After trying for years to leave, he eventually did in 1974 (J.G. Carew 2010, 72–74 and 76; Robinson 1988).

Oliver Golden, the son of ex-slaves raised in Mississippi, was a student of George Washington Carver at Tuskegee Institute. He eventually finished his education in 1928 at the University for the Toilers of the East after joining the Communist Party USA (CPUSA), and,

> in 1931, Oliver left United States with fourteen other African American cotton specialists from various universities and his wife, Bertha Bialek. They were invited by the Soviet government to serve as experts in the cultivation of cotton. They choose to come to Uzbekistan because it was a cotton-growing region and because it was the Soviet Republic of "national minorities" because Uzbeks had faced discrimination in Tsarist Russia because of their skin color.
>
> (Ernst 2018a)

Oliver Golden became a Soviet citizen and raised a daughter, Liya (Lily) Golden (1934–2010), who in turn had a daughter, Yelena Khanga (1962–). Both wrote autobiographical family histories (Golden 2002; Khanga and Jacoby 1994). Liya Golden became a direct link to Black Studies:

> [She] graduated from Moscow State University in 1957 as a historian majoring in African American History. She dedicated her life to teaching and researching that field. After graduating from Moscow State University, she worked for the Institute of Oriental Studies in a department that focused on African Studies. In 1959, the Soviet Academy of Sciences opened the African Institute where Golden worked for over 30 years, publishing books on Africans living in Russia, African music, and over a hundred articles.
>
> (Ernst 2018b)

Liya spent ten years teaching in the USA at Chicago State University. Yelena has become a sensational media star on Moscow television.

African-American communists were active in visiting and studying in the USSR. This included Lovett Huey Fort-Whiteman, Claude McKay, Otto Huiswood, Harry Haywood, Langston Hughes, Paul Robeson, William Patterson, and Louise Thompson Patterson. They were variously embraced as international cultural artists and political allies. The most impactful were their roles at the 1928 Comintern Sixth Congress in formulating and working to adopt the resolution on the African-American (Negro) national question.

Parallel to this political development, there were academic developments. In the main, these programs were focused on Africa (Morison 1964, 59–72; V.G. Solodovnikov 1966; Tokareva 1969). Solodovnikov describes its origins:

> The main impetus to African studies in our country was given by the establishment in 1934 of the Oriental Department of Leningrad University, where four African languages were taught: Swahili, Zulu, Hausa, and Amharic. The African section of the Ethnography Institute was the first centre of the USSR Academy of Sciences organized to study African problems.
>
> (V.G. Solodovnikov 1966, 360)

In 1959–1960, they established the Institute of Africa at the USSR Academy of Sciences. The first director and leading scholar at the Institute of Africa was I.I. Potekhin, a prolific scholar (Holowaty 1969). Potekhin locates the mission of Soviet-based African Studies in line with the politics of African liberation:

> The writing of a truthful history of Africa is a great and honorable task. It has not only a scientific but also a political aspect. European and American imperialists are increasingly employing their poisoned weapon of racialism, and still trying to convince world opinion, and first of all the African Negroid people, that Africans cannot stand on their feet without outside support. … The truth about the historical past of the African peoples is a powerful means for exposing the ideological camouflage used for covering up the "latest" forms of colonialism. A study of Africa's history is therefore part and parcel of the struggle for genuine independence and free choice of roads for further development.
>
> (Potekhin 1968, 141–42)

The Institute of Africa published a comprehensive history of Africa and several studies that have been translated into English (Morison 1964, 59–72; Smirnov 1968; Tarabrin 1974). In addition, many scientific and political studies have been translated into English (Braginskiĭ and Institut

Afriki (Akademiia nauk SSSR) 1966; Vasilij Grigor'evič Solodovnikov 1970; Iskenderov 1972; Starušenko 1975; Tarabrin 1974).

Soviet academicians have also targeted the African-American experience, producing studies and translating African-American authors as well. Ivanov published a survey of African-American history based on a careful reading of US sources as well as Soviet studies (R. Ivanov 1985; R.F. Ivanov 1976). Progress Publishers also published material on the Civil Rights Movement by members of the CPUSA: a good example of this is a study of events from 1957 to 1965 by James Jackson (J.E. Jackson 1967).

The current situation is very different, as there is a small but transgenerational Black community in Russia, estimated to be 50,000 in 2009 (Wikipedia 2020h).

Objectively, it is hard to define in terms of population statistics, since the Russian census does not collect such data. It is clear that a small third generation of Afro-Russians is fully integrated into society. For example, Jean Gregoire Sagbo was born in Benin but is now a Russian citizen. In 2010, he was elected to the local city council in Novozavidovo, a town of approximately 10,000 people located 100 km north of Moscow (Wikipedia 2020f).

As indicated above, Yelena Khanga is a media star on Moscow television. According to Kate Baldwin, her fame is due in part to the suggestive sexual stereotype of Black women and is set in the context of anti-Black violence (2009, 253–62).

The downside of the current situation is that the end of the USSR led to a dramatic change in government policy. A rise in a chauvinistic nationalism has led to racial hostility toward Black people, African immigrants and Afro-Russians alike: "Racial attacks have taken place numerous times in Russia, 49 times in Moscow in one year according to an advocacy group" (Wikipedia 2020f).

Here is how a social service agency describes the case of Afro-Russian children:

> In Moscow Region there are an estimated 4000 black Russian children. Many of them live below the poverty line. Their fathers abandoned them, left for Africa and do not offer them assistance. Their mothers, in most cases, do not have permanent jobs or work low paying jobs. The families live on the pensions of grandmothers and grandfathers who receive an equivalent of 20 US dollars a month. Mothers who

> live outside Moscow and are not Muscovites do not have registration because they were married to African students and therefore cannot enjoy free medical services. Since they lack the money for treatment they suffer from very high rates of illness. They also lack money for clothes and food. Out of despair many of the mothers give their black children to orphanages, which are now overcrowded. Black children in the orphanages live with normal Russian children, where they are far outnumbered by the white Russian children. As a result, black children experience discomfort and pain because of their black skin and their African fathers who abandoned them in a strange country.
>
> (Fund METIS n.d.)

THE CARIBBEAN ISLANDS

The Caribbean islands are historical sites of conflict between four peoples: the indigenous islanders, who suffered genocidal oppression; European colonial settlers; workers imported from Asia; and enslaved African workers. While the African presence has been dominant quantitatively, the subjective self-definition of being African has flourished in many countries, especially Haiti and Jamaica. Cultural development has followed the language prison of colonial history, English, Spanish, French, and Dutch.

JAMAICA

Jamaica's past includes slavery and colonialism, as well as over fifty years of independence. This history also includes a continuous struggle against colonial rule by resistance from Maroons, Africans who established liberated zones of freedom. First, there was colonization by the Spanish (1509–1655), who were followed by the British in 1660. Jamaica became a Black-majority country because of the importation of African labor to work on British sugar plantations in the 1670s. There is a historical process toward freedom that ended slavery and formal colonial control.

The first stage was the formation of Maroon free zones in the Jamaican mountains. One famous instance involved Queen Nanny (1686–1755), who led the Windward Maroons from her base at Nanny Town. She and her forces fought a guerilla war against the British and forced them to sign a peace treaty in 1740. The next advance was the Baptist War Slave Rebellion in 1831 led by Samuel Sharp (1804–1832). This led to the formal end of slavery in Jamaica. The third major figure to emerge in the freedom struggle was Paul Bogle (1820–1865), who led the Morant Bay Rebellion in 1865.

Two institutions were central to how the colonial administration utilized research scholarship to systematize its control in all areas of science and culture. The Institute of Jamaica was founded in 1879, following the model of the Smithsonian Institution in the USA, founded in 1846. The first such comprehensive institution, the British Museum in London, had been established by Hans Sloane in 1759 (Delbourgo 2017). Sloane was a wealthy physician who had married the heiress of sugar plantations in Jamaica, so that his activities were intimately linked to slavery. The Institute of Jamaica comprised several units, including a museum and art gallery.

The second institution was the University of the West Indies (Mona), founded in 1948, initially as a college of the University of London. The first faculty was that of medicine; more subjects were added over time, leading to the achievement of university status and a name change in 1962. This became the most important institution for the social development of a Black professional middle class for Jamaican society. They were shaped with Victorian values and perfected the Western standards of behavior that enabled success in the eyes of the British middle classes and the colonial state apparatus.

This did not become the main tendency among the masses of Jamaican workers and peasants. With the foundation of their African cultural retention, the masses of Afro-Jamaicans developed a political culture of resistance. The best mass expression of this developed under the leadership of Marcus Mosiah Garvey, who formed the Universal Negro Improvement Association and African Communities' League (UNIA-ACL) in 1914, as mentioned above. He continued the tradition of Nanny, Sharp, and Bogle, through his direct connection with Robert Love, a leading Jamaican pan-Africanist (Lewis 1988, 17–53; Grant 2010, 52–72). Garvey took his message to the masses of people:

> From the street corners of Kingston and from the lamp-lit shops and yards of rural Jamaica, Garvey brought his message to the poor. House servants denied knowing what Garvey preached in the homes of their employers, while at night on the stools outside their two-by-four structures, they told their children of the future liberation of Africa and sang the [UNIA] song "Ethiopia, Thou Land of Our Fathers."
>
> (Campbell 1987, 64)

Out of his base in Jamaica, Garvey moved to New York and began building his global mass movement.

The political culture of resistance with a mass base emerged with religious tendencies called Rastafari. This movement took its name from the original name of Haile Selassie, Ras Tafari, after he was crowned Emperor of Ethiopia in 1930. Grassroots activist preachers had been active in the Garvey movement, the UNIA, and they were attracted by the international standing of Ethiopia. This combined a pro-African pan-Africanism with a folk religion around Biblical prophecy, the Book of Revelation (5:2–5; 19:16), the Book of Daniel (7:3), and the Book of Psalms (68:31).

> One of the key leaders that came out of the Garvey movement to organize a Rastafarian community was Leonard Howell. He set up Pinnacle, a commune in the Jamaican mountains, to serve as a living learning center for Rastafarian beliefs and life practices: "Today when one speaks of the Rastafari it is usual to refer to the symbols of locks; the ites (red), green and gold; the symbol of the lion; the distinctive use of the Jamaican language, and the use of ganja. Each of these symbols developed over a period and were not simply an outward mark of identifying the Rasta, but a reflection of a form of resistance, linking these symbols to some concrete struggle among African peoples."
>
> (Campbell 1987, 95)

Howell financed much of Pinnacle with the sale of ganja, and other symbols were taken from Ethiopia to convey the message of direct opposition to the British crown of colonial rule. The use of the dreadlock hairstyle developed after 1953 when photos of the forest fighters of Kenya, called by the British the Mau Mau, appeared on the front page of the Jamaican newspaper the *Gleaner*. There can be little doubt about the anti-colonial pro-Africa orientation of the Rastafari (Campbell 1987, 96).

They were building a base among the Jamaican poor and city ghettoes. Three events led to greater legitimation: first, a university-based research team led by Rex Nettleford demonstrated that the Rastafari community was culturally and religious based and without any criminal or subversive political intention. Of course, ganja was not legal, but it was not the basis of widespread fear of the Rasta. Second, a Rastafarian delegation was sponsored to travel to Africa and was well received. In fact, the Ethiopian government offered to grant them land on which to settle in completing their plans to repatriate (Bonacci and M'Bokolo 2015). And third, Emperor Haile Selassie made a momentous visit to Jamaica and was greeted at the airport by thousands of Jamaicans led by Rastafarians.

The colonial view of the masses of Jamaicans was being challenged by the rising legitimacy of the popular culture and lifestyle of the masses of people. One big example of this was the recognition of the national linguistic behavior of the people as opposed to the colonial state's mandate of the use of standard English language. Louise Bennett led this movement. She brought international recognition of the lived speech of the Jamaican masses (Edmondson 2009).

This focus on the language of the people is common to Black Studies all over the world. This is fundamental to national identity and was necessary to give the 1962 Jamaican independence a solid cultural foundation. It was music that pulled it all together in the form of reggae.

Reggae grew out of the popular soul music of Jamaica, including ska and rocksteady, and embraced the radical cultural expression of the Rastafarians. The film starring Jimmy Cliff, *The Harder They Come* (dir. Perry Henzell, 1972), took reggae to a global audience. That set the stage for the top global star of reggae, Bob Marley.

Again, Horace Campbell helps us to understand the importance of education for the Rastafarians and the generation of youth followers of reggae:

> It was in the school system that many young blacks first became attracted to Rastafari, for the language of black dignity, coupled with the promise of black liberation, seemed a credible alternative to total submission to the Eurocentric and capitalist ideas of the system. ... In order to escape the cultural assault of the racism and ethnocentrism of the society, young black people searched for avenues of self-expression and development, and one of the most compulsive aspects was that of the Rastafari philosophy, which gave them a sense of pride in being black. Through the sound system, which was their primary source of identification and recreation, many were attracted to the lyrics of defiance and love for Africa, which were transmitted through reggae music.
>
> (Campbell 1987, 186)

At the heart of the Rasta educational process, sessions were called alternatively "reasonings" and "groundings." The emphasis was on developing a Black consciousness through collective discussion and close readings of written and oral texts, especially the Bible, the speeches of Haile Selassie, and conversations with Rasta elders. This was well defined by Walter Rodney in his speeches that interpreted the Rastafarian view of Africa through a materialist lens. His focus was on infusing the political dimension of Black Power into the thinking of the Rasta youth:

> Black Power in the West Indies means three closely related things: (1) the break with imperialism which is historically white racist; (2) the assumption of power by the black masses in the islands; (3) the cultural reconstruction of the society in the image of the blacks.
>
> (Rodney 1990, 28)

The contemporary organization of Black Studies continues to be grounded in the popular culture of reggae and Rastafari but has been elevated to formal organizations as well. First, in the year of independence a new Jamaica was being born. In 1962, Rex Nettleford (1933–2010) and Eddy Thomas (1932–2014) formed the National Dance Theatre Company of Jamaica. While Thomas had been part of the Martha Graham Dance Company, the new initiative was oriented to the roots of Jamaica culture and its link to Africa. The language of Miss Lou (Louise Bennett) was connected with full body motion. Nettleford became a force in Jamaican cultural affairs, rising to become vice-chancellor of the University of the West Indies (Nettleford and LaYacona 1970).

In 1972, there was the reorganization of the Institute of Jamaica under the leadership of Neville Dawes (1926–1984). Dawes had been on the faculty of the University of Ghana after earning a degree from Oxford University. While in Ghana, he had been a political cadre for political education in the Convention People's Party led by Kwame Nkrumah. Michael Manley, the Jamaican prime minister, called Dawes back home to lead the Institute of Jamaica in the 1970s.

Among other initiatives, Dawes founded the African Caribbean Institute of Jamaica. This was a formal attempt to link the history of Jamaica to both its African and regional heritages, with a mission: "To collect, preserve, document and facilitate access to information on Africa and African cultural retentions in the Caribbean, through oral and written sources using the latest trends and technology" (Jamaica Memory Bank n.d.).

The National Gallery of Jamaica was established in 1974, with David Boxer (1946–2017) serving as the first director. So the visual arts were added to the cultural transformation of Jamaican culture.

> It was David Boxer's curatorial and scholarly mission to ensure that Jamaica had its own documented and art history, so that Jamaican art could assert its rightful place within the broader context of world art. He started this process in the mid-1970s with several exhibitions that challenged previous understandings about Jamaican art and articulated a new, comprehensive art-historical narrative that continues to be the standard in the field to David Boxer's first exhibition for the National Gallery, *Five Centuries of Art in Jamaica* (1975) [which] challenged the view that what could rightly be called Jamaican art started with the nationalist unrest of 1938 and argued that art in Jamaica had a much longer history, with which modern Jamaican art existed in dialogue. The second such exhibition *The Formative Years: Art in Jamaica 1922–1940* (1978) examined the emergence of modern, nationalist art in Jamaica and identified Edna Manley's *Beadseller* (1922) as its symbolic starting point. The third and perhaps most radical element of Boxer's art history of Jamaica was articulated with *The Intuitive Eye* (1979) exhibition, in which he placed the self-taught, popular artists he designated as Intuitives at the centre of the national canon.
>
> (National Gallery of Jamaica 2017)

In higher education, the major institution for Black Studies is the University of the West Indies at Mona, Jamaica. Three units in particular make it one of the most comprehensive institutions in the entire African Diaspora:

1. Undergraduate degree program in African and African Diaspora Studies
2. Institute of Caribbean Studies
3. Institute of African and Diaspora Studies, Unilag, and UWI

The BA degree program in African and African Diaspora Studies is located in the Department of History and Archeology:

> This programme is dedicated to the study of the intellectual, political, artistic, and social experiences of people of African descent throughout Africa and the African Diaspora. … The objective of this programme is to get students stimulated by a deeper appreciation of the relevance of the past to the present enabling them to develop informed and creative solutions for challenges of the future.
>
> (University of the West Indies n.d.b.)

The Institute of Caribbean Studies (ICS) both supports research and offers classes:

> The Mission of the University of the West Indies is to unlock the potential of the Caribbean Region and contribute to regional integration through the excellence of its scholarship and the education of the region's human resources. A necessary first step in the process of unlocking the region's potential is to understand the complexities of Caribbean culture and society. In line with the University's broad mission, as an academic department the ICS provides undergraduate courses in Cultural Studies, Entertainment and Cultural Enterprise Management (ECEM), Music and Rastafari Studies. The Foundation course FOUN1101 (FD11A) Caribbean Civilization, which is a required course for students in the Faculties of Social, Medical and Science and Technology, is also offered out of the Institute.
>
> (University of the West Indies n.d.c)

The Institute of African and Diaspora Studies was developed as a joint venture with the University of Lagos in Nigeria.

Many scholars at the University of West Indies have made and are making contributions to the study of the African Diaspora. One key person is Rupert Lewis, a professor of political thought in the Department of Government, associate director of the Centre for Caribbean Thought, and associate dean for Graduate Studies in the Faculty of Social Sciences. He is one of the leading scholars on Caribbean intellectuals like Marcus Garvey and Walter Rodney (Lewis 1988; 1998).

Carolyn Cooper is a literary scholar with a special focus on Jamaican popular culture, having published books on reggae and Bob Marley (Cooper 1986; 2004; Wint and Cooper 2003). She also led the founding of the Reggae Studies Unit:

> The Reggae Studies Unit was created based on recognition of the influence of Reggae music on both Jamaican and world cultures. The mandate of the Reggae Studies Unit is to:
>
> 1. increase reggae-related research and teaching in diverse areas such as Film Studies, Musicology and Dance in the Faculty of Humanities.
> 2. establish a Specialist Documentation Centre containing various resources relative to the culture of Reggae music.

3. create partnerships with local and international institutions to promote Reggae Studies.
4. sponsor or cosponsor seminars, conferences, public lectures etc., and assist with the publication of research findings that support its mission.

(University of the West Indies n.d.a)

The Reggae Studies Unit also co-sponsors an annual Walter Rodney Lecture with the Walter Rodney Foundation (Walter Rodney Foundation n.d.).

Jamaican scholars and artists have also contributed to Black Studies throughout the Diaspora. In the UK, these include Stuart Hall and Linton Kwesi Johnson, and in the USA, Lorna Goodison (University of Michigan), Horace Campbell (Syracuse University), Anthony Bogues and Brian Meeks (Brown University), Ekwueme Michael Thelwell (University of Massachusetts Amherst), Jamaica Kincaid and Orlando Patterson (Harvard University), and Sylvia Wynter (Stanford University).

CUBA

Cuba is a major example of the contradiction between the objectivity of African culture, and the subjective suppression of its particularity as autonomous within the national narrative of its heritage from Spain. The US government had historically regarded Cuba as a Black country, but the agency of Black Cubans has always had to struggle to get this recognition within Cuba itself. One powerful example of asserting this identity is when the great Cuban musician Machito named his band "The Afro-Cuban All Stars" in 1940 (Figueroa 2007).

The struggle to understand how Cuban society has dealt with the experience of Afro-Cubans is tied to the national Cuban icons of José Martí and Antonio Maceo. Martí championed the idea that all Cubans were part of one nationality; hence, he was against focusing on the particularity of the Afro-Cuban. Maceo, on the other hand, linked the end of slavery to the independence of Cuba from Spanish colonialism, and by so doing associated the particularity of Black oppression with every step toward the freedom of an independent Cuban country (Alkalimat 2016).

Black Studies in Cuba has been slow to develop because of a national silence on racism, although Afro-Cubans have always sought to find their voice and a way to impact the policies and practices of the country.

The scholar who launched the scientific study of the African factor in Cuban culture was Fernando Ortiz (1881–1969). His career started out with the racist bias of the mainstream, but the intimate connections he made with Afro-Cubans in his field research soon turned him around, and he became an advocate for understanding and appreciating Afro-Cuban culture. In their biography of the Afro-Cuban librarian Marta Terry González, Alkalimat and Williams recount how Ortiz made his debut at the University of Havana:

> One high point for Marta was attending the masterful lecture by Fernando Ortiz in the university's Aula Magna (as they call their large lecture hall) when he first presented his findings, making room on the stage for an unprecedented performance of Afro-Cuban dancing and drumming before the amazed audience. It was one of the most exciting and controversial events concerning new scholarship on the Afro-Cuban experience. While not on the faculty, the great Cuban anthropologist introduced people to his theory of transculturation and invited them to rethink the history and cultural life of Cuba by re-evaluating the role of African-descendant peoples. These lectures were an act of resistance on campus to the popular prejudicial view off campus that devalued and marginalized the role of African culture in Cuba. He introduced a young woman who became a very famous singer and cultural representative of Santeria, Merceditas Valdés. She opened and closed the proceedings, singing in the Yoruba language and dancing all around the lecture hall, which was sacred in its own way to the university community. She danced to Eleggua, god of roads, the one who enables aché (the life force) to flow.
>
> (Alkalimat and Williams 2015, 61)

The artistic and cultural production of many of Cuba's best artists has documented the African foundation of Cuban culture. This is reflected in the poetry of Nicolás Guillén and Nancy Morejón, the art of Wilfredo Lam, and the music from Chano Pozo (drums) to Chucho Valdés (piano).

Currently, there is a new level of interest in the experience of Afro-Cubans. One of most prominent advocates in the national debate is Esteban Morales, a leading scholar on the United States at the University of Havana. He presents a design for Black Studies in Cuba in his book *Race in Cuba* (Morales Domínguez 2013). This is a critical statement by an academic who is also a Communist Party member from an Afro-Cuban point of view. He opens his argument with the observation that the Cuban reliance on proclamations from the revolutionary government in 1959 did not adequately deal with the reality of racism in Cuban society:

> Thinking in 1959 that the racial question would be settled was idealistic. There was confusion between the will to recognize ourselves as equals and to declare the war on inequality, with the objective reality of an inequality imposed by history and thus almost impossible to overcome in so brief a time. … It was an error to believe that by eliminating the basis of capitalism and deploying an equalitarian social policy the racial question would be solved.
>
> (Morales Domínguez 2013, 79 and 88)

Esteban Morales aims his sharpest criticism at the failure to face up to the problem of racism:

> The fundamental problems that we run up against regarding the subject race include ignorance about it, continual avoidance of the topic, as well as insufficient treatment of the subject. … Only by openly dealing with the question of race can we put an end to the ignorance, cynicism, and hypocrisy that still lie below the surface when race is discussed.
>
> (Morales Domínguez 2013, 20 and 27)

On the one hand, great progress has been made, but the final eradication of racism has not been achieved. The Cuban Constitutions of 1901 and 1940 outlawed racism and discrimination, but while no racist policies were allowed officially, hidden below the surface racist practices continued to undermine the unity of the Cuban people. Thus, we have racism surviving in an anti-racist society. This became acute during the Special Period of increased economic hardships. Morales Domínguez notes, "Cuba is no longer a racist society, nor do racial prejudice, racial discrimination, and racism dominate the Cuban social atmosphere, but this discriminatory trilogy survives and relies on situations that feed upon it" (2013, 81); and as proof he points to the absence of Black Studies:

> In Cuba, there is very little in the way of research, degree projects, master's theses or doctoral dissertations on the subject of race. At the University of Havana, like at the other centers of higher education, the subject is practically absent from curriculum and degree programs,

> and only occupies a small space in research activity. Many of the studies that had been conducted on the racial problem in the Cuban context generally ended up being shelved, awaiting publication.
>
> (Morales Domínguez 2013, 89)

After alluding to the growing body of academic work on the Afro-Cuban experience, much of it by scholars in the United States, Morales Domínguez sounds an alarm against allowing others outside Cuba to define the situation:

> Virtually every relevant research work on the race issue published in the last forty years that describes our contemporary problems has been done by people who live abroad. … We just cannot let others be in charge of our own history, because he who controls your past also controls your present and future life.
>
> (Morales Domínguez 2013, 126 and 185)

So moving on to a positive initiative, he proposes a research program methodology for Black Studies in Cuba. Morales Domínguez lists key variables for each of three historical periods of Cuban history: Stage I: Cuban colonial society (from the sixteenth century to the end of the nineteenth century); Stage II: failed independence and the Cuban neocolonial society (1898–1958); and Stage III: Cuban socialist revolutionary society (1959–2001) (Morales Domínguez 2013, 44).

Variables are the stable social phenomena that characterize the system of contradictions at an essential level for each stage in question.

VARIABLES OF HISTORICAL-COLONIAL LEGACY
Colonization–Slavery
Capitalism–Slavery
Slave Trade–Illegal Commerce
Racism–Racial Prejudice–Discrimination
Fear of Blacks
Whitening Policies
Ethnicity–Race–Color of Skin
Slavery–Abolition
Slavery–Annexation
Slavery–Independence Movement

> VARIABLES OF REPUBLICAN FRUSTRATION
> North American Intervention–Frustration of Independence
> Racism–Discrimination during the Republic
> Racism–Cuban Capitalism
>
> VARIABLES OF SOCIALIST REVOLUTIONARY SOCIETY
> Points of Departure for Racial Groups
> Inequality–Social Policy
> Cuban Racialism–Revolutionary Idealism
> Economic Crisis–Welfare Model
> Racial Prejudices–Discrimination–Racism
> Race–National Project
>
> (Morales Domínguez 2013, 45–46)

Today Black Studies is developing in Cuba on several fronts. The public silence on the experience of Afro-Cubans with racism was broken by the *Mesa Redonda* (Round Table) television program on January 20, 2009. This was driven by the work of Afro-Cuban intellectuals and party members at the National Library and Union of Writers and Artists of Cuba (UNEAC). People were unleashed to talk, tell their stories, and openly seek out more information (Farber 2011, 182; Morales Domínguez 2013, 90).

Another major development has been at Casa de las Américas, the national center for the promotion of academic and artistic work on the Western Hemisphere. It has created an African American Studies Program (Programa de Estudios Sobre Afro-America):

> Created in 2015, the program is an academic platform for research and promotion, aimed at deepening the studies of the African legacy in the culture of the continent. It also aims to link to institutions anywhere in the world dedicated to investigating, from a multidisciplinary perspective, the African presence in American art, literature and thought.
>
> The main objective of the program is to promote the exchange of knowledge and knowledge about the African footprint in the American arts and cultures, the consequences of the transatlantic trafficking and slavery and its consequences today, as well as the contributions of the descendants of Africans to the national communities of the Americas.
>
> (Casa de las Américas n.d.)

Under the direction of Zuleica Romay (an Afro-Cuban herself), this program began with a seminar on how the slave experience in Cuba left a legacy that continues today:

> First seminar of the Afro-American Studies Program: International Seminar—130 *Anniversary of the Abolition of Slavery in Cuba—Slavery is not a thing of the past* 2/15/2016 Casa de las Americas: "Commemorate 130 years of the abolition of slavery in Cuba not only expresses the will to remember a fact of great historical significance, it also states the willingness to identify, in the beats of the present, the traces of social relations that deeply marked the culture and psychology of the peoples of America, especially those who, between the sixteenth and nineteenth centuries, forged nationalities nurtured by the forced African diaspora."
>
> (AfroCubaWeb n.d.)

AMERICAS

There are three parts to the Americas: North, Central, and South. The countries of the Americas were once ruled as part of the colonial empires of England, Spain, France, Portugal, and the Netherlands. All were ravaged by genocidal policies against the indigenous population and the enslaved Africans. Historical memory was constructed by the colonial rulers, forcing the indigenous and the African to suffer an induced amnesia. Black Studies in each case has been a movement to restore historical identity, restore memory of a history of oppression and resistance, and to establish the cultural energy to transform society based on principles of social justice.

CANADA

The origin of Black Canada is a historical process that involves three systems of exploitation and resistance:

1. Settler colonialism and genocide of the indigenous Native peoples by the French and British
2. Enslavement of Africans
3. Destination for freedom seekers out of the USA

The fight for Black Studies has been about the full recognition of these three historical experiences and their legacy in institutional racism up to this current period. The main current driving force for Black Studies in Canada is based on settlers from the Caribbean and multigenerational Black Canadians.

The Black Power movement in the USA emerged in 1966 after the assassination of Malcolm X. The Black radical tradition was reborn in study groups and activist discourse in conferences. The Black Canadian experience involved the New World Group, the C.L.R. James Study Group, and the Caribbean Conference Committee. The New World Group was older established intellectuals (e.g., Lloyd Best from Trinidad and Tobago; Austin 2013, 32 and 74). The other two groups were driven by younger students from the Caribbean, who went on to spearhead political and intellectual developments in Canada, the USA, and their Caribbean homes (Austin 2013, 32 and 75).

Three Black Power events in Montreal shook up the ideological landscape and set the stage for Black Studies in Canada. The first was the October 1968 Congress of Black Writers held at McGill University. This event unleashed the Black radical tradition by bringing together an older generation (e.g., C.L.R. James and Richard Moore) with the 1960s generation (e.g., Walter Rodney, Tim Hector, Rosie Douglas, James Foreman, and Stokely Carmichael; Austin 2013, 105–28; 2018).

The second event, the Sir George Williams University struggle, occurred not long afterward in January–February 1969. In April of 1968, six West Indian students at Sir George Williams University had accused a biology professor of racist practices. After petitions, discussions, and community mobilization nothing had happened. The students took action and led about two hundred of their peers to seize and occupy the university computer center. They held it for two weeks and before being forced out trashed it (Austin 2013, 131–42; Forsythe 1971).

The third event was a Black Power confrontation at an October 1969 meeting of the African Studies Association (ASA). This was the emergence of the African Heritage Studies Association (AHSA), which, founded in December 1968, directly followed the line on African history advanced by Walter Rodney in his Black Workers Congress talk (cited in Austin 2018, 127–42). The AHSA rejected the white-dominated ASA and advanced a Black Power mission:

> We intend to use history as a force for our liberation and as a basis of African world unity. We depend on an honest and creative approach to history to tell what we have been, what we are, and what we still must be. And thus, the African Heritage Studies Association was born. (Clarke 1976, 9)

These three events impacted a range of people, from middle-class professionals and students down to the grass roots, reaching out to the diaspora communities linked to every Caribbean country. One key development was the establishment of locally based historical memory institutions, as shown in Table 7.

Table 7 Black Historical Memory Institutions in Canada

Year	*Name*
1975	Amherstburg Freedom Museum
1976	John Freeman Walls Historic Site and Underground Railroad Museum
1977	Black Cultural Society of Nova Scotia
1978	Ontario Black History Society
1992	Chatham-Kent Black Historical Society
1994	British Columbia Black History Awareness Society
2002	Saskatchewan African Canadian Heritage Museum
2007	Black History Month law passed in Quebec (February)
2010	New Brunswick Black History Society
2010	Africville Museum

Black Studies in Canada in its institutional form process as a twenty-first-century activity encompasses the publication of journals, the meetings of professional organizations, and the running of campus programs. *New Dawn* was the first Black Studies journal, publishing two issues, 2006 and 2007, the editor of which was Rinaldo Walcott. In 2006, Jennifer R. Kelly issued the first formal statement:

> Black Canadian studies, if one dares to lay claim to any finite definition, can be viewed as a diverse field that is unified through a heterogeneous exploration of the lived experiences of peoples of African descent residing within a nation-state called Canada.
>
> (Kelly 2006, 90)

Black Canadian Studies took another step forward with two special issues of journals, "Blacks in Canada: Retrospects, Introspects, Prospects" in *Journal of Black Studies* (Thornhill 2008), and "Black Canadian Thought" in the *CLR James Journal* (Henry 2014).

The Black Canadian Studies Association (BCSA) was founded in 2009.

> The BCSA set itself the following interim objectives: To create an institutional infrastructure of Black Canadian Studies in Canada, to support and facilitate interaction and exchange and networking between scholars, community historians and cultural workers of Black Studies here in Canada and abroad, to provide support for Black Canadian Studies scholars, academics, community historians and culture (and those of Black descent regardless of research interests and foci), and to actively encourage and support subsequent generations of scholars, researchers, community historians and cultural workers.
>
> The rest of the objectives are: to encourage the collection, documentation and preservation of a material culture relevant to the study of Blacks in Canada, to encourage a reassessment and activation of existing material cultural collections (or parts thereof) as relevant to Black Canadian Studies, to foster collective action and to challenge the Eurocentrism of Canadian Studies, and to demonstrate the historical and ongoing relevance of Black populations and experiences in Canada.
>
> (BCSA n.d.)

As of 2019, the BCSA Executive Board had representation from seven institutions: Dalhousie University, University of Toronto, McGill University, St Mary's University, York University, Acadia University, and Concordia University.

The first college-level course was introduced at the University of Toronto:

> in the 2014–2015 academic year under the CS Program Director Emily Gilbert, who is cross-appointed between the CS program and the Department of Geography & Planning. Gilbert returned to program's directorship in 2018, after serving a first term between 2010–2015.
>
> "I saw a real need for a course that would examine the experiences of Black Canadians in light of the renewed discussions of anti-Black racism in the wake of the Black Lives Matter movement," wrote Gilbert in an email to *The Varsity*. "While one course will not bring about needed institutional change, it is a small start."
>
> (Chowdhury 2020)

The next major development took place at Dalhousie University in Nova Scotia:

> In 2016, Dalhousie University launched what seems to be the first minor on the subject in this country—and even getting that in place took years. Afua Cooper set about requesting the program after she was named to the James Robinson Johnston Chair in Black Canadian Studies in 2011. According to Dr. Cooper, the first time around, the approval committee said the program's focus was too narrow. So, she rewrote it and brought it back a second time to a newly appointed committee—only to have it rejected, she recalls, for being too broad. The third time was the charm for Dalhousie's interdisciplinary Black and African diaspora studies minor. "Students love it," Dr. Cooper says, "whatever their race or ethnicity." Her intro class takes upwards of 70 people and she says it always has a waiting list.
>
> (Francis 2019, 1)

York University in Toronto followed two years later with another formal program initiative.

> [The] Black Canadian studies certificate and the Black studies and theories of race and racism graduate program stream … marks "an important moment in the advancement of scholarship in Black studies—both with a focus on Black Canada and in relation to the U.S. and the rest of the world." And at the program launch last October, Rhonda Lenton, York president and vice-chancellor, noted that the certificate was born of student advocacy and students' desire to see themselves reflected in the curriculum.
>
> (Francis 2019, 1)

Black Canadian Studies has developed in many other institutions. Two notable research centers have been established: The Harriet Tubman Institute for Research on Africa and Its Diasporas at York University; and The Institute for the Study of Canadian Slavery at the Nova Scotia College of Art and Design. The University of Waterloo has a major, with minors being offered at Ryerson University, Queen's University, and and the University of Guelph. Three institutions have established special research chairs as academic appointments in Black Canadian Studies: York University, Dalhousie University, and NSCAD University.

Katherine McKittrick, Canada Research Chair in Black Studies at Queen's University, is clear about the link between Black Studies and Black Liberation:

> Black Studies is, for me, a field that is invested in understanding the political struggles against different kinds and types of oppression. I'd also add that Black Studies is a creative-intellectual project that builds on, extends, and seeks practices of liberation. The aims of Black Studies differ across time and location, but there is a consistent and sustained commitment to theorizing and enacting social justice within and outside the academy.
>
> (McKittrick, quoted in Chagas 2022)

The field of Black Canadian Studies continues to build a literature, a process that is a dialectical development of local memory projects, public history, and academic research. There is also a battle of ideas that pits the academic scholarship against Black perspectives grounded in a Black liberation framework. This contrasts the work of Robin Winks, *The Blacks in Canada: A History* (1971) and Headley Tulloch, *Black Canadians: A Long Line of Fighters* (1975). There continues to be energy and momentum in the building of Black Canadian Studies (Winks 2008; Tulloch 1975; Walker 1982; Kitossa 2012).

BRAZIL

Beginning in the sixteenth century, enslaved African labor built Brazil under the rule of Portuguese colonialism. Africans were brought mainly from Angola. Afro-Brazilians were able to maintain an independent identity because of their ability to escape and establish autonomous villages of free people. The most famous was the Quilombo dos Palmares, a community that existed from 1630 to 1697 and had a population of over ten thousand at its height (Ramos 1980, 55–65). Brazil was the last country to end the legal slavery of Africans, doing so in 1888. The legacy of this is that in 2010, the official Brazilian census found for the first time that Black people were a majority of the population (T. Phillips 2011).

There have always been two parallel ways of thinking about the Afro-Brazilian experience, that of Afro-Brazilians themselves seeing it as acts of self-determination, and that of mainstream intellectuals mainly pursuing anti-racist reforms in interpreting the Afro-Brazilian experience. The first major development toward a new evaluation of the Black experience by mainstream scholars took place at the First Afro-Brazilian Congress of 1934 with a call to "'lay the foundation for a distinctive Africanology' as Brazilian scholars began to 'break the umbilical cord to Europe [and] suddenly became aware of the value of cultural traits which had come from Africa'" (Roger Bastide, cited in Romo 2007, 34). The purpose was in the invitation to the congress:

> The invitation proclaimed that the purpose of the event was to "study problems of race relations in Brazil and to trace African influence in the cultural development of the Brazilian people." The congress would examine the "problems of ethnography, folklore, art, sociology, and social psychology" and would also include exhibitions by artists.
>
> (Romo 2007, 37)

Following this meeting, Ramos proposed a series of topics that have relevance today for Afro-Brazilian Studies, listing twenty-four topics under the category "Problem of Slavery and Abolition" and twenty-three under "Influence of the Negro on Brazilian Life and Civilization." The list would be revised, however, to include a bolder Black consciousness, targeting institutional racism and all forms of resistance (Ramos 1980, 188–89).

During the decade after the congress, Brazil became a focus for scholars from the USA, among them Melville Herskovits, E. Franklin Frazier, and Lorenzo Dow Turner. Frazier and Turner, two Black scholars, differed on the question of the importance of African cultural retentions in the West. The obvious replication of African cultural practices in Brazil bolstered Turner's position (Sansone 2011).

It must be noted that Afro-Brazilians were active in representing themselves before 1934. The self-determination effort of Afro-Brazilians is exemplified in the life and work of Abdias do Nascimento (1914–2011). In 1931, at the age of seventeen, he joined the Frente Negra Brasileira (Brazilian Black Front), which had been active since the 1920s. His political activity led to his being arrested and incarcerated for a year (1937–1938). Like the US activists, who created Black Studies as a particular thrust of a wider social movement, Nascimento combined his political with his cultural initiatives, as he explains in an autobiographical essay, *Africans in Brazil: A Pan-African Perspective* (Nascimento and Nascimento 1992). Key dates in his life include:

1931 Nascimento joined the Brazilian Black Front (1992, 14–16)
1936 While in prison he formed the Theater of the Convicts (1992, 23–24)
1944 Founded the Black Experimental Theater (1992, 21–29)
1945 Founded the National Convention of Brazilian Blacks (1992, 33–36)
1950 Founded the First National Congress of Brazilian Blacks (1992, 36–37)

Looking back, Abdias do Nascimento notes:

> The Congress was a landmark in Afro-Brazilian history. For the first time, we Africans discussed our concerns publicly, as masters of our own destinies, not only in the form of academic papers or formal oral and written communications, but more importantly in spontaneous improvisation. The spontaneity and self-determination were the accents that marked the radical differences between the First Congress of Brazilian Blacks and the previous Afro-Brazilian Congresses that had been held in the thirties in Recife and Bahia … In these it was the pomp and circumstance of white scholars and scientists that prevailed. They organized and directed everything, while African Brazilians were displayed merely as "ethnographic material," the object of research.
>
> Africans were in charge of the First Congress of Brazilian Blacks, and at various sessions we aggressively confronted the subtle forms of paternalism emanating from "scientists" and other whitenesses.
>
> (Nascimento and Nascimento 1992, 37)

Nascimento went into exile from 1968 to 1981, most of the time holding academic positions in the USA, though he was a visiting scholar at the University of Ife in Nigeria (now Obafemi Awolowo University) for a year. After returning to Brazil, he set up a Black Studies program modeled after his experiences in the USA:

> In 1981, leaving exile behind and coming to live in Brazil, Nascimento founded the Afro-Brazilian Studies and Research Institute (IPEAFRO). At first in São Paulo at the Pontifical Catholic University (PUC), an institution identified with the Liberation Theology and progressive political thought. Unfortunately, PUC was financially unable to sustain the Institute. It was moved to Rio de Janeiro as an indepen-

> dent organization. There, it continued publishing *Afrodiáspora* journal and offering courses at the State University of Rio de Janeiro (UERI) on African and Afro-Brazilian culture, aimed largely at primary and secondary public school teachers.
>
> (Nascimento and Nascimento 1992, 68)

While Nascimento was in exile, some developments did take place even under the military dictatorship ruling Brazil. The Unified Black Movement formed in 1978 as a coalition of forces working together. A main place for this was in Rio de Janeiro, especially within the Institute for the Research of Black Culture (IPCN, Instituto de Pesquisa da Cultura Negra). They were joined by Brasil África Chamber of Commerce, the Rio de Janeiro Art and Folklore Museum, the Center for Afro Asian Studies, the Quilombo Recreation Club for Black Art and Samba, and the Afoxé Filhos de Gandhi dance group (IPCN 2018).

The next major development took place after Luiz Inácio Lula da Silva (Lula), a former trade union activist, became president in 2003. Most notably,

> Federal Law 10.639 of 9 January 2003 was sanctioned by president Luiz Inácio Lula da Silva, making the inclusion of studies of "Afro-Brazilian History and Culture" mandatory in the education system curriculum. In 2004, the National Council of Education approved the National Curriculum Guidelines for the Education of Ethnic and Racial Relations and the Teaching of Afro-Brazilian and African History and Culture.
>
> (Guimarães 2015, 942)

In addition, Lula appointed Gilberto Passos Gil Moreira Minister of Culture (2003–2008), who became the second Afro-Brazilian serving in the presidential cabinet. Gil's policies advanced Afro-Brazilian music into the heart of Brazil's culture.

Two important institutions were created in 2004. Following the US model of HBCU institutions, Brazil created an institution mainly focused on the Afro-Brazilians, the Faculdade Zumbi dos Palmares. This college was named after the great Afro-Brazilian Zumbi (1655–1695), who was the leader of the largest settlement of freed slaves, Palmares. Also, the Museu Afro Brasil was established in São Paulo.

There was an emphasis on improving education attainment for Afro-Brazilians. In 2001, Blacks were 10.2 percent of all students, and by 2011 their percentage had increased to 35.8:

> The number of black students (blacks and browns) in the masters and doctorates more than doubled from 2001 to 2013, from 48,500 to 112,000, according to data from the National Household Sample Survey (Pnad). Considering only the black students, the number went from 6 thousand to 18.8 thousand, an increase of more than three times. Although they represent the majority of the population (52.9%), black students represent only 28.9% of the total number of post-graduates.
>
> (Tokarnia 2018)

Along with this increase were developments that expressed the militant agency of the Afro-Brazilian people. They fought for and gained official recognition of November 20 as a national Black Consciousness Day. This parallels Carter Woodson's achievement of formal recognition of African-American history in February in the USA. To advance research, the Brazilian Association of Black Researchers was established; this organization publishes a journal to make the work of Black researchers readily available (Revista da ABPN n.d.).

Brazil has a strong focus on the country's ties to Africa. The University for International Integration of the Afro-Brazilian Lusophony was founded in 2010 in the first Brazilian city to end slavery, Redenção. It has a global focus and as part of its mission at least half of its students are from African countries that experienced Portuguese colonialism: Brazil, Angola, Cape Verde, Guinea-Bissau, São Tomé and Príncipe, and Mozambique (Sawahel 2013). Elsewhere in Brazil,

> the University of São Paulo offers a masters in education for Angolans, while the federal center of higher studies in Rio Grande do Sul participated in implementing the first course in agronomy at the University of Cape Verde. The collaborative plan also includes granting scholarships to African students to study in Brazilian higher education institutions.
>
> (Sawahel 2013)

A collaborative project with Nigeria is the Center for Afro-Brazilian Studies launched at Lagos State University in 2019 (Lagos State University n.d.).

In the USA, several universities have programs that focus on the Afro-Brazilian experience, as shown in Table 8.

Table 8 US Programs in Afro-Brazilian Studies

Institution	*Program*
University of Massachusetts Dartmouth	PhD in Luso-Afro-Brazilian Studies and Theory
University of Michigan Ann Arbor	Graduate Certificate in Afro-Luso-Brazilian Studies
Howard University	Minor in Afro-Brazilian Studies
Ohio State University	Afro-Brazilian Culture and History (study tour course)
University of Texas	Luso-Afro-Brazilian Literary and Cultural Studies
Vanderbilt University	Capoeira: Afro-Brazilian Race, Culture, and Expression

ASIA

Asia is the most distant region of the world in terms of the African Diaspora. These countries have experienced much the same colonial domination as Africa and the Caribbean. This helps to explain how they have identified with the oppressed in the African Diaspora.

JAPAN

Japan did not have colonial relations with Africa, and never had a large African descendant population, but there were connections to Africa and the African Diaspora:

> The Japanese encounter with black people dates back to 1546, when three Portuguese ships arrived in Japan, carrying a Mozambican. … A Catholic priest reported the incident in a letter to his colleague. "Many," he wrote, "came to see the Negro all the way from as far as a distance of sixty miles. … [T]hey would pay money to see slaves from Ethiopia. Anybody could make money around here merely by showing a Negro."
> (Tsujiuchi 1998, 95)

While Blacks were an object of fascination and exploitation, there is also the story of at least one hero who achieved high status within feudal Japanese society.

Known as Yasuke, the man was a warrior who reached the rank of samurai under the rule of Oda Nobunaga—a powerful sixteenth-century Japanese feudal lord who was the first of the three unifiers of Japan. In 1579, his arrival in Kyoto, the capital at the time, caused such a sensation that people climbed over one another to get a glimpse of him with some being crushed to death, according to historian Lawrence Winkler. Within a year, Yasuke had joined the upper echelons of Japan's warrior class, the samurai. Before long, he was speaking Japanese fluently and riding alongside Nobunaga in battle. "His height was 6 shaku 2 sun (roughly 6 feet, 2 inches, 1.88m) ... he was black, and his skin was like charcoal," a fellow samurai, Matsudaira Ietada, described him in his diary in 1579 (Mohamud 2019).

The Japanese themselves faced two aspects of racism. First, racial hierarchy became regarded as biological fact in the country after the Japanese translation of Darwin's *Descent of Man* in 1881, even while it was clear that they were not at the top. At the same time, faced with US racism and "yellow peril" fear-mongering, many Japanese intellectuals and politicians began to regard African Americans as potential allies in any conflict with the USA (Tsujiuchi 1998, 97).

In the years prior to World War II, Black leaders had positive views of Japan. The Japanese victory over Russia in their 1905 war was viewed as proof that white supremacy over colored people was a myth. Japan carried this image forward in an anti-racist move at the founding of the League of Nations: "[A]t the Paris Peace Conference in 1919 ... the Japanese proposed the introduction of the principle of racial equality in the charter of the League of Nations" (Tsujiuchi 1998, 98).

The USA and its allies voted this proposal down, but it won great admiration among Black people. Horne sums up this widespread belief:

> In the period before World War II, Japan was probably the nation most admired among African Americans. ... Du Bois, Garvey, Booker T. Washington, and others may have had conflicts among themselves, but all looked to Tokyo as evidence for the proposition that modernity was not solely the province of those of European descent and that the very predicates of white supremacy made no sense.
>
> (Horne 2011, 16 and 18)

During and after the Great Depression, there was a working-class awakening in the Black community, and a resurgence of Black nationalism as well. The Japanese government saw an opportunity for coordination, as evidenced by the US activities of Satokata Takahashi (1870–1945), a retired major of the Imperial Japanese Army and member of the Black Dragon Society, a secret paramilitary Japanese organization. In 1932, he began to attend meetings of the UNIA. He married an African-American woman and became close friends with the Nation of Islam leadership. His role was to promote Black support for a future race war between Japan and the USA (Allen 1994).

Hikita Yasuichi (1890–1947) exemplifies a literary expression of this Japanese nationalism. He was around New York at the time of the Harlem Renaissance and invited James Weldon Johnson (1929) and Du Bois (1936) to visit Japan. He translated *Fire in the Flint* (1924) by Walter White, which sold well in Japan as an anti-lynching story (Kato 2013, 831).

There was also a rising Marxist trend in Japanese intellectual circles. Sen Katayama (1859–1933) studied in the USA, earning a degree from Yale Divinity School. He came to know Black left-wing intellectuals like Claude McKay (1890–1948). The two met again in Moscow at the Fourth World Congress of the Communist International in 1922. As a close friend of Lenin, Katayama was active in the conference, and

> McKay was very impressed with the candid way Katayama as an officer of Comintern in charge of racial issues, criticized White comrades from the United States for their unconscious prejudice against Black people due to their upbringings, and asserted that if they really wanted to understand Black people, they should learn about them and be educated among Black peoples like he was educated among them.
>
> (Kato 2013, 832)

The defeat of the Japanese in World War II led to US occupation and that included Black soldiers bringing the US Black experience deep into Japan. This led Nukina Yoshitaka (1911–1985) to establish the Japanese Association of Negro Studies just after the US Supreme Court decision that attempted to end school segregation in 1954.

Yoshitaka, a scholar of American literature, founded the association, called Kokujin Kenkyu no Kai (Association of Negro Studies), in Tokyo, Japan in October 1954. He wrote to Robert Williams in Cuba, explaining the mission of his organization: "Kokujin Kenkyu no Kai is not only an academic research group but [also] moves against [all forms of] racial discrimination and participates in democratization movements in Japan" (Nukina Yoshitaka, cited in Onishi 2013, 98–99).

Kayomi Wada adds:

> Nukina Yoshitaka, a scholar in American literature, wrote that he was motivated to found the Black Studies Association in Tokyo, Japan in October of 1954 because he believed Japanese under United States military control had a commonality with African Americans, as both had their nationalistic/racial pride stripped by American capitalism and imperialism.
>
> (Wada 2008)

The association's journal, *Kokujin Kenkyu* (*Negro Studies*), was launched in 1956.

Fumiko Sakashita has organized a collection of statements by key figures in the Japanese Association of Black Studies, "When and Where We Entered: Intellectual Autobiographies of Japan's Black Studies Scholars" (Onishi and Sakashita 2019, 57–71). Table 9 lists the officers of the association since its inception.

Table 9 Officers of the Japanese Association of Black Studies

Name	*Position*	*Years*
Hiromi Furukawa	President	1992–1996
Nukina Yoshitaka	President	1954–1992
Atsuko Furomoto	Vice-President	1995–2004
Keiko Kusundse	Vice-President	2005–2009
Tsunehiko Kato	President	2010–2015
Gishin Kitajima	President	2005–2010
Toru Kiuchi	President	2020–

In 2009, Hiromi Furukawa recounted the origins of the association:

> At the high school where I taught, the first textbook I chose as a subsidiary reader was Langston Hughes's *One Friday Morning and Other Stories*. The protagonist of the title story, being rejected for a scholarship because of her color, finally came to think "liberty and justice for all" is "the land we must make." This resolution moved my students immensely.
>
> Encouraged by these we organized a research circle in June 1954, then called the Association of Negro Studies. From a group of a dozen

> people or so at the start, the organization has grown to the present membership of about 140 including some foreign scholars. The association, I am sure, has contributed to a lot of enlightenment as well as the studies in Japan of the history and culture of Black Africans and those in the diaspora.
>
> (Onishi and Sakashita 2019, 61)

The members formed around the practice of translating African-American authors. Among the results were translations of works by W.E.B. Du Bois by Nukina Yoshitaka; Langston Hughes, Richard Wright, and Ann Petry by Hiromi Furukawa; Paule Marshall, Octavia Butler, and Alice Walker by Atsuko Furomoto; and Harry Haywood by Tamura Tetsuya. They were determined to introduce Black intellectual production into Japanese political and cultural discourse.

Another major development was an anthology published in 1966, edited by Hiromi Furukawa and Mitsuo Akamatsu, *Amerika Kokujin Kaiho Undo: Atarashi Niguro Gunzo* (*The Black American Liberation Movement: The New Negro Crowd*). The editors included writings by W.E.B. Du Bois, John Henrik Clarke, Julian Mayfield, Robert Williams, Martin Luther King, James Baldwin, Kenneth Clark, Lorraine Hansberry, and Langston Hughes (Onishi 2013, 121–22).

The organization took on new energy with a focus on Black women writers in the 1980s. The key event was its thirtieth anniversary conference, which featured discussions of the writings of Alice Walker, Toni Morrison, and Paule Marshall (Kiuchi 2014, 5).

The organization remains engaged today, as demonstrated by a letter from its current president Toru Kiuchi after the George Floyd murder:

> I have been inspired by protestors against Mr. Floyd's death across the world, and also saddened by the fact that 66 years after the 1954 establishment of the JBSA, a system of institutional racism remains across the United States as well as Asian countries. Including Japan … As I mourn the death of George Floyd, I stand in solidarity with the millions of protestors in American cities and around the world and conclude by stating unequivocally that #black lives matter in the United States and Japan.
>
> (Kiuchi 2020)

One important scholar of Japanese origin is Yuichiro Onishi, working as a tenured professor in the Department of African American and

African Studies at the University of Minnesota. He connects the Asian experience with the Black experience in the USA. In his own words:

> My work specifically centers on the study of Black thought and struggles in relation to Japan and Okinawa. I am continuing the work I started in my first book, *Transpacific Antiracism* (NYU Press, 2013). It rests on the question of liberation, on the one hand, and "the problem of the color line," as W.E.B. Du Bois pronounced at the turn of the twentieth century amid a triumphant rise and expansion of colonial modernity, on the other hand. I explore the relationship between the two: the question of how to be free and learn to live together in a highly unequal and uneven world where race—a marker of difference and a mechanism of differentiation—dynamically imbricates relations of domination and emancipatory strivings.
>
> (Onishi 2020)

CHINA

Black people have had a long history in China. China did not invade Africa as a colonial power, but China was part of an international trade network along with Africa since at least the Tang Dynasty (AD 618–907): "During the Tang Dynasty, Arab traders brought African slaves from east Africa to China. They comprised one of the many commodities in the Arabs' large-scale maritime trade with China" (Lofton 2015).

On the other hand, China experienced colonization and imperialist plunder, thus sharing a historical condition that dominated Africa. The Chinese in the twentieth century identified with African forces fighting for their independence and freedom.

Li Anshan sums up China's relationship with Africa in the twentieth century in four stages:

> 1. Sensing Africa (1900–1949)
> 2. Supporting Africa (1949–1965)
> 3. Understanding Africa (1966–1976)
> 4. Studying Africa (1977–2000)
>
> (Anshan 2005, 59)

However, Mao, recognizing that more needed to be done, made this statement on April 27, 1961:

> An institute of Africa should be established, studying African history, geography and the socio-economic situation. We don't have a clear understanding of African history, geography and the present situation, so a concise book is badly needed. It doesn't need to be big, about one hundred to two hundred pages are enough. We can invite African friends to help and get it published in one or two years. It should include the contents of how imperialism came, how it suppressed the people, how it met people's resistance, why the resistance failed and how it is now rising.
>
> (Mao, cited in Anshan 2005, 62–63)

On July 4, 1961 the School of Asian and African Studies was founded under the leadership of the Communist Party and the Chinese Academy of Sciences (BFSU n.d.). In 1962, in anticipation of a trip to Africa by Premier Zhou Enlai, the book Mao called for was published, *African Introduction*. Following this, the main work was translating books into Chinese. The featured authors included Jamal Abdel Nasser, Kwame Nkrumah, Ahmed Ben Bella, Majhemout Diop, Jack Woodis, Basil Davidson, and W.E.B. Du Bois. A full literature review of African Studies publications is provided by Anshan (2005).

Even before the 1949 revolution, African Americans visited China and began to identify with their struggle. Langston Hughes visited in 1934, meeting with the important innovator of modern Chinese literature Lu Xun. Also, W.E.B. Du Bois made his first visit in 1936.

Du Bois returned to China in 1955, where

> he was received with great acclaim and met with Communist Party leaders. He returned a third time with his wife Shirley Graham Du Bois in 1959 and on this trip met with Mao Zedong, the head of the Communist Party and leader of China. In 1977 Shirley Graham Du Bois died in Beijing, China after a long battle with breast cancer.
>
> (Lofton 2015, 10)

Revolutionary China opened its doors to many African-American delegations, including the Black Panther leaders Huey Newton and Elaine Brown, James Foreman, Bill Epton, Vicki Garvin, and Robert Williams. Garvin played a key role within China:

> Through DuBois Garvin got a job as a "polisher" for the English translations of the *Peking Review* as well as a teaching position at the Shanghai Foreign Language Institute. She remained in China from 1964 to 1970, building bridges between the black freedom struggle, the African independence movements, and the Chinese revolution.
>
> (Kelley and Esch 2008, 105)

Robert Williams was living in China as a guest of the government, while the US government had a warrant for his arrest. He was in contact with Chairman Mao and prompted him to make a statement on August 8, 1963, just weeks before the March on Washington held on August 28, 1963. Here is what Mao said:

> An American Negro leader now taking refuge in Cuba, Mr. Robert Williams, the former President of the Monroe, North Carolina, Chapter of the National Association for the Advancement of Coloured People, has twice this year asked me for a statement in support of the American Negroes' struggle against racial discrimination. I wish to take this opportunity, on behalf of the Chinese people, to express our resolute support for the American Negroes in their struggle against racial discrimination and for freedom and equal rights.
>
> (Mao Tse-Tung 1963)

This was followed by another statement in 1968 after the murder of Martin Luther King. This clear support of the social justice struggle of the African Americans set the stage for Black Studies in China.

The following commentary on Black Studies in China was obtained via a WeChat interview with Professor Yu Zhan from the School of History, Capital Normal University.

> The confrontation and struggle between China and the United States in the 1950s and 1960s led to the first upsurge of the study of the history of African Americans in China, mainly supporting and praising the struggle of African Americans and opposing American imperialism. In 1993, on the 125th anniversary of Dubois's birth, the Chinese authorities held a high-profile seminar, setting up the Dubois Research Institute to conduct in-depth research on Dubois.
>
> In the People's Republic of China, Professors Yang Shengmao, Liu Xuyi, and Liu Zuochang were the founders of the study of American

history in China and also the pioneers of African-American history. They were all students who went to the United States to study before 1949 and then returned to China to start the discipline of American history. In the 1960s, under the direction of Chairman Mao Zedong, American research centers were established at Nankai University and Wuhan University. Because the Civil Rights Movement was in full swing in the United States, one of the focuses of the two centers was African-American history. Mr. Liu Xuyi of Wuhan University mainly studied the Black Civil Rights Movement at that time, while Mr. Yang Shengmao of Nankai University focused on the overall history of black struggle, edited the Civil War data collection, and had a unique understanding of the relationship between Lincoln and the abolition of slavery. Mr. Liu Zuochang of Shandong Normal University has done in-depth research on blacks in the Civil War, Lincoln and slavery, Douglass and the African-American liberation movement, and has written many papers on his own and has written a history of the Civil War. In addition, Professor Tang Taohua of South China Normal University was a pioneer in the study of slavery in the United States.

In the 1950s and 1960s, many American scholars' works on African-American studies were translated and introduced to China. W.E.B. Du Bois, *The Souls of Black Folk*, trans. Wei Qun (Beijing: People's Literature Publishing House, 1959); W.Z. Foster, *The Negro People in American History*, trans. Yu Jiahuang (Beijing: Sanlian Publishing House, 1960); Harry Haywood, *Negro Liberation*, trans. Rong Yilun et al. (Beijing: World Knowledge Press, 1954); Herbert Aptheker, *The Uprising of American Slaves*, trans. Yang Jingyuan (Beijing: Life, Reading, Xinzhi Sanlian Publishing House, 1958); Robert Williams, *Negroes with Guns*, trans. Lu Ren (Beijing: World Knowledge Press, 1962); James Allen, *The African American Problem and the Agricultural Economy of the South*, trans. Zhang Yousong (Beijing: Zhonghua Book Company, 1954). Other famous translations include Robert Allen, *Black Awakening in Capitalist America*, trans. the Sixth Translation Group of the Shanghai May Seventh Cadre School (Shanghai: Shanghai People's Publishing House, 1976); Ann Petry, *The Street*, trans. Liu Xuyi et al. (Changsha: Hunan People's Publishing House, 1984); Joanne Grant, *The Struggle of the Negro in America: History, Literature, and Analysis, 1619 to the Present*, trans. Guo Ying et al. (Beijing: China Social Sciences Press, 1987); John Franklin, *A History of Black America*, trans. Zhang Bingzi et al. (Beijing: The Commercial

Press, 1988); Du Bois, *The Autobiography of W.E.B. Du Bois: A Soliloquy on Viewing My Life from the Last Decade of Its First Century*, trans. Zou Dezhen et al. (Beijing: Encyclopedia of China Press, 1996); B.T. Washington, *Up from Slavery: The Autobiography of Booker T. Washington*, trans. Siguo (Shenyang: Liaoning Education Press, 1997); Eric Foner, *Gateway to Freedom: The Hidden History of the Underground Railroad*, trans. Jiao Jiao (Beijing: China University of Political Science and Law Press, 2017); Eric Foner, *The Fiery Trial: Abraham Lincoln and American Slavery*, trans. Yu Yuzhen (Beijing: The Commercial Press, 2017), etc.

Professor Yu makes these summary comments:

> Some achievements have been made in the study of African-American history in China, but there are still many shortcomings. The research contents and fields are still somewhat poor and narrow, mainly limited to the history of Black oppression, discrimination, resistance and struggle, and other aspects of Black society, culture, including family and religion are relatively few. The character research also mainly focuses on the upper Black leaders, but obviously does not pay enough attention to the lower Black people. The study of the history of Black women in particular needs to be strengthened. In the data mining and application, our defects and deficiencies are obvious. In terms of research methods, there are a few comparative studies, but this is far from enough. As for interdisciplinary studies, there are even fewer, which has seriously restricted the expansion and deepening of the study of Black history. In terms of research theories and perspectives, although there have been some refreshing works and articles published in recent years, generally speaking, the outdated and narrow theories and perspectives are still a prominent problem. In the introduction and reference, digestion, and absorption of American scholars in the latest research results, we also appear very lagging and insufficient. There are few scholars in China who specialize in African-American history, and there has not yet produced a high-level and representative comprehensive treatise. All these deficiencies need to be improved in the future research.

Some recent works have continued to explore the relationship between the Chinese Communist Revolution and the African-American Left, especially W.E.B. Du Bois, Paul Robeson, and Robert Williams (Zhu 2018; Gao 2021).

Professor Yu also compiled a bibliography that provides empirical indicators of the kind of research being done in African-American Studies in China (Table 10).

Table 10 Black Studies Publications in China, by Decades

Decade	*Books*	*Dissertations*
1970s	3	
1980s	1	
1990s	9	
2000s	14	38
2010s	16	30

AFRICA

The greatest expectation for Black Studies focuses on Africa, but the lack of Black Studies in Africa brings with it our greatest disappointment. The legacy of colonial domination remains strong, including the relatively weak development of higher education in Africa. There is some development in every country, but memory institutions (libraries, museums, etc.) remain limited, and academic institutions usually do not have formal units that focus on their national experience or Africa and the African Diaspora in general. The main case to report on is Ghana.

GHANA

Courses and degree-granting programs focusing on African-American history and culture are not found on the African continent. So why stop to examine Ghana? Because it was in Ghana that African and African Diaspora studies was initiated in Africa. It developed not only through the anti-colonial struggle, but also in relation to the African-American experience, in the academy and the community.

Ghana is a West African country that was colonized by the British. The political geography of West Africa is a historical legacy of different colonial systems, so Ghana happens to share borders with only countries colonized by France: Togo, Ivory Coast, and Burkina Faso. Ghana has a history that spans the diverse experiences of the pan-African world: traditional Africa, slavery, colonialism, independence and national development, agency for pan-Africanism, and repatriation from the African Diaspora. The slave trade began its linkage to the USA, the colonial experience to the UK. After its independence, the self-determination of its leadership linked it to all of Africa and the African Diaspora.

The key figure in the origin of Black Studies in Africa is Kwame Nkrumah (1909–1972), the first leader of independent Ghana (1957). Nkrumah was a Diaspora man, in that he studied and was active in both the USA and the UK as a result. He developed a Diaspora-wide network of colleagues and co-workers.

After collaborating with them on the Fifth Pan-African Congress in Manchester, UK in 1945, he maintained the closest ties with W.E.B. Du Bois (1868–1963) and George Padmore (1903–1959). All this led to his leading the fight for Ghanaian independence.

Nkrumah was a student at Lincoln University in Pennsylvania (1935–1939) under the presidency of Horace Mann Bond, who also became a long-time friend and mentor. He enrolled on the advice of Nnamdi Azikiwe, who later became president of Nigeria. Azikiwe, a graduate-student instructor in the history and political science departments at Lincoln University, had created a course in African history at the school with the support of President Bond (Bond 1976, 488–502). While in the USA, Nkrumah spent time in New York and became acquainted with African-American intellectual and political circles (Sherwood 1996, 27–48).

Nkrumah went to London after graduation. George Padmore met him at the train station and took him to get a room at the West African Students' Union (WASU). For the next two years, he built a network of Ghanaian colleagues who were destined to lead the new Ghana. He worked with Padmore to organize the 1945 Pan-African Congress in Manchester (Adi 1998, 125–28; Sherwood 1996, 114–21).

After the congress, he began to plan action for achieving the independence of Africa:

> Perhaps a more effective practical step was the setting up of an organization known as "The Circle." … The need was felt for a vanguard group—a political cadre—to train for revolutionary work in any part of the African continent. I was made chairman of the Circle.
>
> (Nkrumah 1980, 46)

He formulated and published his political views in *Towards Colonial Freedom* (1947). For the next decade, Nkrumah put his practical plan to work so effectively that he led the political movement that liberated Ghana from British colonialism.

Ghana was a beacon of light for African independence in 1957 and Nkrumah its charismatic leader. On the education front, he established the Kwame Nkrumah University of Science and Technology in Kumasi in 1961. This institution was meant to replicate the land-grant institutions in the USA and promote the economic development of Ghana. Related to that, he built the Akosombo Dam in 1965 as a practical example of using self-produced electricity to free African countries from colonial dependence.

Nkrumah was committed to building educational institutions that would help Ghana understand itself and all of Africa. The banner year was 1961, when Nkrumah set up three seminal institutions. The first Black Studies program in Ghana—in all of Africa, in fact—was the Institute of African Studies (IAS), established as part of the University of Ghana:

> From the very beginning the IAS was intended to be Ghana's main focus on Africa as well as its influence and role of her peoples throughout the world. The IAS was established to provide: (i) a focus for research and postgraduate teaching in African Studies in the Universities and Higher Institutions of Ghana, and (ii) a centre for research workers in African Studies in Ghana as well as a base for affiliated scholars and post-graduate students from other universities engaged in field work Kwame Nkrumah did not fail to charge the IAS with the pursuit of pan-African ideals by eliminating colonial influences in African Studies, extending the area of study to peoples of African descent in the Americas and the Caribbean and by co-ordinating with institutes and centres of African studies in other African states to produce an "extensive and diversified Library of African Classics."
>
> (Agbodeka 1998, 169)

This was an intervention in the university to begin the long march of institutional decolonization and Africanization.

He also set up a major library.

> In 1961, when the new research library of African Affairs was opened in Accra, Nkrumah named it The George Padmore Memorial Library.

> This library was to be a centre for research into the life of the peoples of the African continent. In common with most of the new amenities provided during Nkrumah's time, the library was, in his words, to know "no national frontiers: for here shall be stored the cumulative experience, the collective wisdom and knowledge about the entire continent of Africa, and the assessment, re-evaluation and studies of observers from all over the world. … May it be an instrument of scholarship for the study of the African peoples, and an inspiration for those who work towards African freedom and unity."
>
> (Milne 2000, 135)

The third institution, the Kwame Nkrumah Ideological Institute at Winneba, was established in 1961 to implement the plan he had formulated in London for cadre development. This was an educational program to develop agents of change armed with knowledge about Africa and Nkrumah's vision of a united continent based on socialism. He stated as much in his address at the opening of the institute:

> The Kwame Nkrumah Institute will not cater for Ghana alone. Its doors will be opened to all from Africa and the world both who seek knowledge to fit themselves for the great freedom fight against imperialism and colonialism old and new, and the consolidation of peace throughout the world for the progress of mankind.
>
> (Nkrumah 1980, 169)

To help build these institutions for the consolidation of the revolutionary transformation of Ghana, Nkrumah recruited from his network of comrades throughout the African Diaspora. This included, among others, George Padmore, T. Ras Makonnen, and Jan Carew (Guyana), Neville Dawes (Jamaica), and many African Americans from the USA (Gaines 2008).

St. Clair Drake, sociologist, as mentioned above, accepted an offer from Nkrumah to take leave from Roosevelt University in Chicago, where he was based, to head the Department of Sociology at the University of Ghana (1958–1961). W.E.B. Du Bois relocated to Ghana to implement his dream for an "Encyclopedia Africana," work that absorbed him until his death in 1963 (Aptheker 2000; Contee 1971). At the same time, his wife Shirley Graham Du Bois became a central figure in the development of Ghanaian television (Home 2008, 164–96). Alphaeus Hunton, an English professor at Howard University, joined Du Bois in Ghana to help with the encyclopedia project (Hunton 1986, 128–47). Du Bois stated his goal for this Black Studies project:

> My idea is to prepare and publish an Encyclopedia not on the vague subject of race, but on the peoples inhabiting the continent of Africa. I propose an Encyclopedia edited mainly by African scholars. I am anxious that it be a scientific production and not a matter of propaganda. While there should be included among its writers the best students of Africa in the world, I want the proposed Encyclopedia to be written mainly from the African point of view by people who know and understand the history and culture of Africans.
>
> (Du Bois 1962)

By the early 1960s, a community of radical African-American expatriates had moved to Ghana and were active supporters of Nkrumah. This included, among others, Julian Mayfield, Alice Windom, Maya Angelou, Vicki Garvin, Bill Sutherland, Wendell Jean Pierre, William Gardner Smith, Preston King, and Lester Lacy. They were mainly based in the media and at the university. This community was greatly impacted by the visit of Malcolm X in 1964. Malcolm made speeches at the University of Ghana and the Winneba Ideological Institute and to the Ghana parliament. The African-American experience was a featured topic of the day (X et al. 2013, 46–58; Sherwood 2011a, 34–61).

After the end of the Nkrumah regime and Du Bois's death, the project was run by Hunton for a short time and then phased out under Ghanaian leadership. It was taken up years later, but without the leadership that gave it international prominence, so it has not accomplished its original goals. Bright Gyamfi (2021) presents an important analysis of the impact of the Ghanaian diaspora on Black Studies in the Americas.

The major work in Black Studies was continued at the University of Ghana. A course in African Studies is required for all students. More than one thousand international students study there each year, mainly from other African countries and the USA. The university also hosts many study-abroad programs, for instance, from the University of Kansas, the University of California, and State University of New York campuses at Brockport and Stony Brook.

The Ghanaian government has made the major step of offering citizenship to people in the African Diaspora.

African Studies has spread in Africa following the lead of Nkrumah. The following institutions are examples of this trend:

- Egypt: Institute of African Research and Studies, Cairo University
- Ethiopia: Center for African Studies, University of Addis Ababa
- Nigeria: Institute of African Studies, University of Ibadan
- Nigeria: Institute of African and Diaspora Studies, University of Lagos
- Senegal: Institut Fondamental d'Afrique Noire, Cheikh Anta Diop
- South Africa: Centre for African Studies (CAS), University of Cape Town
- South Africa: Centre for Gender and African Studies, University of the Free State
- South Africa: National Heritage and Cultural Studies, University of Fort Hare

A great vision was generated out of liberated South Africa called the African Renaissance by President Thabo Mbeki. The concept was adopted by the African Union in the Charter for African Cultural Renaissance, adopted in 2006:

> African States should strengthen their ties with the African Diaspora worldwide in the areas of culture, education, science and technology, finance and economy. They should support the members of the African Diaspora to better interact with local, regional, and national authorities in their respective countries of residence, capable of seeking solutions to the problems facing their communities. They should also assist them to participate further in the development of Africa.
>
> (African Union 1963)

The next stage has to be setting up African-American Studies programs in Africa. There are none at the present time.

SUMMARY

The African Diaspora has been a focus for Black Studies in the USA at every stage of its development. The post-World War II decolonization process and the global impact of the Black Power movement advanced Black Studies throughout the African Diaspora.

1. Following the spread of the African Diaspora, Black Studies in its many national forms extended to every part of the world;
2. The challenge of Black Studies analysis is the dialectical relationship of analysis in particular cultures and languages, spanning and clarifying differences in culture, language, and historical periodizations, while contextualizing the analysis in the general historical periodization of the African Diasporas;
3. In its totality, Black Studies in the African Diaspora is critical to rethinking the historical experience of the African Diasporas in the context of world history;
4. A major lesson for people in the African Diaspora is to think globally and act locally; the basic footprint for understanding and changing the world is where people live.

PART III

Black Studies as Knowledge Network

The third major aspect of the future of Black Studies is the impact of information technology. It should be obvious by now in this analysis because Afrofuturism and the African Diaspora have been developed precisely because of information technology. This is part of a technological transformation of society in all its aspects. Education is a primary part of this change. The Covid-19 pandemic, that forced a shutdown of normal social life, including schooling at all levels, has led to the normalization of information technology at a high level of everyday use.

Our concern is to begin by reviewing key examples of how technological change has made a great import on the Black experience, from the rural experience in the South, picking cotton, to the urban industrial throughout the country, mainly the example of auto production. This change of the work experience was transformative in terms of family structure, education opportunities, and social norms of everyday life.

On the basis of the new technologies, scholars have started researching and theorizing on what it means for the Black experience. We are terming this new area of Black Studies theories of eBlack, how digital technology is transforming the Black experience and how we can study and think about that experience.

Finally, we are proposing that the model developed at the University of Toledo is a good starting place for redesigning Black Studies programs based on incorporating information technology.

8

Science and Technology in Black History

Black people have a long history of great accomplishment in science and math stretching back to ancient Africa (Van Sertima 1994; Lumpkin 1987). Lumpkin writes the following to refute the idea that Africa made no contribution, especially in the area of mathematics:

> However, Africa played a special role in the foundation of school mathematics. The widely accepted Greek tradition credited Egypt as the source of Greek mathematics, and the Egyptian priests with being the teachers of Thales and Pythagoras. The rich culture, prosperous economy, and geographical closeness for water travel made Egypt and North Africa the source and the conduit to Europe for the ancient knowledge of Africa and Asia, including the period of high Islamic culture.
>
> (Lumpkin 1987, 2)

More broadly, scholars have investigated the use of mathematical principles to structure traditional African cultures (Zaslavsky 1999; Gerdes 1998; Eglash 2005). Zaslavsky notes that:

> applications of mathematics are to be found in market transactions, art, architecture, games, religious practices, and many other aspects of African life, dating all the way back to evidence of a lunar calendar notched in a bone about nine thousand years ago.
>
> (Zaslavsky 1973, 532)

Africans also contributed to math and science through cultural performance.

Black Studies scholars have called for this history to be included in Black Studies curriculum development (S.E. Anderson 1974; 1970; 1990;

King 1992; Young and Young 1977). The critical issue is to keep both qualitative and quantitative methods in research and teaching and to link both to the Black experience. Science is often divorced from the Black experience and discussed only using a Eurocentric lens. This has become a barrier to Black youth entering scientific fields, including computer science. Scholars have argued that we need to include the contributions of ancient Africa and traditional African culture, as well as to survey the contributions of African-American scientists and mathematicians. Scott Williams at the University of Buffalo maintains a comprehensive website, *Mathematicians of the African Diaspora* (S. Williams n.d.); and Mitchell Brown at Princeton has a comprehensive website, *The Faces of Science: African Americans in the Sciences* (Brown n.d.).

Of course, incorporating science and technology into Black Studies curriculum development should take into account the social and economic historical dynamics of the African-American experience. There are two critical examples of this in the history of agriculture and industry: first, technology changed cotton production in Southern US agriculture in the nineteenth century; and second, technology changed auto production in Northern US industry in the twentieth century (Alkalimat 1996b).

The cotton gin increased productivity in a very dramatic way. By hand, it took one enslaved person a full day to clean one pound of cotton. The hand-powered cotton gin increased this productivity to 150 pounds per day. With steam power driving the gin, one enslaved person could produce one bale or 1,000 pounds per day. So, the statistics speak for themselves. In 1790, before the cotton gin, the USA produced 6,000 bales of cotton; by 1810, this was up to 178,000 bales, and by 1860 the annual output was 4 million. By 1820, cotton was more than 50 percent of all US exports and, after 1825, US-produced cotton was 80 percent of the commercial supply on the entire world market. Cotton had become king, meaning that from 1830 to 1860 more money was invested in land and enslaved people for cotton production than in all the rest of the US economy put together! In 1790, there were 700,000 enslaved persons and by 1860 there were 4 million, of whom more than 70 percent were in cotton production (Alkalimat 1996b).

The second breakthrough came in 1944 with the work of International Harvester, working with a plantation in Clarksdale, Mississippi. Here is how one account sums up the introduction of the first commercially viable version of the mechanical cotton picker:

> An estimated 2,500 to 3,000 people swarmed over the plantation on that one day. 800 to 1,000 automobiles leaving their tracks and scars throughout the property. The pickers, painted red, drove down the white rows of cotton. Each one had mounted in front a row of spindles, looking like a wide mouth, full of metal teeth that had been turned vertically. The spindles, about the size of human fingers, rotated in a way that stripped the cotton from the plants; then a vacuum pulled it up into the big wire basket that was mounted on top of a picker. In an hour, a good field hand could pick twenty pounds of cotton; each mechanical picker, in an hour picked as much as a thousand pounds. ... Picking a bale of cotton by machine cost ... $5.25, and picking it by hand cost ... $39.41. Each machine did the work of fifty people.
>
> (Lemann 2008, 4–5)

The result of this technological innovation was that the sharecroppers were literally driven off the land in the great migration of Black people out of the rural South into the urban industrial North. From 1910 to 1970, more than 6.5 million Black people migrated from the South; 5 million left after 1940, showing the impact of the mechanical cotton picker. Now only half of the Black community was in the South, and only 25 percent remained rural. Everything began to change. The historical mass Black experience of cotton production, under slavery and sharecropping, was bracketed by two technological innovations: it began with the cotton gin and ended with the mechanical cotton picker.

Auto manufacturing is another good example. The moving assembly line was created in 1913, which turned out to be the end of a long process of technological innovation. In 1908 automobiles were put together by assemblers, people who performed a whole series of tasks, gathering up parts and then fitting them together. The Ford Company became the leader in US auto manufacturing by introducing three kinds of innovations related to auto parts and assembly: interchangeability, simplicity, and ease of attachment.

Henry Ford was clear on what this could mean for his profits. Workers, especially Black workers, could see what it meant for them in wages. In 1917, when agricultural work yielded less than one dollar per day in wages in Mississippi, Ford was paying five dollars a day. In 1910, there were 6,000 Black people in Detroit and by 1920 there were 41,000, making Detroit the fastest-growing Black community of the major US cities. In 1916, there were 50 Black people working for Ford Motor Company in

Detroit, and by 1920 there were 2,500. This means that if people were living in families of four each, then from 1910 to 1916 about 3 percent of the Detroit Black community was connected to Ford, but by 1920 that was up to 25 percent (Alkalimat 1996b, 9).

But good things don't always last. The mass production techniques of Ford were challenged and overcome by the lean production system of Toyota, the Japanese auto company. Ford had the idea for his endless chain conveyor assembly line from the meat packing industry. Toyota got its idea of lean production from US supermarkets, especially how they handled inventory control and work assignments and maximized economy of time and space. These new management techniques for the social organization of production in later decades were linked to the increased use of computers and robots to initiate a revolutionary transformation of manufacturing. Once again, the auto industry was leading the way for all industrial activity.

Technological change was becoming a major issue in reshaping the economy, and in that respect was going to be an obstacle for Blacks entering the workforce. This was taken up by Congressman Adam Clayton Powell and labor leader A. Philip Randolph, who collaborated to advance the adoption of the Manpower Development and Training Act of 1962 that was designed to retrain workers because of the impact of automation and technological change (McIlwain 2019, 174–75).

A decade later Black professionals began to organize to respond to the technological revolution. Two organizations were formed in 1975: the National Society of Black Engineers (NSBE) and Black Data Processing Associates (BDPA). The NSBE was initiated at the college level:

> In 1974, Edward Coleman, Anthony Harris, Brian Harris, Stanley L. Kirtley, John W. Logan Jr., and George Smith, the "Chicago Six," along with a host of other Purdue Engineering students and professor Arthur J. Bond, PhD formed the first chapter of the, then, Society of Black Engineers. After contacting the other 288 accredited engineering schools, the Purdue SBE held its first annual meeting in April 1975 with 48 students from 32 schools. It was at that meeting that they unanimously voted to form the National Society of Black Engineers (NSBE). (NSBE n.d.)

The BDPA targeted youth at the high school level, setting up training programs and annual competitions to test skill levels at programming computers. Currently, they have forty-five chapters that train between 800 and 1,200 high school youth per year (BDPA n.d.).

Two decades later, innovations established the basis for the Internet. John Berners-Lee invented the World Wide Web (WWW) in 1990, followed by Marc Andreessen's invention of Mosaic in 1993, a graphical web browser developed at the University of Illinois Super Computer Center. The explosion of content on the web following these developments made the Internet the new library on a global scale. Black innovators jumped into the process with the major goal of making web-based Black content accessible. Central were Black graduate students: at San Diego State University, Ken Onwere established Afronet in 1993, and at Georgia Technology University, the Black Graduate Students Association developed the Universal Black Pages in 1994.

On the commercial side of things, Malcolm CasSelle worked with AOL to establish NetNoir in 1994 (McIlwain 2019, 91–121):

> On its website, NetNoir describes itself as the "leading media destination connecting people and business to Black culture and lifestyle." Further its goal is to "be the premier location where anyone interested in Black culture, heritage and lifestyle can come for information, products, and interaction ... [and] a portal into the global Black experience." On its home page, NetNoir features several information and activity sections.
>
> (Mack 2002, 96)

A systemic technological transformation took place when digital tools began to dominate the productive forces and activities of everyday life. An example of how deep and pervasive the rise of this technology is, is in personal home ownership of computers. The home computer was introduced in 1977, and by 1984, 8.2 percent of homes had computers. Thirty-two years later, 81 percent of white homes had computers, compared to 64 percent of Black homes.

During this time, the digital transformation of knowledge became a major topic of discussion in higher education.

CONFERENCES

One of the ways that Black Studies as a digitally based knowledge network has developed is through the gathering of cyberactivists in conferences. While until recently, this has not been initiated in the main by people in Black Studies, it has greatly contributed to the transformation of the academic discipline. There have been many smaller seminars and symposia; we will chart this history by mentioning only certain conferences that have had national impacts (Table 11).

Table 11 Selected Conferences on Black Studies in the Digital Age

Year	*Institution*	*Conference Title*
1995	Schomburg Center	Africana Libraries in the Information Age
1998	MIT	Race and Cyberspace
1999	University of Toledo	Afro Cyber Tech Seminar
2001	MIT	Race in Digital Space
2002	University of Virginia	Building an African-American Digital History Archive
2002	New York City Technical College	Digitizing the Discipline
2004	UC Santa Barbara	AfroGEEKS: From Technophobia to Technophilia
2005	UC Santa Barbara	AfroGEEKS: Global Blackness and the Digital Public Sphere
2008	University of Maryland	Digital Humanities and African American/African Diaspora Studies
2012	Duke University	Black Thought 2.0: New Media and the Future of Black Studies
2015	Central Pennsylvania Consortium's Africana Studies Conference	Envisioning Black Digital Spaces
2016	University of Maryland	Synergies: Digital Humanities and African American History and Culture
2016	Rutgers University	Digital Blackness
2016	Purdue University	Space and Place in Africana/Black Studies
2018	University of Maryland	Intentionally Digital, Intentionally Black

Howard Dodson, then head of the Schomburg Center library, points up the importance of the information revolution in designing the library's 1995 conference:

> Recognizing the potential implications of this fact, the Schomburg Center convened a national conference entitled "Africana Libraries

> in the Information Age." The conference was held on January 28–29, 1995. Representatives from libraries, museums and other repositories as well as scholars in African American, African Diasporan and African Studies gathered at the Schomburg Center to assess the current state of information on the Internet on the Black experience and to explore strategies for ensuring that there would be a robust presence of Africana resources there in the 21st century. The major findings were that there was relatively little material on the Black experience on the web and relatively few institutions were planning to create such content. A decade or so later, the Internet is literally brimming full of Africana-related resources.
>
> (Alkalimat 2004, viii)

MIT has been a leader in technological innovations since it was established in 1861. They held their first conference of interest in 1998, "Race in Cyberspace":

> The Race and Cyberspace Symposium, April 23, 1998 was jointly sponsored by the Media in Transition Project and the Women and Cyberspace Lecture Series. ... The goal of the symposium was to foreground the various ways that digital media are shaping our conceptions of and experience of race in America. ... The program was designed to be far-reaching, touching on such topics as the digital representation of racial difference; the role of the internet and the web in building and maintaining minority communities; the challenge of providing greater access to digital media for disadvantaged groups; the role of hate groups and community activism online.
>
> ("Race and Cyberspace Symposium" n.d.)

They followed this with a conference in 2001, "Race in Digital Space: A National Conference on Race and New Media Technologies." This conference featured Black agency in the arts and was held jointly with an art exhibit.

The next major conference focused on the digitization of African-American history in 2000. This conference at the University of Virginia convened under the title "Building African American History Digital Archives: A Workshop for Principal Investigators and Project Teams." The Carter G. Woodson Institute for African Americana and African Studies sponsored the conference under the leadership of Reginald Butler and Scott French.

Anna Everett organized the next conferences at the University of California at Santa Barbara under the category of the Afro-Geek: in 2004, AfroGEEKS: From Technophobia to Technophilia; and in 2005, AfroGEEKS: Global Blackness and the Digital Public Sphere. These two conferences featured reports on actual projects that showcased the agency of digital scholar-activists that she named the Afro-Geeks. Everett summed up the conferences and her research in *Digital Diaspora: A Race for Cyberspace* (A. Everett 2009).

Three institutions held conferences that focused specifically on the overall changes of the discipline of Black Studies: University of Toledo (1999), New York City Technical College (2002), and University of Maryland (2008, 2016, 2018). At the 2002 New York conference, Steven Panford stated the mission of the conference:

> The Conference is part of an attempt to bring the latest technology to the teaching of Africana Studies. Conference workshops, lectures, seminars, and panel discussions will revolve around issues, knowledge, and techniques of distance learning, use of software (Power Point presentations), the role of the Internet, website development and interactive technologies as pedagogic tools. It should be interesting.
>
> (Panford 2002, 6)

Over a ten-year period, the University of Maryland, along with major funding from the Mellon Foundation, established what are now the leading institution tools and training for the transformation of Black Studies based on information technology:

> African American History, Culture and Digital Humanities (AADHum) was awarded to the College of Arts and Humanities (ARHU) and is being co-directed by MITH and the Arts and Humanities Center for Synergy (Center for Synergy). The project was funded by a $1.25 million grant from the Andrew W. Mellon Foundation for research, education and training at the intersections of digital humanities and African American studies, and will help to prepare a diverse community of scholars and students whose work will both broaden the reach of the digital humanities in African American history and cultural studies, and enrich humanities research with new methods, archives and tools.
>
> (Maryland Institute for Technology in the Humanities n.d.)

9
Theories of eBlack

Theoretical reflection on the development of digital tools and cyberspace brought discussions of a utopian future into popular discourse. There were idealist projections of robotic production, universal consciousness, and a revolutionary era that would end global scarcity. There were also dystopian projections of the autonomous development of robots and artificial intelligence that would come into conflict with human society. Being stronger and smarter, they would create a nonhuman future. These future projections of negation or affirmation of life are idealist fantasy. The actual experience thus far is that the human experience of cyberspace is a reproduction of actual lived experience.

Cyberspace is the digital reproduction of the actual into virtual representation. When this happens, there are identifying notations that link the two, the actual and the virtual, so it is highly unlikely that cyberspace will ever delink from the actual humans who create and control it. What is happening is that the contradictions of how people live and have lived are reflected in the form and content of cyberspace. So, for African Americans, cyberspace is full of oppression and exploitation, as well as struggle and resistance.

Given this, one of the first questions to be explored has been to identify the content of cyberspace and to map it. Just as printed texts are located by a bibliography, a listing of information to identify and locate each text, for cyberspace one develops a webliography, a digital identification and location of material in cyberspace.

As mentioned earlier, the first webliography to identify and locate Black content in cyberspace was the Universal Black Pages, prepared by graduate students at Georgia Institute of Technology in 1994. The second major webliography was produced in 1996 by Stafford L. Battle and Rey O. Harris, The African American Resource Guide to the Internet & Online Services. The last comprehensive printed guide to Black content of cyberspace, *The African American Experience in Cyberspace: A Resource Guide to the Best Web Sites on Black Culture and History*, an annotated webliography, was published in 2004 by Abdul Alkalimat. This guide is based on the author's textbook for an introductory course in Black Studies (Alkalimat 2004; 1986).

The content of cyberspace was expanding at such a high rate that printed guides could hardly keep up. Such guides were replaced by algorithm-based search engines. Google search was launched in 1997, and as of 2020 it maintained about a 90 percent share of all US internet searches. But this is not without serious problems.

A natural language search is usually based on the architecture of knowledge it seeks to explore. Therein is the inherent weakness of the process, as it can only serve up what has been digitized. A racist bias shows up in general library classifications as well as in the results from a Google search. Noble demonstrates how the main search engines, especially Google, are biased against. (Noble 2018) Searching on terms about Black people often yields search results informed by a racist filter. We have yet to have an accurate Black-oriented way to search the full content of cyberspace.

However much this is the case, most of us are in the practical bind of having to negotiate our way through multiple searches to get the information that we need. We can, however, explore alternative theoretical frameworks for understanding the general experience of Black people in confronting the digital realm of knowledge. This will provide a general orientation to how the actual experiences in society are being replicated in the cyberspace experience. We will discuss four such frameworks:

1. Inequality: As in all aspects of society, inequality creates fundamental differences in how people experience their lives. The digital divide is a concept used to discuss inequality in owning, having access to digital tools and connectivity, and using digital tools.
2. Racism: Prejudice and discriminatory practices used against Black people are the content of systemic racism in society. This is being replicated in cyberspace by advocates of white supremacy, who are being confronted by Black liberation cyberactivists and eBlack Studies scholars.
3. Culture: Much of cyberspace reflects Eurocentrism as practiced in society in general. African Americans use their own cultural resources to affirm a Black identity and to construct digital resources that reflect the autonomous force of self-determination.

4. Power: Digital inequality, racism, and Eurocentrism all are enforced by the power of who owns digital tools, hardware and software, and who dominates organizations that control the production of digital information. In opposition to this, digital tools are being used to consolidate resources for an anti-racist struggle for social justice, for digital Black power.

These four frameworks set the theoretical focus for eBlack studies.

INEQUALITY

Digital technology platforms have become institutional norms, so to be online is to be a participating member of mainstream society. Of course, this is not the case for everyone, because class inequality produces digital inequality, which is summed up by the term "digital divide." The main focus of efforts to end the digital divide is on evaluating three kinds of access: machines, connectivity, and bandwidth. The first major measure of this was undertaken by the National Telecommunications and Information Agency (NTIA) in the Department of Commerce in 1995. NTIA was founded in 1978 to research telephone use and was reprogrammed to examine digital activity. The focus was on developing markets for companies selling equipment and connectivity. The key questions targeted what kinds of digital equipment people owned, mainly computers. The data that were generated pointed to a divide between Blacks and whites, but when controlling for class, for example those making the same high salaries, the difference disappeared.

This led to the notion that there was a divide between the information rich and the information poor. The bias in this formulation was based on the notion that the information worth noting was that available through digital technology. In fact, everyone is full of information, based on language and the necessary travails of everyday life, whatever the circumstances. The actual information divide is based on what kind of information is being discussed. This is very important.

The digital divide is critical in a society undergoing a paradigm shift from the industrial age to the information age. The fundamentals of literacy have added to the 3 Rs (reading, writing, arithmetic) the big D (digital). While this is true in the activities of everyday life, in a crisis the digital divide becomes the most important critical issue of inequality.

If Black people are not adapting their lives to digital practices, they are not able to fully participate in any of the major institutional processes. This includes banking, moving from face-to-face exchanges with the bank teller to interfacing with a web page for digital transactions, and accessing the news on a real-time basis as opposed to the once-a-day print newspaper or the television/radio versions.

The digital divide is the twenty-first-century inequality that forces all Black agency to move forward in cyberspace as well as actual space.

> Black and Hispanic adults in the United States remain less likely than White adults to say they own a traditional computer or have high-speed internet at home, according to a Pew Research Center survey conducted Jan. 25 to Feb. 8, 2021.
>
> (Atske and Perrin 2021)

When people are off-line, they are being left behind as society is moving forward. So Black Studies scholars and activists are required to understand, to confront, and to eliminate the digital divide crisis of the Black community.

RACISM

What is clear is that cyberspace reflects the experience we live in society. Cyberspace is not a utopia, but simply another representation of who people are—sometimes who they actually are, and sometimes who they pretend to be. One of the harsh realities is that cyberspace is a place where Black people are confronted with racism. This is a profound manifestation of the systemic racism that pervades all aspects of society.

There is a white supremacist movement that is active in cyberspace. Each movement maintains organizational activities for membership, as well as active outreach via social media platforms. They mobilize for specific campaigns, targeting key places for confrontation and conflict. One of the most aggressive forms of this are the militias, armed and based on recruitment from military and police veterans. Jessie Daniels presents a comprehensive analysis of what she labels "cyber racism":

> White supremacy in the print-only era included the voices of a few white men who represented the leadership of the movement. Now, as the message has been converted into digital media, white supremacy

> online is increasingly multivocal and less one dimensional than when it relied primarily on printed newsletter for communication.
>
> (Daniels 2009, 111)

The white supremacists also disguise their message by pretending to be a progressive voice in what Daniels calls "cloaked websites":

> Cloaked websites represent a unique new form of white supremacy online because they disguise white supremacy in the rhetoric of multiculturalism and civil rights. David Duke and others attempted to mimic the discourse of civil rights in print (e.g., the National Association for the Advancement of White People), the deception inherent in cloaked sites is a new twist, made all the more effective because of the medium of the Internet.
>
> (Daniels 2009, 133)

In a more general sense, Nakamura investigates the tendencies of how race is portrayed in cyberspace. She coined the term "cybertype" as a way to discuss race identity in cyberspace:

> The study of racial cybertypes brings together the cultural layer and the computer layer; that is to say, cybertyping is the process by which computer/human interfaces, the dynamics and economics of access, and the means by which users are able to express themselves online interacts with the 'cultural layer' or ideologies regarding race that they bring with them into cyberspace.
>
> (Nakamura 2002, 3)

Nakamura also identifies a digital process by which people take on an ethnic identity when they surf within the "others" digital space. She calls this "identity tourism," by which the Internet allows one to access a multicultural world without taking the risks of crossing divides that are socially restricted. This covers the white liberal tendency to consume a multicultural experience without having to confront racist disapproval. Personal experience of multiculturalism is no alternative to facing up to the demonic social force of white supremacy.

All of this is the reason Black agency to advance an anti-racist agenda has developed as a vital part of the eBlack experience. Black digital activity mobilizes Black people to advance the "Black Lives Matter" slogan as a fundamental challenge to all racist aggression.

CULTURE

When Black people represent themselves in cyberspace, they bring forth a digital Black cultural reality. The three most general aspects of this are Black discourse, musical appreciation, and representation of community culture. Digital discourse activity that Black people practice with each other often takes the form of cultural autonomy. Banks calls this the work of digital griots:

> The griot has survived the middle passage, slavery, and centuries of American apartheid and has been diffused into many different spaces and figures: storytellers, preachers, poets, standup comics, DJs, and even everyday people all carry elements of the griot's role in African American culture … The "digital griot," an amalgamation of all these figures, offers a useful model for conceptualizing black rhetorical excellence bridging print, oral, and digital communication.
>
> (Banks 2011, 25)

At a personal level, this translates into digital practice by Black people owning and using cell phones at rates comparable to mainstream trends. There is no digital divide on this, including the tendency of Black people to use cell phones the most when it comes to jobs, health, and education (M. Anderson 2015).

Roderick Graham in his analysis of *The Root* sums up aspects of Black digital discourse:

> Content analysis of the politics section of *The Root* shows that at least three themes present themselves: counterhegemonic interpretations of current events, a reliance upon historical context, and an understanding that African Americans are often the moral conscious of the nation. As a whole, these three themes help construct a uniquely African American discourse, one that is in opposition to mainstream discourse.
>
> (Graham 2014, 108)

This focus on discourse is also relevant to Black women in particular. Catherine Knight Steele makes this clear.

> A Black feminist epistemology centralizes the conversations of Black women that occur in settings that are often excluded as valid by academic researchers. This study seeks to examine the online gossip of Black women for its potential to contribute to a discourse of resistance. ... This discourse analysis examines the content of two popular celebrity gossip blogs that were established by and are written by Black female authors: The Young, Black, and Fabulous (theybf.com), started by Natasha Eubanks; and Necole Bitchie (NecoleBitchie.com) founded by Necole Kane.
>
> (Steele, cited in Noble and Tynes 2016, 74, 77)

Steele's findings identify key topics: beauty, mothering, relationships, the Black male hero, sister friends, Black lover relationships, fighting institutional power, and defending Black men.

As has been noted, music is the foundation of African-American culture. Of course, there is a technological component of how music is created and consumed by its audience. One of the major relationships has been how Black musicians have impacted technology. Rayvon Fouché demonstrates this with the role of hip-hop legend Grandmaster Flash.

> As hip-hop became an important part of American culture, the electronics industry embraced the technological tweaks of early hip-hop. DJ legend and hip-hop pioneer Grandmaster Flash was instrumental in creating a set of new technological objects and practices that incorporated black cultural interests. For example, in 2002 the Rane Corporation, a leading manufacturer of DJ equipment, introduced the Empath mixer. Grandmaster Flash played a key role in this device's design. He presented Rane design engineer Rick Jeffs with a series of technical challenges that would extend his performance capabilities. Many of the suggestions pushed Rane's team to its technical limits. But through the collaborative efforts of Rane's innovative engineering and Grandmaster Flash's musical creativity, they produced an amazing new device. Grandmaster Flash and Rick Jeff brought together technology and black musical styles to extend the limits of technology and expand the ways black cultural priorities influence technological design and innovation.
>
> (Fouché 2009)

The most inclusive example of culture as a mode of cyber activism is the representation of the Harlem Renaissance in virtual reality. As a project for teaching Black history, Bryan Carter began using virtual reality to take his students into the Harlem of that time.

> The Virtual Harlem project allows students not only to visualize a historical context for the Harlem Renaissance, circa 1921–1930, which is the setting of several fictional texts, but also to navigate through streets and to interact with historical characters through questions and audio cues. ... To date, approximately ten square blocks of Harlem have been reconstructed in a VR learning environment. This environment gives students an unprecedented view of the cultural history of one of the most productive periods in African American culture.
>
> (Carter cited in Sosnoski, Harkin, and Carter 2006, 45, 46)

Andre Brock presents a summary analysis. He posits the following concepts as central to his understanding of Black online digital practice: Blackness, intersectionality, America, Invention/style, Modernity, The future.

> The Black technocultural matrix neither supplants nor propounds the same ideologies of dominance and control over nonwhite bodies. Instead, I am theorizing a Black cultural relationship with technology, drawing on the Black experience in the West—an experience that is shaped by relationships with whiteness and with technology from a social and political subject position.
>
> (Brock 2020, 228)

As digital tools become more of the norm Black expressive culture is exploding online. What began as self-publishing with the inexpensive availability of printers and scanners, the freedom for digital cultural production extends down to elementary school students as well as all forms of aspiring professionals. There are two important contradictions that are critical to this cultural production. The first is the contradiction between free distribution and commodification. Both are possible and widely being used. The issue is whether culture is best developed as free expression or as it is distributed in a market. Another aspect is between universal digital tools versus proprietary tools. This is also a market question. This is clearly the case in music making. The proprietary tools cost money, like Pro-Tools. But there are several free alternatives, like Audacity.

Even when something appears to be free lurking in the system is a market function. Many people approach software like Facebook, Twitter, or Google as a free service, and pour their cultural content in them. So far so good, but these "free" donations of culture are then used by these companies to build algorithms that build market strategies that harness us back into their distribution schemes. Our gifts to them help them make us consumers of what they are selling.

CYBERPOWER

The Black digital experience is not simply about representation, but also it is aimed at changing society to improve the quality of life for Black people in general. This raises the question of power. The concept of cyberpower was introduced by Tim Jordan (Jordan 1999). The focus is on how digital online tools can be used to influence, organize, mobilize, and activate people. In this way, the Black Liberation Movement and Black political action in general are in play in the twenty-first century. Cyberpower is the way politics is being played out.

Political education is taking place online. There has been an expanded opportunity for individuals to blast their ideas as blogs, listservs, or any other number of social media formats. The Zoom format is a popular format for group presentations. In addition, websites have become the norm for presenting and archiving material for individuals and organizations. Social media postings have replaced leafletting for mass outreach to mobilize for any kind of protest action. In some cases, these actions can be streamed live on cell phones.

The African-American community is less equipped with laptop or desk top computers, but not so with cell phones. It is with the cell phone technology that Black political action is being maintained at a very high level.

The main aspect of cyberpower is the ability to use digital tools to gather together people to have a common point of view, or to take a common action.

Of course, to the extent that there is a freedom struggle, in any form, people reach out for the tools that can help them communicate, organize, and mobilize. Every community organization and organizer, every social movement organization and political activist are nowadays expected to be online. One to many contact tools enables cyberpower to be measured quantitatively. This contact can arrange more formal actions like a study process via a webinar, a seminar online, or a movement action like a flash mob.

There is considerable debate about the relative importance of maintaining face-to-face interaction as part of a process, even one that leans mostly on virtual formats. While the virtual cuts back on the cost of travel and other expenses to gather folks who are dispersed, there is also the issue of the digital divide and who is online and able to use advanced tools. Many people access online material on their cell phone and that works to an extent but without full capabilities.

SUMMARY

These four points of emphasis are not separate from each other—they are connected and should be understood within a common framework. The precondition for digital activity is overcoming the digital divide. Everything is based on having access and skill, motivation, and practice. One of the main obstacles to face is racism in cyberspace, and the greatest asset for resisting and advancing Black agency is based on Black culture, both form and content. And, finally, the need to change society requires that digital activity produce cyberpower.

10

Toledo Model for eBlack Studies

We will use a model first developed at the University of Toledo to demonstrate how Black Studies is being transformed by the use of information technology. Upon my appointment as Director of the Black Studies Program in 1996, I stated the following at a welcoming reception given by faculty and community leaders:

> Our program will be innovative as we plan on building our Africana Studies Program in cyberspace. Our students will be experts with computer technology and the Internet. But more than that we will be coming after many of you as we want to assist in the "wiring of the Black community" here in Toledo but also in South Africa and Jamaica. The key to the 21st century is the Internet where all of us can travel at warp speed. Either we get moving or we get left behind. You can count on the Africana Studies Program and the University of Toledo to be your gateway to the future.
>
> (Alkalimat 1996a)

This declaration of intent started a process involving four key stages. The innovation of digital technology was a disruption that began to change all aspects of work in higher education. New skill sets were required. These new skills were more likely to be taken up first by younger scholars, so a generational conflict developed. This led to a period of experimentation, finding ways to embrace digital tools that would include as many people as possible, and not create too big a digital divide on campus. Not surprisingly the engineers, computer scientists, and the professional schools were the first to more fully adopt the new technologies, in keeping with their professions.

Out of this period of experimentation, institutions began to adopt digital tools and associated software as a normative part of how they functioned. They became a measure of institutional literacy. Higher education as a whole began to move in the direction of standardization.

Partly this was driven by the computer market, as companies began to develop machines and a marketing focus on higher education. This was also facilitated by software developers targeting specific issues, so library needs and research needs began to be met, and solutions were generally adopted across institutions and disciplines.

The Toledo model of eBlack was based on a conceptual framework that summed up the aspects of how academic work was being standardized in digital terms. This was possible, because I was the only full-time staff person in Black Studies at the time, plus I was a full professor and did not have any power struggles to wage to formally institutionalize digital practices.

We developed a fully digital approach to Black Studies (Table 12).

Table 12 The Toledo Model of eBlack Studies

Academic Practice	*Black Studies*	*eBlack Studies*	*The Toledo Model*
Administrative identity	College catalog	Website	Website
Professional discourse	FTF conference	Listserv discussion	H-Afro-Am
Curriculum	FTF classrooms	Distance learning	Collaboration with University of Ghana
Research	Hard-copy publication	Research websites	Malcolm X: A Research Site
Public policy	Consulting and internships	Advocacy websites and online petitions	1998 Black Radical Congress
Community service	Service learning	Community informatics	eBlack Champaign Urbana

INSTITUTIONAL IDENTITY

The historical identity of each institution, as well as those of all specific academic units, was established by the published college catalogue. This document along with department bylaws and course syllabi are official legal documents constituting a contract with all enrolled students. The exchange is tuition for courses and degrees as stipulated in the official documents. The first digital impact was simply the digitization of the college catalogue. But soon thereafter the dynamic possibilities of the technology moved institutions to take on a more interactive format, putting a more improvisational format on top of the remaining legal contractual information.

Digital skills first became the basis for a new professional role, a digital expert, the webmaster. The work was done as piecework, a skilled professional working for a department doing specific tasks. The main goal was to be consistent with their institutional norm, but eventually, as more and more people began to use the technology in their work, departments had their own webmasters who handled all digital tasks for the department and individual faculty.

Web identity has become so important that many institutions no longer print and distribute college catalogues. Faculty are identified by their URL, both linking to their departmental site and their personal homepage.

DISCOURSE

The digitization of discourse has been a major development. Email has been the dominant form of digital communication, especially for formal institutions. It is immediate, global, archival, available on most digital devices, and simultaneously archived. Beyond one-to-one communication is the LISTSERV, software that allows for easy one-to-many communication. Both email and LISTSERVs are available as commercial products or as part of what institutions provide to their faculty, students, and staff. A full menu of social media has diversified discourse to use all file types (text, image, sound, and video).

The main LISTSERV from 1998 to 2014 in Black Studies was H-Afro-Am, which I edited during that time, seventeen years of building a community to share a conversation every weekday. Sometimes there was a conversation thread that several joined in. Other email posts were just a statement to the LISTSERV. Figure 2 gives a sample of the discourse. Over the seventeen years there were more than 21,000 messages covering more than 12,000 topics. Readers were diverse and writers were, too. Close to one in five of the topics (18 percent) generated two or more messages, that is, a thread, a conversation. Two percent of all topics had ten or more messages. The longest thread was sixty-nine messages on the topic of "passing."

H-Afro-Am demonstrated that Black Studies was becoming a digitally based discourse community, something that could operate on a global level. National conferences that enable face-to-face meetings once a year are important, but this listserv was an everyday service to more people than attend any Black studies conference face-to-face.

2013-05-21		
@hotmail.com	Identities of "the slaves"	View
@tarleton.edu	Re: Were "the slaves" Africans or "Americans"	View
@sandiego.edu	Re: Were "the slaves" Africans or "Americans"	View
@albanylaw.edu	Re: Were "the slaves" Africans or "Americans"	View
@yahoo.com	Re: Were "the slaves" Africans or "Americans"	View
@juno.com	Re: Were "the slaves" Africans or "Americans"	View
@orange.sn	Were "the slaves" Africans or "Americans": 4 REPLIES	View
@orange.sn	Were "the slaves" Africans or "Americans": 2 REPLIES	View
@utep.edu	Re: Query re: "high-toned"	View
@gmail.com	Re: Query re: "high-toned"	View

2013-05-20		
@MAIL.H-NET.MSU.EDU>	H-Net, Public History and Independent Scholars	View
@morehouse.edu	The Racial Wealth Gap As Deliberate Public Policy	View
@yahoo.com	2013 National Underground Railroad Conference-Little Rock, Arkansas (June 19-22)	View
@gmail.com	Social Security Changes Could Hurt Blacks Most	View
@gmail.com	REGISTRATION OPEN: Black German Heritage and Research Association Convention, Amherst College, Aug. 8-10, 2013	View
@gmail.com	YouTube: James Turner: Pioneer of Africana Studies and Freedom Activist	View
@gmail.com	Jamaica Kincaid: "People Only Say I'm Angry Because I'm Black and I'm a Woman"	View
@yahoo.com	2013 SAMLA Conf CFP- Women's Studies Panel	View
@vcu.edu	research on women and social media	View
@gmail.com	College diploma gap widens between rich and poor	View
@nsu.edu	Call for Papers: 1619:Making of America--Deadline Extended	View
@temple.edu	Postwar Civil Rights History	View
@hood.edu	Query re: "high-toned"	View
@internationalmediatv.com	Former Black Panther Party leader Elaine Brown at Marcus Books!	View
@gmail.com	Towards a Black Aesthetic (essay by Hoyt Fuller)	View
@vcu.edu	cfp: "Cultural History in the United States: Past, Present, and Future Trajectories"	View
@gmail.com	William "Nick" Nelson (d 2013)	View

Figure 2 An Example of Daily Discussion on the LISTSERV H-Afro-Am

H-Afro-Am was and is part of H-Net, a service organization based at Michigan State University that offers virtual communities for academic fields of study based on the work of volunteer academics. From the start in 1992 until 2014, it was based on the simple and yet effective use of email. They then made what I consider to be the mistake of fixing what was not broke, hiring consultants to migrate all the discussions from LISTSERVs to a Drupal content management system, and then H-Net "discussions" as they call them really declined in importance. The new technology was too complicated for almost everyone to post messages. A big lesson is we have to safeguard our platforms. In Sankofa terms, freedom of the press is for those who own the presses.

All professional associations have an annual face-to-face conference. The 2020 Covid-19 pandemic has seriously disrupted this norm. The alternative for face-to-face meetings has become the Zoom software, which enables groups to gather with face-to-face visualizations and a package of other capabilities including PowerPoint, video recording, a chat box, being able to raise one's hand to a moderator, archiving, and more. Zoom has likely become a permanent part of social life, expanding beyond FaceTime telephony to embrace group interaction.

CURRICULUM

The curriculum of Black Studies has focused on finding the Black content in many of the courses spread throughout all of the liberal arts departments. The most fundamental unifying course has been the course that introduces the students to the general subject of African-American Studies. Our experience has served one of the earliest models for an introductory course.

INTRO: EVOLVING FORM AND CONTENT, PRODUCTION AND DISTRIBUTION

There have been four technological stages in our curriculum development efforts for the course Introduction to Afro-American Studies, which are shown in Table 13. This covers the last forty years of professional collaboration in Black Studies.

The first stage involved four changes. *Intro* began in Fisk University's Afro-American Studies Program as the course syllabus for Modern Culture and Black People, a course offered to first-year students in a new

Table 13 Technological History of *Introduction to Afro-American Studies: A People's College Primer*

Year	*Format*	*Production*	*Distribution*
1970	Study guide, hand folded and stapled	Typing stencils for mimeograph	Hand delivered and mailed
1978	Two-volume anthology, paper bound	Typed copy, offset printing, photo slides	Direct mail, campus and movement bookstores
1984	Single-volume text, cloth and paper bound	Computer-generated text for photo offset	Direct mail, campus and movement bookstores
2000	eBook	Conversion from printed pages to html via scan and optical character recognition	Web
2007	Online lecture series	PowerPoint, digital video, mp3 audio	Web

Freshman Interdisciplinary Program (FIP). This first experience was a forced march to bring the intensity of the Black Liberation Movement into the classroom. The students revolted and our class process became a site for struggle and education. They took the challenge and did excellent work, and we still have their papers in the archive.

Our use of slides in the classroom was an important addition, as the visuals of historical experience were more engaging than the spoken word by itself. However, the downside was keeping the slides organized after putting them in and taking them out of the apparatus used for projection. There was a high utility, but with a high cost to maintain.

After experimentation and broad discussion of various versions, *Intro* Green emerged as the fourth edition, a study guide and handbook that served both the campus classroom environment and community-based study groups. Throughout this project, *Intro* was self-produced by faculty, students, and staff with financing from the supplies budget of the Black Studies program. This was an act of self-determination, building on the intellectual tradition started by Dr. Charles Johnson, Fisk's first Black president, who established People's College as a campus-based community education program.

This approach was based on our conception of the historical periodization of the Black experience. The first part was a survey of the historical periods in broad strokes, with a series of chapters devoted to each period and a series of chapters exploring the development of social classes, pivotal social and cultural developments, and key social movements. For the second part of the course—equivalent to a second semester of study—we developed a concept of what would constitute "classics" in the field, our sense of what the basic canon for a foundational understanding would be, comprising a few texts that everyone would read. There were five criteria: A work of Black social analysis is considered a classic when it: (1) definitively summarizes the existing knowledge of a major Black experience; (2) represents a model of methodology and technique that serves to guide future investigation; (3) draws from the analysis theoretical concepts and propositions that contribute to our general theoretical grasp of the socio-economic and political history of the USA and African-American people; (4) stands the test of time by not being proven incorrect or inadequate and replaced by a superior work; and (5) guides one to take an active role in the struggle to liberate Black people and fundamentally change the nature of American society.

Based on these criteria, we selected texts that we deemed important discussions of several critical themes—selections that could be and were critiqued and criticized, and hopefully used to develop lists of other criteria, themes, and texts:

1. W.E.B. Du Bois, *Black Reconstruction in America, 1860–1880* (1935)
2. St. Clair Drake and Horace Cayton, *Black Metropolis: A Study of Negro Life in a Northern City* (1945)
3. Charles S. Johnson, *Shadow of the Plantation* (1934)
4. Abram Harris and Sterling D. Spero, *The Black Worker: The Negro and the Labor Movement* (1931)
5. E. Franklin Frazier, *Black Bourgeoisie: The Rise of a New Black Middle Class in the United States* (1957)
6. Booker T. Washington, *Up From Slavery: The Autobiography of Booker T. Washington* (1901)
7. Malcolm X, *Autobiography of Malcolm X* (1965)

One of the important events that gathered the users of the study guide was the 1975 Fisk conference to "Pull the Covers Off Imperialism." This was a critical moment of consensus that brought together both the intellectual and militant leaders of the Black Liberation Movement. The conference ratified a declaration that was then distributed nationally to Black Studies academics and Black liberation activists. It can be used today by Black Studies faculty and students to rethink how to relink with the Black Lives Matter Movement (Alkalimat 2021).

> WE DECLARE that a primary task of black intellectuals today is to study the character and historical development of U.S. imperialism, especially its impact on black people, and to promote this study throughout schools, publications, conferences, and organizations;
>
> WE DECLARE that the main objective of our study must be to expose the essence of imperialism and provide the intellectual tools necessary for combating every imperialist assault on the people;
>
> WE DECLARE that our immediate goal is to establish a new unity between black intellectuals and the black liberation movement in which intellectuals function to serve the interests of the people with humility based on compassion, strength, based on science, and a revolutionary optimism that the people will triumph over all enemies and prosper.
>
> (Alkalimat 1975)

A heightened demand for a more in-depth survey of Black intellectual history within the framework of the historical periodization of the paradigm of unity led to the next stage of *Intro*. We created a comprehensive collection, one thousand pages of primary-source material for the historical study of the African-American experience. This was typed and proofed before being formatted in the design of two 8½ x 11 inch volumes.

These volumes were part of a reprint impulse in Black Studies to bring back the major texts of the African-American intellectual tradition, since most were out of print. The strength was the access they gave to primary sources, but this also raised the bar in terms of the intensity of reading required.

Our third stage was the editorial transformation of the anthology into one coherent text. This was accomplished by a grant from The Fund for the Improvement of Postsecondary Education (FIPSE) to the University of Illinois at Urbana-Champaign. A team of five people provided the research and editorial work. This was a major technological leap: in 1984, we used a dial-up connection from one of our basements to send digital text files to the campus mainframe. The floppies in those days could only hold one half of one chapter of text, but we did it. On this basis, we then could assemble and design a digital file to be sent to a printer. At this stage, production was computerized for hard-copy text.

One of the important events in this stage was a 1991 working conference hosted by Northeastern University for colleagues from around the USA who had used *Intro* in their institutions. Represented were colleagues from the following institutions: Howard University, Jackson State, University of Mississippi, Atlanta Metropolitan College, Wayne State University, Olive Harvey College, Northeastern University, and People's College.

Our fourth stage, in 2000, moved the project into an entirely digital format, also maintained as a digital archive. Up until then, we had been committed to following the self-determination path of self-publishing—in print—of Carter G. Woodson and J.A. Rogers and others. But as we struggled to maintain this, and the new technological revolution swept us up, it became clear that we needed a radical break. Alkalimat walked into his lab and put three graduate students on the task of scanning and editing the book. It was a "stop on a dime" learning moment—they finished the task of scanning the four-hundred-page book, making corrections to the optical character output, and then formatting for HTML in one week! We formatted the text so that it could be printed and bound into a useable 8½ x 11 inch volume and then launched it as a free online text.

The fifth stage of *Intro* began in 2007, when I returned to Illinois after more than twenty years, taught *Intro* as a series of ninety-minute lectures, videotaped them, and posted videos, syllabus, slides, and a link to the listserv H-Afro-Am. Again, this is available online for free.

Intro has been transformed in sync with major technological changes in printing and word processing over the last half of the twentieth century. This has not only included the use of digital technology, but also the study of the impact of digital technology on the Black experience.

We started out using the production capacity of a campus-based office (typewriters, copiers, mimeograph machines) and then moved to offset printing, both in-house and outsourced. What has been consistent is our control over content and design. Our control over the production process has increased in the digital stage, because we continue to own the tools we use. In the end, there is one major remaining problem: ownership and control of the servers, the machines where the buck stops. Owning and administering one's own servers in the digital age is comparable to owning a printing press in the industrial age.

Our future is in the clouds, with the eternal choice replication of the commodified cloud of a commercial operation like Google, versus a free commons cloud based on D-Space technology and hosted on a campus. So choices are emerging as to what kind of server control will define our digital being in the world.

Three contributions should be highlighted by this summary of the historical development of our work on the *Intro* text in Black Studies: (a) the emphasizing of the importance of intellectual history; (b) the linking of the academy to the historical concerns of the Black community; and (c) the reiterating of the need for developing interdisciplinary scholarship.

First, the *Intro* text, and Black Studies more generally, emphasize that a necessary topic for discussion is the intellectual history of all disciplines and fields as they study the Black experience. Black Studies has always stated in no uncertain terms that the Black experience is as worthy of study as any other human experience. And, further, it has fought against the historical invisibility of Black people in higher education by insisting that Black intellectuals and scholars were necessary if such studies were to be authentic.

Second, African-American Studies, by its very title and its subject matter, has kept in front of us the historical and contemporary realities of people of African descent, and focuses attention on the historical dynamics of the slave trade, slavery, colonialism and imperialism, poverty, the "triple oppression" of Black women (patriarchy, racism, and class exploitation), and other social issues. It does so even when doing so is uncomfortable, perhaps, in the polite company of the academy. African-American Studies thus keeps in front of us the story of resilience and achievement against the odds, both by individuals and by communities. The reality of this continuing challenge is what is best captured by the phrase "Academic Excellence and Social Responsibility."

Third, African-American Studies has pioneered the development of interdisciplinary scholarship in US higher education and spurred similar developments in other fields, and more attention must be paid to this aspect. This approach has been a crucial and forward-looking aspect of intellectual history and current practice. For example, in the field of urban studies, *The Philadelphia Negro*, published by W.E.B. Du Bois in 1899, is widely regarded as the first and pioneering study of America's cities. Margaret Walker's novel of historical fiction, *Jubilee*, demonstrates her mastery of literature as well as the study of history and other fields (Walker 2016).

A critical turning point in the discipline was the adoption of the 1980 Report of the Curriculum Studies Commission by the National Council for Black Studies. The authors proposed an interdisciplinary model that contributed to the shape of the final report. Chaired by Perry Hall, the report proposed a standardized approach to the Black Studies curriculum that mandated courses in three fields—historical studies, social and behavioral studies, cultural studies—and an interdisciplinary introductory course and a capstone seminar for seniors. There is an urgent need to revisit and refine this model, especially to be more inclusive of the African Diaspora.

A face-to-face lecture course can be documented via video and then made available as an online file. There are examples from the University of Illinois, Yale, and Stanford of videoed courses being made free to the public (Ponder n.d.).

Curriculum has usually been delivered in a face-to-face lecture hall or seminar room. Now there are online alternatives. Some syllabi are made available online. The major innovation in online courses was initiated by MIT:

> OCW is a free and open publication of material from thousands of MIT courses, covering the entire MIT curriculum. That's every MIT department and degree program, and ranging from the introductory to the most advanced graduate level. Each OCW course includes a syllabus, some instructional material (such as lecture notes or a reading list), and some learning activities (such as assignments or exams). Many courses also have complete video lectures, free online textbooks, and faculty teaching insights. While some OCW content is custom-created for online use, most of it comes straight from the MIT classroom.
>
> (Massachusetts Institute of Technology n.d.)

RESEARCH

Digital tools have had a major impact on research in Black Studies. Our conceptual framework for this is called the D-7 method as in Table 14.

In the first step, D1, Definition, one identifies a problem to address and then asks, what specific research question will the research seek to answer? The *Sankofa Principle* requires us to first investigate this research question by engaging in an intensive review of the literature. The Black librarian is an invaluable collaborator at this step.

The library is the most universal memory institution in society: not only do books and print media circulate as part of contemporary information dissemination, but the library also has a reference section of documents that are secure and maintained to provide the memory of history, culture, and scientific knowledge. Although all library collections

Table 14 D7 Method

D1. Definition	Defining the problem, summing up the relevant literature, formulating the research question and/or hypothesis
D2. Data collection	Operationalizing the variables, drawing a population sample, collecting data regarding the variables
D3. Digitization	Inputting, scanning, otherwise putting the data on a computer, organized in a useful way
D4. Discovery	Analyzing the data to test the hypothesis or answer the research question
D5. Design	Laying out the data and analysis in text, tables, and figures to convey the findings to various audiences
D6. Dissemination	Sharing the findings with the various audiences as widely and effectively as possible
D7. Difference	Using the research to make a difference in your research community or the larger world

do not serve to maintain the memory of knowledge about the Black experience, Black people themselves have documented this memory, so it is possible to recover it in a library. The librarian as a professional is key to preserving the memory of a society. And Black librarians are key for preserving the memory of the Black experience.

The main point here is to locate our research in the multigenerational production of knowledge, never failing to consult our history, because important information is always there. Each field of scholarship has a history; each major research question also has a history that usually has been taken up by several disciplines. All research either confirms what is known, challenges and replaces what has been known, or adds something entirely new. These are the only three results from all scholarship, but we cannot know which will be produced by our research until we have conducted a historical review of the literature.

D2, Data collection, gathers the information needed to answer a research question. It is important in all cases that we think of our population of people as not only objects for our analysis, but also as thinking subjects who can always contribute to the design and implementation of research, as well as to the analysis. Now some data is born digital, and it requires its own methodology. For instance, I used born-digital data to make the first comprehensive survey of Black Studies academic units.

My first attempt was in the 1990s, when many academic units did not have a web presence; today, having a web presence is a norm, and it has the value of being self-reported data. In 2013, I found that 76 percent of 1,777 US colleges and universities had Black Studies in some form: 20

percent had established formal Black Studies units, and 56 percent had changed the curriculum of their existing units to include Black Studies courses. Since this survey, the annual *New York Times* and the *Chronicle of Higher Education* articles proclaiming the end of Black Studies on campus have stopped, but, of course, not the attacks.

The next step, D3, Digitization—building our data and analysis in digital form—is a new feature of eBlack Studies research. One of its main benefits is that it enables us to embrace research as a collective activity bridging time and space. For us as individuals, this means that our research is with us whenever we have our laptops at hand. Those who use larger datasets will need network connectivity to that data. But more than this, we have the possibility to develop what might be called a Black Studies Collaboratory, a "center without walls, in which the nation's researchers can perform their research without regard to physical location, interacting with colleagues, accessing instrumentation, sharing data and computational resources, [and] accessing information in digital libraries" ("Collaboratory" 2020).

Digitization takes three forms: (1) digitization of discourse (the virtual community of scholars and activists); (2) digitization of scholarship (secondary data); and (3) digitization of experience (primary data). The digitization of discourse has been done in at least two main ways: first, aggregating voices that are already online, creating a virtual community; and second, building an intentional community based on shared interests. One example of the latter is H-Afro-Am.

The digitization of scholarship is taking new forms that provide new functionality: enhancing data collection and creating comprehensive datasets on each major topic being studied. Examples include a dataset that attempts to document every slave ship of the transatlantic trade, a dataset for every African-American novel, and the many sites digitizing key works, from the Project Gutenberg ebooks to the Gilder Lehrman Center's online document collection on slavery at Yale University. These datasets add unprecedented memory that is accessible to scholars and, in many cases, the general public.

A major advance in the digitization of scholarship is the dSpace software developed at MIT in 2002. This is an open source tool for archiving scholarship that has been adopted by more than one thousand institutions, including Deep Blue at the University of Michigan, IDEALS at the University of Illinois, and the Purdue University Research Repository. The National Science Foundation subsequently proposed that this type of archiving be formally instituted as national policy. The crisis facing Black Studies is that the neoliberal paradigm of commodifying research has become so pervasive that little Black Studies scholarship has been posted in these free-access archives. Most historically Black colleges and universities do not use dSpace and therefore are being excluded from cyberspace archives. There is a crisis of budget around maintaining library collections to support curriculum without the resources to train or hire new digitally skilled staff. In fact, this absence goes even deeper: most Black Studies scholars and departments also ignore institutional archives in all too many cases.

One of the developments in the digitization of scholarship is the collected works project. There are now volumes of collected works on or by Frederick Douglass, Booker T. Washington, Marcus Garvey, and Martin Luther King Jr. These volumes are hard-copy commodity products in the main, although the University of Illinois did make the Booker T. Washington volumes available online for free for some time. I have begun making the material by and about Malcolm X on the Brother Malcolm website available to the public without any barriers of institutional affiliation or cost. (Alkalimat n.d.) The Shabazz family owns his works, but in a much greater historical sense, they belong to all of us.

For years I have advocated a political solution to this issue of individuals having a financial interest in personal archives of great public importance. In matters of intellectual property, we need a policy whereby, just as with eminent domain for real estate, the government can take property in the public interest and adequately compensate the owner. Without such a policy, in a fundamental sense, we are commodifying our history, and that is not a good prospect. The most exciting aspect of digitization is its ability to preserve experience, especially that of everyday life, in the here and now and in any other historical time-frame.

Black Studies teachers have made digitization of everyday experience part of classroom pedagogy. Using digital tools, we turn the classroom from a site of intellectual consumption via our syllabi, reading lists, and lectures into a site of intellectual production in the digital age. The main tool we emphasize is the smart cellphone that can handle text, audio, video, and photographs. Based on data collected through students' phones, we work with them to build websites that target, for example, all of the churches or all of the hair-care institutions in a local community.

In working on these classroom projects at the University of Illinois, we found that the archives were full of material, but it was not within easy reach of the community—or scholars, for that matter. There is a great deal of campus research on the local community that has never been shared with the community. Meanwhile the community has been uploading its own material regarding the family, the church, the neighborhood, and many other aspects of social life onto social media platforms. At the University of Illinois, I helped build a website—a digital library, really—called eBlack CU (Champaign-Urbana) that contains 10 days of video/audio, 50,000 pages of text, and 1,000 photographs; it boasts 58,000 users to date (Lenstra n.d.). One side note: in the process we found a local woman who had uploaded 9,000 community photos to Facebook in one year, which made her what we called a "Facebook archivist"—doing a lot with a little.

D4, Discovery, is the stage is which one answers the key research question by analyzing the data. The text of the research report is strongest when it is argued back into the context—the review of the literature created when defining the research question. As mentioned, there are three basic types of findings: affirming what is known from previous research, contesting or resynthesizing what has been recorded in the research literature, or addressing a new question that has not yet been investigated. In digital humanities, we have great opportunities to raise new research questions, but only after their novelty has been validated by an exhaustive review of the literature. This ensures that our work is special and makes a contribution. There is nothing special about our work unless we can prove it is novel.

D5, Design, speaks to the need for every presentation to make contact with its particular audience. For scholars, this means committing to making multiple iterations of your work based on listening to the comments of reviewers and having a thick skin to avoid being discouraged. The best way to maintain that energy to keep revising your work is to have, as your first audience, some colleagues close to you who support you and whom you trust. We cannot afford to work in isolation. It also means presenting works-in-progress at conference sessions, not only to get suggestions for revision but also to make contact with possible venues for publication. The main target for scholarly articles is a journal. The Black community can be reached through the mass media—radio, television via cable channels, and the Internet, especially Facebook and sharing within networks. Here our language is key. We must accept the challenge of speaking in plain language, remembering what people said when Malcolm X spoke: "Make it plain brother, make it plain."

D6, Dissemination, recognizes that findings do not speak for themselves: they have to be presented in a comprehensible form to whomever is the target audience. And the audience matters. For eBlack Studies, it includes Black Studies scholars, the Black community, and the broader global network of scholars in digital humanities. Digital dissemination includes video, audio, and graphics of all kinds, so we have a great opportunity to be creative in maximizing who we can speak to: we are motivated to increase the reach of our work, both out of our desire for academic excellence and as the historical necessity of social responsibility. In a 1977 conference, it was my good fortune to invent the slogan that became the mission statement of the National Council for Black Studies: "Academic Excellence and Social Responsibility."

Finally, D7, Difference, means that we have to make sure we do not get caught in the self-serving process of seeking approval from academic gatekeepers and ignoring the change we need to foster on so many levels. Research is about finding out what is real and true, and as we continue to do this over time, we change ourselves and then stand on this knowledge that we know so well. In sharing our work with our colleagues, we also seek to change research in general. Research on Black people always has some policy implications for the USA and indeed other parts of the world. This is our responsibility—academic excellence and social responsibility together.

But a word of caution: do not expect one research paper to change the world. It is our task to design research programs, a process involving the development of many specific research projects, amassing large quantities of data, and critiques of alternative explanations before we can have a serious impact and make a difference.

POLICY

Black Studies as an academic program always exists in relationship to the Black community. Just as the College of Agriculture maintains a relationship to farming, and Labor Studies with the trade union movement and the concerns of civil society. Black social institutions are linked to the research and teaching of Black Studies. In this context, policy regarding the quality of life of the Black population is a fundamental issue. Several institutions have programs that serve as national centers.

The University of Chicago has the Race and Capitalism Project led by Michael Dawson and Megan Ming Frances (at the University of Washington) (Dawson and Frances n.d.). This project serves as a think tank for scholars on how the capitalist crisis intersects with racist practices. In addition to bringing together working research groups, they sponsor an online podcast for scholars to discuss their work and its policy implications (Dawson n.d.). These scholars are based in many different departments and thus demonstrate how a Black Studies initiative is transdisciplinary.

Brown University has a Center for the Study of Race and Ethnicity in America under the leadership of Tricia Rose. She has set up a series of conversations on key policy questions regarding the Covid-19 coronavirus called "Underlying Conditions" (Rose n.d.). She also recruited Cornel West to join her in more wide-ranging discussions called "Tight Rope," an "in-depth yet accessible conversations about race, social justice and African American arts and culture" (Brown University 2000).

The latest development is that Boston University has set up a Center for Anti-Racist Research founded by its new director, Ibram X. Kendi.

> The mission of the Boston University Center for Antiracist Research is to convene researchers and practitioners from various disciplines to figure out novel and practical ways to understand, explain, and solve seemingly intractable problems of racial inequity and injustice. We foster exhaustive racial research, research-based policy innovation, data-driven educational and advocacy campaigns, and narrative-change initiatives. We are working toward building an antiracist society that ensures equity and justice for all.
>
> (Kendi 2012)

This center is being financed by a $1.3 million grant from the Rockefeller Foundation (CBS News 2020). One of the main projects being supported is a race data dashboard called the COVID Racial Data Tracker, a tool enabling one to get trend data on virus infections from the national down to the local level.

These policy initiatives are important ways that Black Studies professionals are representing the interests of the Black community. But more needs to be done. Black Studies has yet to return to its roots by reconnecting to the Black Liberation Movement. Many individual faculty and students are involved in social movements, but the radical Black tradition does not presently have a home on a mainstream campus.

There are also organizations active in the Black Liberation Movement that draw on the participation of students and faculty as agents of their missions. Table 15 lists just a few.

Table 15 Current Organizations Active in the Black Liberation Movement

Organization	*URL*
Black Lives Matter	https://blacklivesmatter.com/
Black Youth Project 100	www.byp100.org/
Left Roots	https://leftroots.net/
Project South	https://projectsouth.org/
Black Workers for Justice	https://blackworkersforjustice.com/
Southern Workers Assembly	https://southernworker.org/
Cooperation Jackson	https://cooperationjackson.org/
Movement for Black Lives	https://m4bl.org/
Black Liberation Collective	www.blackliberationcollective.org/
Dream Defenders	https://dreamdefenders.org/
Scholars for Social Justice	http://scholarsforsocialjustice.com/
Black Alliance for Peace	https://blackallianceforpeace.com/

COMMUNITY SERVICE

Black Studies is primarily about knowledge, the production and distribution of knowledge about the Black experience. This is linked to the agency of advocacy in support of the well-being of the Black community. Again, we refer to our slogan "Academic Excellence and Social Responsibility." Taking another step, Black Studies, both faculty and students, have a role of hands-on service to the immediate Black community in which they are located. This kind of activity has been institutionalized under the rubric "service learning," a process by which students can get credit for such activity (Jones et al. 1994).

Community service can be a function of knowledge production about the community. Our work in Urbana-Champaign, the twin cities that are home to the University of Illinois, was served by our work in community informatics. Led by a graduate student, Noah Lenstra (now on the faculty of University of North Carolina at Greensboro), we developed a website, eBlack Champaign, Urbana that aggregated information about the Black community.

> The eBlack Champaign-Urbana project is a collaborative portal on African-American history and culture that draws on multiple public and private collections of information on the African-American community in Champaign-Urbana.
>
> The goals of eBlackCU are to: 1) Centralize information on local African-American history and culture and create new knowledge through this centralization; 2) Collaborate with past and present community residents in the production of knowledge by soliciting their contributions, both in the form of personal memories and in the form of digitized personal archives; 3) Contribute to a community of scholars, activists and citizens interested in learning more about various aspects of local African-American history and culture; and 4) Develop best-practices for other, similar projects to build on our experiences.
>
> (Lenstra n.d.)

Another approach moves knowledge from the campus to the community. This was the research to performance process created at Brown University by Rhett S. Jones and George Bass. They created the Rites and Reason Theatre to transform academic research into dramatic productions, thus sharing knowledge with the community in innovative, culturally transmittable ways.

> **The Mission**
>
> The Department of Africana Studies' Rites and Reason Theatre's mission is to develop new creative works which analyze and articulate the phenomenal and universal odyssey of the African Diaspora. Through this commitment, Rites and Reason has developed creative works that have explored the experiences and expressions of peoples and cultures from across the world.
>
> **The Research-to-Performance Method (RPM)**
>
> The Research-to-Performance Method (RPM) is Rites and Reason's signature method. RPM teams consisting of scholars, writers and community persons collaborate in creating and developing significant new works. A magical and wonderful thing happens when scholars become artists and artists become scholars within the RPM process.
>
> (Brown University 2000)

Other key projects that reflect community service are listed in Table 16. Another service learning project we have practiced is having students become cybernavigators in community institutions, helping people with their computer skills. Digital literacy is the new challenge that eBlack Studies can help the community overcome.

Table 16 Key Projects that Reflect Community Service

Website	Scholars	Institutional Host / URL
eBlack Champaign-Urbana	Noah Lenstra, Abdul Alkalimat	University of Illinois-Urbana Champaign http://eblackcu.net/portal/
Virtual Harlem Renaissance	Bryan Carter	University of Illinois-Chicago www.evl.uic.edu/cavern/harlem/
Race and Place: An African American Community in the Jim Crow South	Scott French, Reginald Butler, William Thomas	University of Virginia www2.vcdh.virginia.edu/afam/raceandplace/
Bronx African American History Project	Mark Naison	Fordham University www.fordham.edu/info/25190/bronx_african_american_history_project

Epilogue

We are approaching the end of the founding generation of Black Studies in the 1960s, as people go into retirement and make their life transitions. We need a comprehensive history to hand off to the coming generations, with as many lessons as possible that we can get from our historical experience. This study contributes to the filling of this need. It is a start.

The most basic question is still asked: what is Black Studies? Many studies assume that what something is called is the key to what it is. But there is that old saying about a rose being what it is, no matter what one calls it. I suppose that I feel the same way about Black Studies—it is what it is, no matter what one calls it. Black Studies is the study of the Black experience tied to the intellectual refutation of racism and the advocacy for improvement in the lives of Black people. It is study, pedagogy, and knowledge for change. We captured this position in the main mission of Black Studies adopted by the National Council for Black Studies: Academic Excellence and Social Responsibility.

In two volumes, we have tried to be as comprehensive as possible in discussing Black Studies in six main ways: as intellectual history, social movement, academic profession, studies about the future of Black people, Diaspora Studies, and as knowledge networks. These manifestations reflect study to gain new knowledge, the organization of teaching materials, cultural performance, and protest advocacy. Each manifestation has a record and has been researched, but has never before been brought together as part of a Black Studies history. We want to be respectful of all these manifestations and not succumb to the notion that knowledge production belongs only to institutions of higher education.

There are two main concerns for this history: knowledge production and supporting Black people's struggle for a better life. This has required the people whom the Italian Marxist philosopher Antonio Gramsci calls:

> the "organic" intellectuals, the thinking and organizing element of a particular fundamental social class. These organic intellectuals are distinguished less by their profession, which may be any job characteristic of their class, than by their function in directing the ideas and aspirations of the class to which they organically belong.
>
> (Gramsci 1999, 131)

My intention in connecting these two concerns is to return to the basic experience of the 1960s, linking Black Studies back to its origin as part of the Black liberation movement. When we examine the Black intellectual history of the HBCUs and the insurgent institutions in the Black community and its movements, we find this connection as well. Reason has always required resistance by the oppressed. It makes sense.

As a member of the founding generation, I have concerns about the state of Black Studies today, but I am keenly aware that these concerns have to be contextualized in the current economic, social, and political situation we face.

Marx and Engels point to our fundamental economic situation in *Preface to a Critique of Political Economy*:

> The mode of production of material life conditions the social, political and intellectual life process in general. It is not the consciousness of men that determines their being, but, on the contrary, their social being that determines their consciousness.
>
> At a certain stage of their development, the material productive forces of society come in conflict with the existing relations of production, or—what is but a legal expression for the same thing—with the property relations within which they have been at work hitherto. From forms of development of the productive forces these relations turn into their fetters.
>
> Then begins an epoch of social revolution. With the change of the economic foundation the entire immense superstructure is more or less rapidly transformed.
>
> (Marx and Engels 1969, 503)

The technological revolution has disrupted the economic foundation of class relations, and raised even more profoundly than ever the question: "Who needs the Negro?" Willhelm (1971) and Yette (1972) raised this question in the 1970s, but it is now more urgent than ever. What was then a choice, whether to continue to employ the masses of workers both Black and white, is now a question being answered by labor-replacing technology. The capitalists are planning an economy without workers. Robots and other smart machines, for example, driverless cars, have become a permanent part of economic development all over the world.

Given this decline in the demand for Black labor, mass education has been declining as well. Now there is a great polarity developing. Higher education, especially in engineering and computer science, is now being transformed toward the new economy. Public schools do not work like they used to, when they were training workers for the old industrial economy. Cities that were once the prosperous communities of industrial works are pockmarked with vacant lots, Single Room Occupancy hotels, and food deserts. Police killings of unemployed youth are at record levels, with few if any prosecutions or convictions of any wrongdoing.

On the other hand, a new professional class of Black Studies academics has been developed, based on the struggles against institutional racism and the battle of ideas to legitimate Black intellectual history. The crisis is the contradiction between careerism and commitment to academic excellence and social responsibility. As the class polarity increases, this contradiction will expose a fault line in Black Studies. Will there continue to be a betrayal, about which Houston Baker (2010) has written so eloquently? He uses Martin Luther King as a standard to judge the current public intellectuals:

> My hypothesis is that post-Civil Rights era black public intellectuals have been far more interested in serving as self-promoters than as thinkers committed to black majority interests. Much of what they have proclaimed, postulated, and published of their personal deliberations on the great problem of race, particularly race in the contemporary United States, has been profitably tailored to the tastes of conservative black and white audiences.
>
> (Baker 2010, 15)

Baker deals with nationally popular neoconservatives, but his point applies to a much wider portion of Black academics, including those who are foul-weather friends of the community and the movement. The critical issue is about using the money and resources of the campus, often the most resource-rich institution to which Black people have any access in any given community.

On the other hand, there is much to celebrate and support. Black Studies is a permanent part of higher education, including doctoral-degree granting programs. Rational reflection on the Black experience and the corresponding cultural celebration impact the vast majority of students and faculty at all levels, from kindergarten to twelfth grade and on into undergraduate- and graduate-level programs. We present to the reader this reflection on the future to help them stay on the path covered by those who have come before us. We study this history so we can repeat it, not as it was, but as it can be in the new times in which we live.

We have been presenting an analysis of the future of Black Studies. There is an old saying: if you don't know where you are going any road can take you there. So while it is critical to have historical understanding, it is our responsibility to develop a collective agreement on a path into the future toward a goal. The main goal that has had a central position guiding the motion of Black history has been freedom. In the most abstract sense, freedom has been on the one hand the end of oppression and exploitation, and on the other the social, political, and economic conditions facilitating the full development of one's human potential via education and culture. So Black Studies has a purpose—it is not neutral and without a value orientation.

We have discussed the future of Black Studies in three main ways, and out of these analyzes we can draw three main lessons.

1. The future we need must be fought for, can only come about through struggle. This means that Black Studies is part of the battle of ideas, against racism, about the freedom struggle, and for the reorganization of society to facilitate the realization of freedom. We need the fullness of our imagination grounded in the motion of the masses of Black people to do what must be done.
2. The world has now become one arena for politics, so while Black Studies must maintain its foundation in the African-American experience, it is essential that our research and teaching embrace Africa and the African Diaspora in a global historical context. This includes monitoring how Black Studies is being researched and taught in countries all over the world.
3 These two goals on the march to freedom can be achieved with the tools of digital technology. Black Studies can become eBlack Studies by continuing the process of utilizing the tools of digital technology.

This is the most progressive future for Black Studies, but of course this will by itself not be enough to change society. On an academic level, this will have to also be embraced by other academic disciplines, all the diverse ethnic studies programs as well as labor and working-class studies. But in the end this is only an intervention at the level of consciousness, theory, and moral beliefs. The connection has to be with social motion.

We must remember the profound insight from Karl Marx: "Material force can only be overthrown by material force, but theory itself becomes a material force when it has seized the masses" (Marx 1843). This truth requires that Black Studies return to its origin as a tool of the Black liberation movement. So, my final comment on the future of Black Studies is summed up in the slogan I created for NCBS, "Academic Excellence and Social Responsibility." Our future is on campus with academic excellence, and in the movements for justice, social responsibility. I call on the rising generation of Black Studies scholar-activists to take up the baton and carry on to create the future we need.

Bibliography

Adi, Hakim. 1998. *West Africans in Britain: 1900–1960: Nationalism, Pan-Africanism, and Communism*. London: Lawrence and Wishart.

Adi, Hakim. 2013. *Pan-Africanism and Communism: The Communist International, Africa and the Diaspora, 1919–1939*. Trenton, NJ: Africa World Press.

Adi, Hakim. 2017. "MRes—The History of Africa and the African Diaspora." University of Chichester. May 23. www.chi.ac.uk/department-humanities/postgraduate/mres-history-africa-and-african-diaspora.

Adi, Hakim. 2018. *Pan Afrikanism: A History*. London: Bloomsbury.

Adi, Hakim, and Marika Sherwood. 2007. *Pan-African History: Political Figures from Africa and the Diaspora Since 1787*. London: Routledge.

Adi, Hakim, Marika Sherwood, and George Padmore. 1995. *The 1945 Manchester Pan-African Congress Revisited*. London: New Beacon Books.

African American Research Center. 2019. "African Cultural Survivals in America: University of Illinois Library Bibliography." www.library.illinois.edu/afx/subject-bibliographies/africanisms/.

African Union. 1963. "Organization of African Unity Charter." May 25. https://au.int/en/treaties/charter-african-cultural-renaissance.

AfroCubaWeb. n.d. "Zuleica Romay Guerra." www.afrocubaweb.com/zuleicaromay.htm#Afro_American. Accessed October 31, 2020.

Agbodeka, Francis. 1998. *A History of University of Ghana: Half a Century of Higher Education (1948–1998)*. Accra: Woeli Publishing Services.

AIEUT (Ahmed Iqbal Ullah Education Trust). 2020. "Ahmed Iqbal Ullah Race Relations Resource Centre and Education Trust." www.racearchive.org.uk/.

Aitken, Robbie John Macvicar. 2015. *Black Germany: The Making and Unmaking of a Diaspora Community, 1884–1960*. Cambridge: Cambridge University Press.

Akuno, Kali. 2012. "The Jackson–Kush Plan: The Struggle for Black Self-Determination and Economic Democracy." Jackson, MS: Malcolm X Grassroots Movement, New Afrikan People's Organization. https://mronline.org/wp-content/uploads/2020/07/Jackson-KushPlan.pdf.

Alexandrov, Vladimir. 2013. *The Black Russian*. n.p.: Grove/Atlantic, Inc. http://rbdigital.oneclickdigital.com.

Alkalimat, Abdul. 1975. "People's College. Report from National Planning Conference: Year to Pull the Covers Off Imperialism Project. *Black Scholar* (January–February): 54–56.

Alkalimat, Abdul. 1986. *Introduction to Afro-American Studies: A Peoples College Primer*. Chicago, IL: Twenty-First Century Books & Publications.

Alkalimat, Abdul. 1996a. "Speech at the Welcome Reception at University of Toledo on the Appointment of Dr. Abdul Alkalimat as Director of Africana Studies." http://alkalimat.org/210%201996%20welcome%20reception%20university%20toledo.pdf.

Alkalimat, Abdul. 1996b. "Technological Revolution and Black Liberation in the 21st Century." *Cy.Rev: A Journal of Cybernetic Revolution, Sustainable Socialism and Radical Democracy*, no. 4 (Summer–Fall): 6–14.

Alkalimat, Abdul. 2004. *The African American Experience in Cyberspace: A Resource Guide to the Best Websites on Black Culture and History*. London: Pluto.

Alkalimat, Abdul. 2006. *Africana Studies in New York State*. Toledo, OH: University of Toledo Africana Studies Program.

Alkalimat, Abdul. 2007. "Africana Studies in California." University of Toledo. http://alkalimat.org/353%20alkalimat%202007%20africana%20studies%20in%20calif.pdf.

Alkalimat, Abdul. 2016. *Rethinking Afro-Cuba*. Urbana, IL: Twenty-First Century Books & Publications.

Alkalimat, Abdul. 2021. *The History of Black Studies*. London: Pluto.

Alkalimat, Abdul. n.d. "Brother Maclolm X: A Research Site." http://brothermalcolm.net/. Accessed November 1, 2020.

Alkalimat, Abdul. n.d. "Festac: The Second World Black and African Festival of Arts and Culture." http://alkalimat.org/festac/.

Alkalimat, Abdul, Ronald William Bailey, Sam Byndom, Desiree McMillion, LaTasha Nesbitt, Kate Williams, and Brian Zelip. 2013. *African American Studies 2013: A National Web-Based Survey*. Urbana, IL: University of Illinois at Urbana Champaign. https://katewill.web.ischool.illinois.edu/work/53-alkalimat-et-al-2013-black-studies-survey.pdf.

Alkalimat, Abdul, and Kate Williams. 2015. *Roots and Flowers: The Life and Work of Afro-Cuban Librarian Marta Terry González*. Sacramento, CA: Library Juice Press.

Allen, Ernest. 1994. "Satokata Takahashi and the Flowering of Black Messianic Nationalism." *The Black Scholar: Journal of Black Studies and Research* 24 (January): 23–46. https://doi.org/10.1080/00064246.1994.11413118.

Alleyne, Brian. 2007. "Anti-Racist Cultural Politics in Post-Imperial Britain: The New Beacon Circle." In *Utopian Pedagogy: Radical Experiments Against Neoliberal Globalization*, edited by Mark Coté, Richard J.F. Day, and Greig de Peuter, 207–26. Toronto: University of Toronto Press.

American Bible Society. 2010. *Holy Bible: Containing the Old and New Testaments: King James Version*.

Anderson, Monica. 2015. "Racial and Ethnic Differences in How People Use Mobile Technology." *Pew Research Center* (blog). April 30. www.pewresearch.org/fact-tank/2015/04/30/racial-and-ethnic-differences-in-how-people-use-mobile-technology/.

Anderson, Reynaldo, and Charles E. Jones. 2017. *Afrofuturism 2.0: The Rise of Astro-Blackness*. Lanham, MD: Lexington Books.

Anderson, Samuel E. 1970. "Mathematics and the Struggle for Black Liberation." *The Black Scholar* 2(1): 20–27.

Anderson, Samuel E. 1974. "Science, Technology, and Black Liberation." *The Black Scholar* 5(6): 2–8.

Anderson, Samuel E. 1990. "Worldmath Curriculum: Fighting Eurocentrism in Mathematics." *The Journal of Negro Education* 59(3): 348–59. https://doi.org/10.2307/2295569.

Andrews, Kehinde. 2013. *Resisting Racism: Race, Inequality, and the Black Supplementary School Movement*. London: Institute of Education Press.

Andrews, Kehinde. 2016. "The Black Studies Movement in Britain." *The Black Scholar*, October. www.theblackscholar.org/black-studies-movement-britain/.

Andrews, Kehinde. 2018a. *Back to Black: Retelling Black Radicalism for the 21st Century*. London: Zed Books.

Andrews, Kehinde. 2018b. "The Black Studies Movement in Britain." *African American Intellectual History Society* (blog). June 22. www.aaihs.org/the-black-studies-movement-in-britain/.

Anshan, Li. 2005. "African Studies in China in the Twentieth Century: A Historiographical Survey." *African Studies Review* 48(1): 59–87.

Anyaso, Hilary Hurd. 2013. "Jan Carew, Leader in Black Studies, Dies at 92." January 10. https://news.northwestern.edu/stories/2013/01/obituary-jan-carew/.

Appiah, Kwame Anthony, and Henry Louis Gates, Jr. eds. 2005. *Africana: The Encyclopedia of the African and African American Experience*. Oxford: Oxford University Press.

Aptheker, Herbert. 2000. "Notes on Du Bois's Final Years." *Souls* 2(4): 76–79.

Asante, Molefi Kete. 2007. *Cheikh Anta Diop: An Intellectual Portrait*. Los Angeles, CA: University of Sankore Press.

Asante, Molefi Kete. 2009. *Maulana Karenga: An Intellectual Portrait*. Cambridge: Polity.

Association for African Studies in Germany. n.d. "Vereinigung für Afrikawissenschaften in Deutschland." http://vad-ev.de/en/. Accessed October 31, 2020.

ASWAD (Association for the Study of the Worldwide African Diaspora). 2020. "Mission and Constitution." www.aswadiaspora.org/mission-and-constitution.

Atske, Sara, and Andrew Perrin. 2021. "Home Broadband Adoption, Computer Ownership Vary by Race, Ethnicity in the US." *Pew Research Centre*, July 16. www.pewresearch.org/fact-tank/2021/07/16/home-broadband-adoption-computer-ownership-vary-by-race-ethnicity-in-the-u-s/.

Austin, David. 2013. *Fear of a Black Nation: Race, Sex, and Security in Sixties Montreal*. Toronto, ON: Between the Lines.

Austin, David, ed. 2018. *Moving against the System: The 1968 Congress of Black Writers and the Shaping of Global Black Consciousness*. London: Pluto Press.

Ayim, May, Katharina Oguntoye, and Dagmar Schultz, eds. 2018. *Farbe bekennen: afro-deutsche Frauen auf den Spuren ihrer Geschichte*. Berlin: Orlanda.

Babu, Abdul Rahman Mohamed. 1981. *African Socialism or Socialist Africa?* London: Zed Press.

Bailey, Anne Caroline. 2007. *African Voices of the Atlantic Slave Trade Beyond the Silence and the Shame*. Kingston: Ian Randle.

Baker, Houston A. 1993. *Black Studies, Rap, and the Academy*. Chicago, IL: University of Chicago Press.

Baker, Houston A. 2010. *Betrayal: How Black Intellectuals Have Abandoned the Ideals of the Civil Rights Era*. New York: Columbia University Press.

Baldwin, Kate. 2009. *Beyond the Color Line and the Iron Curtain: Reading Encounters between Black and Red, 1922–1963*. Durham, NC: Duke University Press.

Ball, Sharon. 2006. "Octavia Butler: Eye on the Stars, Feet on the Ground." *NPR: Obituaries*, March 4. www.npr.org/2006/03/04/5245686/octavia-butler-eye-on-the-stars-feet-on-the-ground.

Banks, Adam J. 2011. *Digital Griots: African American Rhetoric in a Multimedia Age*. Carbondale, IL: Southern Illinois University Press.

Baptiste, Fitzroy André, and Rupert Lewis. 2009. *George Padmore: Pan-African Revolutionary*. Kingston: Ian Randle Publishers.

Baraka, Amiri, and LeRoi Jones. 1969. "A Black Value System." *The Black Scholar* 1(1): 54–60.

BASA (Black and Asian Studies Association). n.d. Wikipaedia. "Black and Asian Studies Association." https://en.wikipedia.org/wiki/Black_and_Asian_Studies_Association.

BASA (Black and Asian Studies Association). "Black and Asian Studies Association: A 27 Year Review." November 3. YouTube. www.youtube.com/watch?v=ZEdxy_az-B4.

BCSA (Black Canadian Studies Association). n.d. "Black Canadian Studies Association." https://bcsa.wordpress.com/. Accessed October 31, 2020.

BDPA (Black Data Processing Associates). n.d. "About BDPA: National BDPA." www.bdpa.org/page/About_BDPA. Accessed October 31, 2020.

Bell, Howard Holman. 1969a. *A Survey of the Negro Convention Movement, 1830–1861*. New York: Arno Press.

Bell, Howard Holman. 1969b. *Minutes of the Proceedings of the National Negro Conventions 1830–1864*. New York: Arno Press.

BFSU (Beijing Foreign Studies University). n.d. "School of Asian and African Studies." https://global.bfsu.edu.cn/pl/info/1181/1414.htm.

BGCS (Black German Cultural Society). n.d. "History: Black German Cultural Society™." http://afrogermans.us/bgcs-history/. Accessed October 31, 2020.

Bhambra, Gurminder K., Dalia Gebrial, and Kerem Nişancioğlu, eds. 2018. *Decolonizing the University*. London: Pluto Press.

Black Central Europe. n.d. "Black Central Europe." https://blackcentraleurope.com/. Accessed October 31, 2020.

Black Cultural Archives. 2020. "Black Cultural Archives." Black Cultural Archives. https://blackculturalarchives.org/about.

Black History in America. n.d. "Black Nationalism." *My Black History*. www.myblackhistory.net/Black%20Nationalism.htm/.

Black History Month Bordeaux. 2018. *1er Black History Month, Bordeaux (3–25 February 2018)*. YouTube. www.youtube.com/watch?v=Q-vs3M_CQYw&t=332s.

Black History Month Bordeaux. n.d. "Black History Month Bordeaux." www.facebook.com/BlackHistoryMonthBordeaux/. Accessed November 1, 2020.

Blackshire-Belay, C. Aisha. 2001. "The African Diaspora in Europe: African Germans Speak Out." *Journal of Black Studies* 31(3): 264–87.

Blain, Keisha N. 2016. "The Ruth Simms Hamilton African Diaspora Series: An Interview with Quito Swan and Glenn Chambers." *AAIHS* (blog). October 25. www.aaihs.org/the-ruth-simms-hamilton-african-diaspora-series-an-interview-with-quito-swan-and-glenn-chambers/.

Blakely, Allison. 1976. "The Negro in Imperial Russia: A Preliminary Sketch." *The Journal of Negro History* 61(4): 351–61. https://doi.org/10.2307/2717002.

Bloom, Joshua, and Waldo E. Jr Martin. 2016. *Black Against Empire The History and Politics of the Black Panther Party*. Berkeley, CA: University of California Press.

Bonacci, Giulia, and Elikia M'Bokolo. 2015. *Exodus! Heirs and Pioneers, Rastafari Return to Ethiopia*. Translated by Antoinette Tidjani Alou. Kingston: University Press of the West Indies.

Bond, Horace Mann. 1976. *Education for Freedom: A History of Lincoln University, Pennsylvania*. Lincoln, PA: Lincoln University.

Braginskiĭ, M. I and Institut Afriki (Akademiia nauk SSSR). 1966. *Africa Wins Freedom*. Translated from the Russian by G. Ivanov-Mumjiev. Moscow: Progress Publishers.

British Association for American Studies. 2020. "African-American Studies Archives." *British Association for American Studies* (blog). www.baas.ac.uk/project-category/afam/.

British Black Studies. n.d. "British Black Studies List." www.jiscmail.ac.uk/cgi-bin/webadmin?A0=BRITISHBLACKSTUDIES. Accessed October 29, 2020.

Brock, André, Jr. 2020. *Distributed Blackness: African American Cybercultures*. New York: New York University Press.

Brown, Mitchell. n.d. "The Faces of Science: African Americans in the Sciences." https://tinyurl.com/y4ms8p5c.

Brown University. n.d. "Rites and Reason Theatre | Africana Studies." www.brown.edu/academics/africana-studies/rites-and-reason-theatre. Accessed November 1, 2020.

Brown University. 2000. "Podcast by Tricia Rose, Cornel West Explores African American Arts, Culture, History and Politics." Brown University. www.brown.edu/news/2020-06-12/tightrope. Accessed October 31, 2020.

Brutus, Dennis. 1973. *A Simple Lust*. London: Heinemann.

Brutus, Dennis. 1991. *Stubborn Hope: New Poems and Selections from China Poems and Strains*. Oxford: Heinemann.

Bryan, Beverley, Stella Dadzie, and Suzanne Scafe. 1985. *The Heart of the Race: Black Women's Lives in Britain*. London: Virago.

Buhle, Paul. 1989. *C.L.R. James: The Artist As Revolutionary*. London: Verso.

Busby, Margaret. 1992. *Daughters of Africa: An International Anthology of Words and Writings by Women of African Descent from the Ancient Egyptian to the Present*. New York: Ballantine Books.

Busby, Margaret, ed. 2019. *New Daughters of Africa: An International Anthology of Writing by Women of African Descent*. Oxford: Myriad Editions.

Bush, Rod. 2000. *We Are Not What We Seem: Black Nationalism and Class Struggle in the American Century*. New York: New York University Press.

Butler, Octavia E. 2007. *Parable of the Sower*. New York: Grand Central Publishing.

Butler, Octavia E. 2019. *Parable of the Talents*. New York: Grand Central Publishing.

Butler, Octavia E. 2020. "Earthseed." https://godischange.org/the-destiny-of-earthseed/.

Campbell, Horace. 1975. "Socialism in Tanzania: A Case Study." *The Black Scholar* 6(8): 41–51.

Campbell, Horace. 1987. *Rasta and Resistance: From Marcus Garvey to Walter Rodney*. Trenton, NJ: Africa World Press.

Carew, Jan. 1961. *The Last Barbarian*. London: Secker & Warburg.

Carew, Jan R. 2006. *The Rape of Paradise: Columbus and the Origins of Racism in the Americas*. Astoria, NY: Seaburn Publishing Group.

Carew, Jan R., and Kwame Senu Neville Dawes. 2009. *Black Midas*. Leeds: Peepal Tree Press.

Carew, Jan, and Malcolm X. 1994. *Ghosts in Our Blood: With Malcolm X in Africa, England, and the Caribbean*. New York: Lawrence Hill Books.

Carew, Joy Gleason. 2010. *Blacks, Reds, and Russians: Sojourners in Search of the Soviet Promise*. New Brunswick, NJ: Rutgers University Press.

Carson, Clayborne. 1995. *In Struggle: SNCC and the Black Awaking of the 1960s*. Cambridge, MA: Harvard University Press.

Carter, Martin. 1997. *Selected Poems*. Revised ed. Georgetown, Guyana: Red Thread Women's Press.

Casa de las Américas. n.d. "Programa de Estudios Sobre Afroamérica." http://casadelasamericas.org/afro.php. Accessed October 31, 2020.

CBS News. 2020. "Boston University's Center For Antiracist Research Gets 'Game Changing' $1.5 Million Gift." October 1. https://boston.cbslocal.com/2020/10/01/boston-university-antiracist-research-center-ibram-kendi-grant-covid/.

CSRPC (Center for the Study of Race, Politics, and Culture, University of Chicago). 2016. "'The Minority Paradox: Blackness in France,' with Historian Pap NDiaye." November 10. https://csrpc.uchicago.edu/programs/partnerships/2016_17/pap_ndiaye/.

Césaire, Aimé. 2001 (1955). *Discourse on Colonialism*. New York: Monthly Review Press.

Chagas, Catarina. 2022. "Shaping the Future of Black Studies." *Queen's Gazette*, Queen's University. February 2. www.queensu.ca/gazette/stories/shaping-future-black-studies.

Cha-Jua, Sundiata Keita. 1998. "The Black Radical Congress and the Reconstruction of the Black Freedom Movement." *The Black Scholar* 28(3/4): 8–21.Chowdhury, Ibnul. 2020. "'We Unearth the Unheard Histories of Black Canadians': CDN335 Returns to U of T." *The Varsity* (blog). January 13. https://thevarsity.ca/2020/01/12/we-unearth-the-unheard-histories-of-black-canadians-cdn335-returns-to-u-of-t/.

Clarke, John Henrik. 1976. "The African Heritage Studies Association (AHSA): Some Notes on the Conflict with the African Studies Association (ASA) and the Fight to Reclaim African History." *Issue: A Journal of Opinion* 6(2/3): 5–11. https://doi.org/10.2307/1166439.

Clarke, John Henrik. 1977. "The University of Sankore at Timbuctoo: A Neglected Achievement in Black Intellectual History." *The Western Journal of Black Studies* 1(2).

"Collaboratory." 2020. *Wikipedia*. https://en.wikipedia.org/w/index.php?title=Collaboratory&oldid=937501221.

Cone, James H. 1984. *For My People: Black Theology and the Black Church*. Maryknoll, NY: Orbis Books.

Contee, Clarence G. 1971. "The Encyclopedia Africana Project of W.E.B. Dubois." *African Historical Studies* 4(1): 77–91.

Cooper, Carolyn. 1986. "Chanting Down Babylon: Bob Marley's Song as Literary Text." *Jamaica Journal* 19(4): 2–9.

Cooper, Carolyn. 2004. *Sound Clash: Jamaican Dancehall Culture from Lady Saw to Dancehall Queen*. New York: Palgrave Macmillan.

Cooperation Jackson. 2020. "Social Transformation." https://cooperationjackson.org/principles.

Cornforth, Maurice Campbell. 1975. *Science Versus Idealism: In Defence of Philosophy Against Positivism and Pragmatism*. Westport, CT: Greenwood.

Council for the Development of Social Science Research in Africa. 2020. "CODESRIA." https://codesria.org/spip.php?

CRAN (Conseil Répresentatif des Associations Noires). n.d. "CRAN: Cartographie Des Mémoires de l'Esclavage." www.mmoe.llc.ed.ac.uk/en/association/conseil-r%C3%A9presentatif-des-associations-noires-cran. Accessed January 28, 2022.

Dadie, Bernard Binlin Dadié / Bernard Binlin. 1984. *An African in Paris*. Champaign, IL: University of Illinois Press.

Dadzie, Stella. 2000. *Toolkit for Tackling Racism in Schools*. Stoke-on-Trent: Trentham.

Dadzie, Stella. 2020. *A Kick in the Belly: Women, Slavery and Resistance*. London: Verso.

Daniels, Jessie. 2009. *Cyber Racism: White Supremacy Online and the New Attack on Civil Rights*. Lanham, MD: Rowman & Littlefield.

Davies, Carole Boyce. 2008. *Left of Karl Marx: The Political Life of Black Communist Claudia Jones*. Durham, NC: Duke University Press.

Davis, John Aubrey, ed. 1958. *Africa Seen by American Negro Scholars*. Paris: Présence Africaine; New York: American Society of African Culture.

Dawson, Michael C. n.d. "New Dawn." *Listen Notes*. www.listennotes.com/podcasts/new-dawn-michael-dawson-UWHreGXMViQ/. Accessed November 1, 2020.

Dawson, Michael C., and Megan Ming Frances. n.d. "The Race and Capitalism Project." Center for the Study of Race, Politics, and Culture, University of Chicago. https://csrpc.uchicago.edu/programs/projects/race_and_capitalism_project/. Accessed November 1, 2020.

Delbourgo, James. 2017. *Collecting the World: Hans Sloane and the Origins of the British Museum*. Cambridge, MA: Belknap Press.

Dhondy, Farrukh. 2001. *C.L.R. James*. London: Weidenfeld & Nicolson.

Diedrich, Maria I. 2016. "Black 'Others'? African Americans and Black Germans in the Third Reich." In *Remapping Black Germany: New Perspectives on Afro-German History, Politics, and Culture*, edited by Sara Lennox, 135–48. Amherst, MA: University of Massachusetts Press.

Digging Deep. 2020. "Black Coal Miners." www.blackcoalminers.com/.

Diop, Cheikh Anta. 1962. *The Cultural Unity of Negro Africa: The Domains of Patriarchy and of Matriarchy in Classical Antiquiry*. Paris: Presence Africaine.

Diop, Cheikh Anta. 1991. *Civilization Or Barbarism: An Authentic Anthropology*. New York: Lawrence Hill Books.

Diop, Cheikh Anta. 1997 (1974). *The African Origin of Civilization: Myth or Reality*. Chicago, IL: Lawrence Hill Books.

Diop, Cheikh Anta, Harold J. Salemson, and Marjolijn De Jager. 1991. *Civilization or Barbarism: An Authentic Anthropology*. New York: Lawrence Hill Books.

Diouf, Sylviane A. 2009. *Dreams of Africa in Alabama: The Slave Ship Clotilda and the Story of the Last Africans Brought to America*. Oxford: Oxford University Press.

Donovan, Patricia. 2000. "Showing Their Colors: Afro-Germans Beginning to Carve a Place for Themselves in German Society." News Center, University of Buffalo, September 21. www.buffalo.edu/news/releases/2000/09/4879.html.

Drake, St. Clair. 1987. *Black Folk Here and There: An Essay in History and Anthropology*. Los Angeles, CA: Center for Afro-American Studies, University of California.

Du Bois, W.E.B. 1899. *The Philadelphia Negro: A Social Study*. Philadelphia, PA: University of Pennsylvania Press.

Du Bois, W.E.B. 1915. "The African Roots of War." *Atlantic Monthly*, May.

Du Bois, W.E.B. 1962. "A Statement Concerning the Encyclopaedia Africana Project." April. www.endarkenment.com/eap/legacy/620401duboisweb.htm.

Du Bois, W.E.B. 1972. *The World and Africa: An Inquiry into the Part Which Africa Has Played in World History*. New York: International Publishers.

Du Bois, W.E.B. 2001 (1915). *The Negro*. Philadelphia, PA: University of Pennsylvania Press.

Du Bois, W.E.B. 2010 (1896). *The Suppression of the African Slave Trade to the United States of America, 1638–1870*. Cambridge, MA: Harvard University Press.

Edmondson, Belinda. 2009. "Gentrifying Dialect, or the Taming of Miss Lou." In *Caribbean Middlebrow: Leisure Culture and the Middle Class*, 86–109. Ithaca, NY: Cornell University Press.

Eglash, Ron. 2005. *African Fractals: Modern Computing and Indigenous Design*. New Brunswick, NJ: Rutgers University Press.

Emory University. 2007. "Michel Fabre Archives of African American Arts and Letters, 1910–2003." Emory University. December 17.

Equiano, Olaudah. 2012. *The Interesting Narrative of the Life of Olaudah Equiano: or Gustavus Vassa, the African*. n.p.: Emereo Publishing.

Ernst, Alina. 2018a. "Oliver Golden (1887–1940)." *Black Past*, April 1. www.blackpast.org/global-african-history/golden-oliver-1887-1940/.

Ernst, Alina. 2018b. "Lily Golden (1934–2010)." *Black Past*, July 7. www.blackpast.org/global-african-history/golden-lily-1934-2010/.

Everett, Anna. 2009. *Digital Diaspora: A Race for Cyberspace*. Albany, NY: SUNY Press.

Everett, Kim. 2015. "Audre Lorde's Germany." *Mädchenmannschaft*, January 20. https://maedchenmannschaft.net/audre-lordes-germany/.

Fabre, Michel. 1970. *Les Noirs Americains*. Paris: A. Colin.

Fabre, Michel. 1993. *From Harlem to Paris: Black American Writers in France, 1840–1980*. Urbana, IL: University of Illinois Press.

Fabre, Michel. 2009. *The World of Richard Wright*. Jackson, MS: University Press of Mississippi.

Fabre, Michel, and Paul Oren. 1971. *Harlem, ville noire*. Paris: Colin.

Falola, Toyin. 2014. *The African Diaspora: Slavery, Modernity and Globalization*. Rochester, NY: University of Rochester Press.

Fanon, Frantz. 1965. *The Wretched of the Earth*. New York: Grove Press.

Fanon, Frantz, and Charles Lam Markmann. 1967. *Black Skin, White Masks*. New York: Grove Press.

Farber, Samuel. 2011. *Cuba since the Revolution of 1959: A Critical Assessment*. Chicago, IL: Haymarket Books.

Fawcett, Kirstin. 2014. "Watch George Clinton's P-Funk Mothership Get Reassembled For Its Museum Debut." *Smithsonian Magazine*. June 10. www.smithsonianmag.com/smithsonian-institution/watch-george-clintons-mothership-get-reassembled-for-its-museum-debut-180951685/.

FESTAC 77. 1977. Second World Black and African Festival of Arts and Culture, January 15–February 12, Lagos, Nigeria. www.festac77.net/.

Figueroa, Frank M. 2007. *Machito and his Afro-Cubans*. Oldsmar, FL: Pillar Publications.

Fleming, Beatrice J., and Marion J. Pryde. 1946. *Distinguished Negroes Abroad*. Washington, DC: Associated Publishers.

Forman, James. 1972. *The Making of Black Revolutionaries: A Personal Account*. New York: Macmillan.

Forsythe, Dennis. 1971. *Let the Niggers Burn! The Sir George Williams University Affair and Its Caribbean Aftermath*. Montreal: Our Generation Press.

Fouché, Rayvon. 2009. "Following the Artifacts: Hip Hop, Japan, and Technological Knowledge." *Studies of Urban International Society: Compilation of Seminar Papers*, September 15, 59-85.

Francis, Angelyn. 2019. "The Growing Field of Black Canadian Studies." *University Affairs* (blog). August 7. www.universityaffairs.ca/news/news-article/the-growing-field-of-black-canadian-studies/.

Frazier, E. Franklin. 1957. *Black Bourgeoisie: The Rise of a New Middle Class in the United States*. New York: Free Press.

Freedom Archives. 2020. "Presence Africaine." https://freedomarchives.org.

Fuente, Alejandro de la, and George Reid Andrews, eds. 2018. *Afro-Latin American Studies: An Introduction*. Cambridge: Cambridge University Press.

Fuller, Howard, and Lisa Frazier Page. 2014. *No Struggle, No Progress: A Warrior's Life from Black Power to Education Reform*. Milwaukee, WI: Marquette University Press.

Fund METIS. n.d. "Who We Are." www.fundmetis.ru/en/who-we.html. Accessed October 31, 2020.

Gaines, Kevin Kelly. 2008. *American Africans in Ghana: Black Expatriates and the Civil Rights Era*. Chapel Hill, NC: University of North Carolina Press.

Gao, Yunxiang. 2021. *Arise, Africa! Roar, China! Black and Chinese Citizens of the World in the Twentieth Century*. Chapel Hill, NC: University of North Carolina Press.

Garvey, Marcus, Robert A. Hill, and Barbara Bair. 1987. *Marcus Garvey: Life and Lessons: A Centennial Companion to the Marcus Garvey and Universal Negro Movement Association Papers*. Berkeley, CA: University of California Press.

Gavrilov, Igor. 1969. *Africa in Soviet Studies: 1968 Annual*. Moscow: Central Department of Oriental Literature.

Gellman, Erik S. 2012. *Death Blow to Jim Crow the National Negro Congress and the Rise of Militant Civil Rights*. Chapel Hill, NC: University of North Carolina Press.

Gendzier, Irene L. 1985. *Frantz Fanon: A Critical Study*. New York: Grove Press.

Gerdes, Paulus. 1998. *Women, Art and Geometry in Southern Africa.* Trenton, NJ: Africa World Press.

German Studies Association. n.d. "German Studies Association." www.thegsa.org/. Accessed October 31, 2020.

Gilman, Sander L. 1983. *On Blackness without Blacks: Essays on the Image of the Black in Germany.* Boston, MA: Hall.

Gilroy, Paul. 2020. "Sarah Parker Remond Centre for the Study of Racism & Racialisation." Sarah Parker Remond Centre. February 25. www.ucl.ac.uk/racism-racialisation/about-us.

Gilroy, Paul. 2007 (1993). *The Black Atlantic: Modernity and Double Consciousness.* London: Verso.

Golden, Lily. 2002. *My Long Journey Home.* 1st edn. Chicago, IL: Third World Press.

Gomez, Michael A. 2008. *Reversing Sail: A History of the African Diaspora.* Cambridge: Cambridge University Press.

Graham, Roderick. 2014. *The Digital Practices of African Americans: An Approach to Studying Cultural Change in the Information Society.* New York: Peter Lang.

Gramsci, Antonio. 1999. *Selections from the Prison Notebooks of Antonio Gramsci.* Translated by Quentin Hoare and Geoffrey Nowell Smith. London: ElecBook.

Grant, Colin. 2010. *Negro with a Hat: The Rise and Fall of Marcus Garvey.* New York: Oxford University Press.

Greenidge, Kerri K. 2019. *Black Radical: The Life and Times of William Monroe Trotter.* New York: Liverlight.

Griffith, Donald Muldrow. 2017. "A Complexion Change: 'I Know a Way Exists….'" 32nd Black International Cinema Berlin, program, May 12–14. Fountainhead Tanz Théâtre. http://black-international-cinema.com/BIC17/html/bic17_press_en.html.

Griggs, Sutton E. 1899. *Imperium in Imperio: A Study of the Negro Race Problem. A Novel.* www.gutenberg.org/cache/epub/15454/pg15454-images.html.

Guimarães, Selva. 2015. "The Teaching of Afro-Brazilian and Indigenous Culture and History in Brazilian Basic Education in the 21st Century." *Policy Futures in Education* 13(8): 939–48. https://doi.org/10.1177/1478210315579980.

Gyamfi, Bright. 2021. "From Nkrumah's Black Star to the African Diaspora: Ghanaian Intellectual Activists and the Development of Black Studies in the Americas." *The Journal of African American History* 106(4): 682–705. https://doi.org/10.1086/716492.

Haley, Alex. 2016. *Roots: The Saga of an American Family.* Boston, MA: Da Capo Press.

Hall, Stuart, Paul Gilroy, and Ruth Wilson Gilmore. 2021. *Selected Writings on Race and Difference.* Durham, NC: Duke University Press.

Hall, Stuart, and David Morley. 2019a. *Essential Essays Volume 1.* Durham, NC: Duke University Press.

Hall, Stuart, and David Morley. 2019b. *Essential Essays Volume 2.* Durham, NC: Duke University Press.

Harris, Abram, and Sterling D. Spero. 1931. *The Black Worker: The Negro and the Labor Movement.* New York: Columbia University Press.

Harris, Joseph E. 1993. *Global Dimensions of the African Diaspora.* Washington, DC: Howard University Press.

Haywood, Harry. 1976. *Negro Liberation*. Chicago, IL: Liberator Press.

Haywood, Harry. 1978. *Black Bolshevik: Autobiography of an Afro-American Communist*. Chicago, IL: Liberator Press.

Henry, Paget, ed. 2014. "Special Issue: Black Canadian Thought." *CLR James Journal* 20(1–2). www.jstor.org/stable/e26752052.

Henzell, Perry, dir. 1972. *The Harder They Come*. International Films, USA. www.imdb.com/title/tt0070155/.

Herskovits, Melville J. 2017 (1941). *The Myth of the Negro Past*. n.p.: Andesite Press.

Herskovits, Melville J., and Frances S. Herskovits. 1969. *The New World Negro: Selected Papers in Afroamerican Studies*. New York: Minerva Press.

Hill, Adelaide Cromwell, and Martin Kilson, eds. 1969. *Apropos of Africa: Sentiments of Negro American Leaders on Africa from the 1800s to the 1950s*. London: Frank Cass.

Hill, Robert A., Marcus Mosiah Garvey, and Emory J. Tolbert. 1983. *The Marcus Garvey and Universal Negro Improvement Association Papers Vol. II, Vol. II*. Berkeley, CA: University of California Press.

Hill, Robert A, Marcus Garvey, and Universal Negro Improvement Association. 2006. *The Marcus Garvey and Universal Negro Improvement Association Papers*. Berkeley, CA: University of California Press.

Hine, Darlene Clark, Trica Danielle Keaton, and Stephen Small. *Black Europe and the African Diaspora*. Urbana, IL: University of Illinois Press, 2009.

H-Net. n.d. "H-Black-Europe." https://networks.h-net.org/h-black-europe. Accessed October 31, 2020.

Holloway, Jonathan Scott. 2002. *Confronting the Veil: Abram Harris, Jr., E. Franklin Frazier, and Ralph Bunche, 1919–1941*. Chapel Hill, NC: University of North Carolina Press.

Holloway, Jonathan Scott, and Ben Keppel. 2007. *Black Scholars on the Line: Race, Social Science, and American Thought in the Twentieth Century*. Notre Dame, IN: University of Notre Dame Press.

Holloway, Joseph E. 2005. *Africanisms in American Culture*. Bloomington, IN: Indiana University Press.

Holowaty, Luba A. 1969. "Selected Bibliography of the Works of I.I. Potekhin, Soviet Africanist, 1947–1964." *African Studies Bulletin* 12(3): 315–22. https://doi.org/10.2307/523210.

Hopkins, Leroy T. 1992. "Expanding the Canon: Afro-German Studies." *Die Unterrichtspraxis/Teaching German* 25(2): 121–26. https://doi.org/10.2307/3531905.

Horne, Gerald. 2011. "Tokyo Bound: African Americans and Japan Confront White Supremacy." *Souls* 3(3): 16–28.

Horne, Gerald. 2012. *Negro Comrades of the Crown: African Americans and the British Empire Fight the U.S. before Emancipation*. New York: New York University Press.

Hughes, C. Alvin. 1984. "The Negro Sanhedrin Movement." *The Journal of Negro History* 69(1): 1–13.

Humanities and Social Sciences Online 2018. 2018. "5th Congress of African Historians Association (AHA)." https://networks.h-net.org/node/73374/announcements/2138102/5th-congress-african-historians-association-aha.

Hunter College. 2020. "Department of Africana and Puerto Rican/Latino Studies." http://www.hunter.cuny.edu/afprl.

Huntington, Samuel P. 2004. *Who Are We? America's Crisis of National Identity*. London: Free Press.

Huntington, Samuel P. 2011 (1996). *The Clash of Civilizations and the Remaking of World Order*. New York: Simon & Schuster.

Hunton, Dorothy. 1986. *Alphaeus Hunton: The Unsung Valiant*. Richmond Hill, NY: D.K. Hunton.

Hurston, Zora Neale. 2019. *Barracoon: The Story of the Last "Black Cargo."* New York: Amistad Press.

IAAW (Institut für Asien- und Afrika-Wissenschaften). 2020. "Institute of Asian and African Studies." www.iaaw.hu-berlin.de/en/region/africa/africa/profile.

"The International Books Fairs 1970–2005". n.d. The George Padmore Institute. www.georgepadmoreinstitute.org/collections/the-international-book-fairs-1970-2005.

IPCN (Instituto de Pesquisa da Cultural Negra). 2018. "Institute for the Research of Black Culture." Rio de Janeiro, Brazil. *Artememoria*, October 20. http://artememoria.org/artememoria_map_poi/2/.

Iskenderov, A.A. 1972. *Africa: Politics, Economy, Ideology*. Moscow: Central Books.

Ivanov, R.F. 1976. *American History and the Black Question*. Moscow: Novosti Press Agency Publishing House.

Ivanov, Robert. 1985. *Blacks in United States History*. Moscow: Progress Publishers.

Jackson, James E. 1967. *U.S. Negroes in Battle: From Little Rock to Watts; a Diary of Events, 1957–1965*. Moscow: Progress Publishers.

Jackson, Joseph D. 2013. *The Black Commandos: Warriors Forged from Blood, Sweat, and Tears...* 2nd edn. n.p.: Julian Jackson and Commando Publishing.

Jamaica Memory Bank. n.d. "The African Caribbean Institute of Jamaica." www.facebook.com/JamaicaMemoryBank/about/?ref=page_internal. Accessed October 31, 2020.

James, C.L.R. 1969. *A History of Pan-African Revolt*. Oakland, CA: PM Press.

James, C.L.R. 1993. *Beyond A Boundary*. Reprint edition. Durham, NC: Duke University Press Books.

John, Gus. 2006. *Taking A Stand: Gus John Speaks on Education, Social Action, and Civil Unrest*. Croydon: Gus John Books.

Jones, Rhett S., Alexander W. Astin, Doris Y. Wilkinson, and J. Blaine Hudson. 1994. "The Lasting Contributions of African-American Studies." *The Journal of Blacks in Higher Education* 6: 91–94. https://doi.org/10.2307/2962476.

Jordan, Tim. 1999. *Cyberpower: The Culture and Politics of Cyberspace and the Internet*. London: Routledge.

Karenga. 1980. *Kawaida Theory: An Introductory Outline*. Inglewood, CA: Kawaida Publications.

Karenga. 2008. *Kwanzaa: A Celebration of Family, Community and Culture*. Los Angeles, CA: University of Sankore Press.

Karim, Aisha, and Lee Sustar. 2006. *Poetry & Protest: A Dennis Brutus Reader*. Chicago, IL: Haymarket Books.

Kato, Tsunehiko. 2013. "The History of Black Studies in Japan: Origin and Development." *Journal of Black Studies* 44(8): 829–45.

Kaya, Dou, ed. 2000. *Cheikh Anta Diop*. Paris: L'Harmattan.

Kelley, Robin D.G. 2014. "The Third International and the Struggle for National Liberation in South Africa." *Ufahamu: A Journal of African Studies* 38(1): 245–66. https://doi.org/10.5070/F7381025031.

Kelley, Robin D.G., and Betsy Esch. 2008. "Black Like Mao: Red China and Black Revolution." In *Afro Asia: Revolutionary Political and Cultural Connections Between African Americans and Asian Americans*, edited by Fred Ho and Mullen, Bill, 97–154. Durham, NC: Duke University Press.

Kelly, Jennifer R. 2006. "Black Canadian Studies: A Move towards Diasporan Literacy." *New Dawn, Journal of Black Canadian Studies* 1(1): 204.

Kendi, Ibram X. 2012. *The Black Campus Movement: Black Students and the Racial Reconstitution of Higher Education, 1965–1972*.

Khanga, Yelena, and Susan Jacoby. 1994. *Soul to Soul: A Black Russian American Family 1865–1992*. 1st edn. New York: W.W. Norton.

King, Jr., Martin Luther. 1968. "The Role of the Behavioral Scientist in the Civil Rights Movement." *Journal of Social Issues* 24(1): 1–12. https://doi.org/10.1111/j.1540-4560.1968.tb01465.x.

King, William M. 1992. "The Importance of Black Studies for Science and Technology Policy." *Phylon (1960–)* 49(1/2): 23–32. https://doi.org/10.2307/3132614.

Kitossa, Tamari Kitossa. 2012. "Black Canadian Studies and the Resurgence of the Insurgent African Canadian Intelligentsia." *Southern Journal of Canadian Studies* 5 (December): 255–84.

Kiuchi, Toru. 2014. "Japan Black Studies Association at Sixty: Recent Thirty Years, 1984–2014." Tokyo: Nihon University. http://home.att.ne.jp/zeta/yorozuya/jbsa/Japan_Black_Studies_Association_at_Sixty--Recent_Thirty_Years_1984-2015.pdf.

Kiuchi, Toru. 2020. "Letter on George Floyd." https://kmmtshuji.wixsite.com/jbsa.

Lagos State University. n.d. "Center For Afro-Brazilian Studies." https://www.facebook.com/LASUCAS.ng/. Accessed October 31, 2020.

La Rose, Michael. 2015. "History of the Caribbean Carnival." *Charleston Carifest*, January 23. https://charlestoncarifest.com/information/history-of-the-caribbean-carnival/.

Lemann, Nicolas. 2008. *The Promised Land The Great Black Migration and How It Changed America*. Paw Prints.

Lenin, Vladimir Ilyich. 1914. "The Left Narodniks." May 14. www.marxists.org/archive/lenin/works/1914/may/14.htm.

Lenstra, Noah. n.d. "EBlack Champaign-Urbana." http://eblackcu.net/portal/. Accessed November 1, 2020.

Lewis, Rupert. 1988. *Marcus Garvey: Anti-Colonial Champion*. Trenton, NJ: Africa World Press.

Lewis, Rupert. 1998. *Walter Rodney's Intellectual and Political Thought*. Barbados: Press University of the West Indies; Detroit, MI: Wayne State University Press.

Liebenow, J. Gus. 1969. *Liberia: The Evolution of Privilege*. Ithaca, NY: Cornell University Press.

Lofton, Robin. 2015. "Africans and African Americans in China: A Long History, A Troubled Present, and A Promising Future?" *Black Past*, March 9. www.

blackpast.org/global-african-history/africans-and-african-americans-china-long-history-troubled-present-and-promising-future/.

Logan, Rayford Whittingham. 1969. *Howard University: The First Hundred Years, 1867–1967*. New York: New York University Press.

Lozès, Patrick. 2012. "The Invention of Blacks in France." In *Black France/France Noire: The History and Politics of Blackness*, edited by Trica Danielle Keaton, Tracy Denean Sharpley-Whiting, and Tyler Stovall, 103–109. Durham, NC: Duke University Press.

Lumpkin, Beatrice. 1987. "African and African American Contributions to Mathematics." Geocultural Baseline Essay Series. Portland, OR: Portland Public Schools.

McClellan, Woodford. 1993. "Africans and Black Americans in the Comintern Schools, 1925–1934." *The International Journal of African Historical Studies* 26(2): 371–90. https://doi.org/10.2307/219551.

McEachrane, Michael. 2021. "On Conceptualising African Diasporas in Europe." *African Diaspora* 13(1–2): 160–82. https://doi.org/10.1163/18725465-bja10014.

Mchunu, Vusi. 1988. "Editorial." *AWA-FINNABA*, no. 12 (March).

McIlwain, Charlton D. 2019. *Black Software: The Internet and Racial Justice, from the AfroNet to Black Lives Matter*. Oxford: Oxford University Press.

Mack, Raneta Lawson. 2002. *The Digital Divide: Standing at the Intersection of Race & Technology*. Durham, NC: Carolina Academic Press.

McKissick, Floyd B. 1969. *Three-Fifths of a Man*. New York: Macmillan.

McWorter, Gerald A., ed. 1968. "Black University Part 1." Special issue. *Negro Digest* 5(17) (March). http://freedomarchives.org/Documents/Finder/DOC513_scans/Negro_Digest/513.NegroDigest.NegroDigest.March.1968.pdf.

McWorter, Gerald A., ed. 1969. "Black University Part II." Special issue. *Negro Digest* 5(18) (March). http://freedomarchives.org/Documents/Finder/DOC513_scans/Negro_Digest/513.NegroDigest.NegroDigest.March.1969.pdf.

McWorter, Gerald A., ed. 1970. "Black University Part III." Special issue. *Negro Digest* 19 (March). https://www.freedomarchives.org/Documents/Finder/DOC513_scans/Negro_Digest/513.NegroDigest.NegroDigest.March.1970.pdf.

Madhubuti, Haki, and Herb Boyd. 2019. *Black Panther Paradigm Shift or Not?* Chicago, IL: Third World Press.

Manning, Patrick. 2010. *The African Diaspora: A History Through Culture*. New York: Columbia University Press.

Mao Tse-Tung. 1963. "Oppose Racial Discrimmination By US Imperialism." August 8. www.marxists.org/reference/archive/mao/selected-works/volume-9/mswv9_04.htm.

Marable, Manning, and Leith Mullings. 2000. *Let Nobody Turn Us Around: Voices of Resistance, Reform, and Renewal: An African American Anthology*. Lanham, MD: Rowman & Littlefield.

Martin, Tony. 1986. *Race First: The Ideological and Organizational Struggles of Marcus Garvey and the Universal Negro Improvement Association*. Dover, MA: Majority Press.

Martin, Tony. 2008. *Amy Ashwood Garvey: Pan-Africanist, Feminist and Mrs Marcus Garvey Number 1, or, A Tale of Two Armies*. Dover, MA: Majority Press.

Marx, Karl. 1843. *Contribution to the Critique of Hegel's Philosophy of Right*. www.marxists.org/archive/marx/works/1843/critique-hpr/intro.htm.

Marx, Karl, and Friedrich Engels. 1969. *Selected Works, Volume 1*. Moscow: Progress Publishers.

Marx, Karl, and Friedrich Engels. 1973. *Karl Marx and Frederick Engels Selected Works in Three Volumes: Volume 3*. Moscow: Progress Publishers.

Marxist Internet Archive. n.d. "South African Communist Party Documents. 1928." www.marxists.org/history/international/comintern/sections/sacp/1928/comintern.htm. Accessed October 31, 2020.

Maryland Institute for Technology in the Humanities. n.d. "African American History, Culture and Digital Humanities." *Maryland Institute for Technology in the Humanities* (blog). https://mith.umd.edu/research/aadhum/. Accessed October 31, 2020.

Massachusetts Institute of Technology. n.d. "MIT OpenCourseWare | Free Online Course Materials." https://ocw.mit.edu/index.htm. Accessed October 31, 2020.

Massaquoi, Hans J. 2014. *Destined to Witness: Growing up Black in Nazi Germany*. n.p.: HarperCollins e-Books. http://rbdigital.oneclickdigital.com.

MESEA (Society for Multi-Ethnic Studies: Europe and the Americas). n.d. https://mesea.org.

Michigan State University. n.d. "Department of African American and African Studies." Department of African American and African Studies. https://aaas.msu.edu/.

Milne, June. 2000. *Kwame Nkrumah: Biography*. London: Panaf.

Minchin, Timothy J. 2005. "'A Brand New Shining City': Floyd B. McKissick Sr. and the Struggle to Build Soul City, North Carolina." *The North Carolina Historical Review* 82(2): 125–55.

Mohamud, Naima. 2019. "Yasuke: The Mysterious African Samurai." *BBC News*, October 13. www.bbc.com/news/world-africa-48542673.

Morales Domínguez, Esteban. 2013. *Race in Cuba: Essays on the Revolution and Racial Inequality*. New York: Monthly Review Press.

More, Thomas. 1900. *Utopia*. New York: F.M. Lupton.

Morison, David. 1964. *The USSR and Africa, 1945–1963*. London: Oxford University Press.

Mosley, Walter. 2018. *47*. New York: Little, Brown and Co.

Nakamura, Lisa. 2002. *Cybertypes: Race, Ethnicity, and Identity on the Internet*. New York: Routledge.

Nascimento, Abdias do, and Elisa Larkin Nascimento. 1992. *Africans in Brazil: A Pan-African Perspective*. Trenton, NJ: Africa World Press.

National Gallery of Jamaica. 2017. "In Memoriam Dr. the Hon. David Boxer, O.J. (1946–2017)." National Gallery of Jamaica (Blog), May 30. https://nationalgalleryofjamaica.wordpress.com/tag/david-boxer/.

National Museums Liverpool. 2020. "International Slavery Museum." www.liverpoolmuseums.org.uk/international-slavery-museum.

Ndiaye, Macodou, and Florence Alexis. 2019. *Les Noirs en France: du XVIIIème siècle à nos jours*. Paris: Paari.

Ndiaye, Pap. 2009. *Les Noirs américains: en marche pour l'égalité*. Paris: Gallimard.

Ndiaye, Pap. 2011. *La condition noire: Essai sur une minorité française*. Paris: Gallimard.

Nelson, Alondra. 2002. "Introduction to Afrofuturism." *Social Text* 20(2): 1–16.

Nettleford, Rex M., and Maria LaYacona. 1970. *Roots and Rhythms; Jamaica's National Dance Theatre.* New York: Hill and Wang.

New York Public Library. n.d. "About the Schomburg Center for Research in Black Culture." www.nypl.org/about/locations/schomburg. Accessed October 26, 2020.

Nkrumah, Kwame. 1945. *Towards Colonial Freedom.* Accra: Guinea Press.

Nkrumah, Kwame. 1980. *Revolutionary Path.* London: Panaf.

Noble, Safiya Umoja. 2018. *Algorithms of Oppression: How Search Engines Reinforce Racism.* New York: New York University Press.

Noble, Safiya Umoja, and Brendesha M. Tynes. 2016. *The Intersectional Internet: Race, Sex, Class and Culture Online.* New York: Peter Lang.

Noe-Bustamante, Luis, Antonio Flores, and Sono Shah. n.d. "Facts on Latinos of Dominican Origin in the U.S." *Pew Research Center's Hispanic Trends Project* (blog). www.pewresearch.org/hispanic/fact-sheet/u-s-hispanics-facts-on-dominican-origin-latinos/. Accessed November 1, 2020.

Northamptonshire Black History Association. 2020. www.facebook.com/NorthamptonshireBlackHistory/.

NSBE (National Society of Black Engineers). n.d. "National Society of Black Engineers." www.nsbe.org/home.aspx.

Obadele, Imari Abubakari. 1974. "The Struggle of the Republic of New Africa." *The Black Scholar* 5(9): 32–41. https://doi.org/10.1080/00064246.1974.11431428.

Obadele, Imari Abubakari. 1975. *Foundations of the Black Nation.* Detroit, MI: House of Songhay.

Obadele, Imari Abubakari. 1984. *Free the Land! The True Story of the Trials of the RNA-11 in Mississippi and the Continuing Struggle to Establish an Independent Black Nation in Five States of the Deep South.* Washington, DC: House of Songhay.

Ogbar, Geoffrey O.G. 2004. *Black Power: Radical Politics and African American Identity.* Baltimore, MD: Johns Hopkins University Press.

Okpewho, Isidore, Carole Boyce Davies, and Ali A. Mazrui, eds. 2002. *The African Diaspora: African Origins and New World Identities.* Bloomington, IN: Indiana University Press.

Olaniyan, Tejumola, and James H. Sweet, eds. 2010. *The African Diaspora and the Disciplines.* Bloomington, IN: Indiana University Press.

Olusanya, G.O. 1982. *The West African Students' Union and the Politics of Decolonization, 1925–1958.* Ibadan: Daystar.

Onishi, Yuichiro. 2013. *Transpacific Antiracism: Afro-Asian Solidarity in 20th-Century Black America, Japan, and Okinawa.* New York: New York University Press.

Onishi, Yuichiro. 2020. "Q&A with Yuichiro Onishi." College of Liberal Arts, Minneapolis. May 28. https://cla.umn.edu/aaas/news-events/story/qa-yuichiro-onishi.

Onishi, Yuichiro, and Fumiko Sakashita, eds. 2019. *Transpacific Correspondence Dispatches from Japan's Black Studies.* Cham: Palgrave Macmillan.

Ortiz, Paul. 2018. *An African American and Latinx History of the United States.* Boston, MA: Beacon Press.

Padmore, George. 1931. "American Imperialism Enslaves Liberia." *The Communist* X(2): 133–46.

Painter, Nell Irvin. 1992. *Exodusters: Black Migration to Kansas after Reconstruction*. New York: W.W. Norton.

Panford, Steven. 2002. "Digitizing the Discipline Conference Program." New York City Technical College.

Pappademos, Melina. 2011. *Black Political Activism and the Cuban Republic*. Chapel Hill, NC: University of North Carolina Press.

Pattieu, Sylvain, Emmanuelle Sibeud, and Tyler Stovall, eds. 2022. *The Black Populations of France: Histories from Metropole to Colony*. Lincoln, NE: University of Nebraska Press.

People's College. 1977. "Black Liberation and the United Front Against Imperialism: Some Lessons for Our Continunig Support for the Struggle in Southern Africa." 1–14. Detroit, MI. https://tinyurl.com/y5zbvkns.

Phillips, Jerry. 2002. "The Intuition of the Future: Utopia and Catastrophe in Octavia Butler's 'Parable of the Sower.'" *NOVEL: A Forum on Fiction* 35(2/3): 299–311. https://doi.org/10.2307/1346188.

Phillips, Tom. 2011. "Brazil Census Shows African-Brazilians in the Majority for the First Time." *The Guardian*, November 17. www.theguardian.com/world/2011/nov/17/brazil-census-african-brazilians-majority.

Plummer, Brenda Gayle. 2013. *In Search of Power: African Americans in the Era of Decolonization, 1956–1974*. New York: Cambridge University Press.

Ponder, Erik. n.d. "LibGuides: African American Studies Research Guide: African American Online Courses and Lectures." https://libguides.lib.msu.edu/c.php?g=95622&p=624416. Accessed November 1, 2020.

Potekhin, I.I. 1968. *African Problems: Analysis of Eminent Soviet Scientist*. Moscow: Nauka.

Preston Black History Group. 2020. www.prestonblackhistorygroup.org.uk/.

"Race and Cyberspace Symposium." n.d. MIT Program in Women and Gender Studies. https://stuff.mit.edu/afs/athena.mit.edu/org/w/wgs/pdf/race-cyberspace.pdf. Accessed March 27, 2019.

Ramos, Arthur. 1980 (1939). *The Negro in Brazil*. Philadelphia, PA: Porcupine Press.

Rediker, Marcus. 2008. *The Slave Ship: A Human History*. New York: Penguin Books.

Rediker, Marcus, and Cornell Womack. 2005. *Villains of All Nations: Atlantic Pirates in the Golden Age*. 1st edn. Boston, MA: Beacon Press.

Revista da ABPN. n.d. *Revista da ABPN (Journal of the Brazilian Association of Black Researchers)*. http://abpnrevista.org.br/revista.

Rhodes, Jane. 2017. *Framing the Black Panthers: The Spectacular Rise of a Black Power Icon*.

Robinson, Robert. 1988. *Black on Red: My 44 Years inside the Soviet Union*. Washington, DC: Acropolis Books.

Rodney, Walter. 1981 (1972). *How Europe Underdeveloped Africa*. Washington, DC: Howard University Press.

Rodney, Walter. 1990 (1969). *The Groundings with My Brothers*. London: Bogle-L'Ouverture Publications.

Rolinson, Mary J. 2008. *Grassroots Garveyism: The Universal Negro Improvement Association in the Rural South, 1920–1927*. Chapel Hill, NC: University of North Carolina Press.

Romo, Anadelia A. 2007. "Rethinking Race and Culture in Brazil's First Afro-Brazilian Congress of 1934." *Journal of Latin American Studies* 39(1): 31–54. www.jstor.org/stable/4491775.

Rose, Tricia. n.d. "Underlying Conditions | Center for the Study of Race and Ethnicity in America | Brown University." www.brown.edu/academics/race-ethnicity/programs-initiatives/signature-series/underlying-conditions. Accessed November 1, 2020.

Rout, Leslie B. 1976. *The African Experience in Spanish America: 1502 to the Present Day*. Cambridge: Cambridge University Press.

Rutgers University, Camden. 2012. "Black German Cultural Society of New Jersey: Mid-Atlantic Regional Center for the Humanities." February 10. https://march.rutgers.edu/cfp-black-german-cultural-society-of-new-jersey/.

Rutgers University–Camden. 2020. "Black Germany and Beyond: Africana Studies." April 3. https://africanastudies.camden.rutgers.edu/bghra/.

Sansone, Livio. 2011. "Turner, Franklin and Herskovits in the Gantois House of Candomblé: The Transnational Origin of Afro-Brazilian Studies." *The Black Scholar* 41(1): 48–63. https://doi.org/10.5816/blackscholar.41.1.0048.

Saunders, Frances Stonor. 2013. *The Cultural Cold War: The CIA and the World of Arts and Letters*. New York: New Press.

Sawahel, Wagdy. 2013. "Brazil Launches African Higher Education Collaboration." *University World News*, June 15. www.universityworldnews.com/post.php?story=20130615100438 40.

Secretariat for an Encyclopedia Africana. 1963. "Messages on the Death of Dr. W.E.B. DuBois." *Encyclopedia Africana Information Report* 7: 2. Accra: Ghana Academy of Sciences. https://credo.library.umass.edu/view/pageturn/mums312-b287-i015/#page/1/mode/1up.

Sherwood, Marika. 1996. *Kwame Nkrumah: The Years Abroad, 1935–1947*. Legon: Freedom Publications.

Sherwood, Marika. 2011a. *Malcolm X Visits Abroad: April 1964–February 1965*. Oare, Kent: Savannah Press.

Sherwood, Marika. 2011b. *Origins of Pan-Africanism : Henry Sylvester Williams, Africa and the African Diaspora*. New York: Routledge.

Sherwood, Marika. 2015. *Claudia Jones: A Life in Exile*. London: Lawrence & Wishart. https://muse.jhu.edu/books/9781910448250/.

Shivji, Issa G. 1979. *The Silent Class Struggle*. Dar es Salaam: Tanzania Publishing House.

Small, Stephen. 2018. *20 Questions and Answers on Black Europe*. The Hague: Amrit.

Smirnov, S.R., ed. 1968. *A History of Africa: 1918–1967*. U.S.S.R. Academy of Science: Institute of Africa.

Sollers, Werner, ed. 1972. *A Bibliographic Guide to Afro-American Studies: (Based on the Holdings of the John F. Kennedy Institut Library)*. Berlin: John F. Kennedy-Institut für Nordamerikastudien, Freie Universität Berlin.

Solodovnikov, V.G. 1966. "African Studies in the U.S.S.R." *The Journal of Modern African Studies* 4(3): 359–66. https://doi.org/10.1177/0011325568001001 05.

Solodovnikov, Vasilij Grigor'evič. 1970. *Africa Fights for Independence*. Moscow: Novosti Press Agency Publishing House.

Sonebeyatta, Yusufu, and Joseph F. Brooks. 1971. "Ujamaa for Land and Power." *The Black Scholar* 3(2): 13–20.

Soske, Jon. 2004. "The Dissimulation of Race: 'Afro-Pessimism' And the Problem of Development." *Qui Parle* 14(2): 15–56. https://doi.org/10.1215/quiparle.14.2.15.

Sosnoski, James J., Patricia Harkin, and Bryan Carter. 2006. *Configuring History: Teaching the Harlem Renaissance Through Virtual Reality Cityscapes*. New York: Peter Lang.

"*Squid Game*." 2022. *Wikipedia*. https://en.wikipedia.org/w/index.php?title=Squid_Game&oldid=1070142710.

Stalin, Joseph. 1954. *Marxism and the National Question 1913*. Moscow: Foreign Languages Publishing House.

Starušenko, Gleb. 1975. *Africa Makes a Choice: The Development of Socialist-Oriented States*. Moscow: Novosti Press Agency Publishing House.

Stovall, Tyler. 2012. *Paris Noir African Americans in the City of Light*. Boston, MA: Houghton Mifflin.

Strain, Christopher. 2004. "Soul City, North Carolina: Black Power, Utopia, and the African American Dream." *The Journal of African American History* 89(1): 57–74. https://doi.org/10.2307/4134046.

Stringer, Chris, and Robin McKie. 1998. *African Exodus: The Origins of Modern Humanity*. New York: Henry Holt.

Stuckey, Sterling. 1987. *Slave Culture: Nationalist Theory and the Foundations of Black America*. New York: Oxford University Press.

Szwed, John F. 2012. *Space Is the Place: The Lives and Times of Sun Ra*. New York: Pantheon.

Tarabrin, E.A. 1974. *The New Scramble for Africa*. Moscow: Progress.

Taylor, Ula Yvette. 2002. *The Veiled Garvey: The Life & Times of Amy Jacques Garvey*. Chapel Hill, NC: University of North Carolina Press.

Tetteh, Benjamin. 2018. "2019: Year of Return for African Diaspora." *Africa Renewal*, December. www.un.org/africarenewal/magazine/december-2018-march-2019/2019-year-return-african-diaspora.

Thompson, Robert Farris. 1984. *Flash of the Spirit: African and Afro-American Art and Philosophy*. New York: Vintage Books.

Thompson, Vincent Bakpetu. 1977. *Africa and Unity: The Evolution of Pan-Africanism*. Harlow: Longmans.

Thornhill, Esmeralda M.A., ed. 2008. "Special Issue: Blacks in Canada: Retrospects, Introspects, Prospects." *Journal of Black Studies* 38(3). www.jstor.org/stable/i40001816.

Tokareva, Z. 1969. "The Africa Institute of the USSR Academy of Sciences." *Nauka Publishing House*, Africa in Soviet Studies 1968 Annual, 153–62.

Tokarnia, Mariana. 2018. "Racism Harms Scientific Production of Black Researchers in Brazil." *Medium*, March 5. https://medium.com/@tokarnia/racism-harms-scientific-production-of-black-researchers-in-brazil-1c9669a3b688.

Tolbert, Emory J. 1980. *The UNIA and Black Los Angeles: Ideology and Community in the American Garvey Movement*. Los Angeles, CA: Center for Afro-American Studies, University of California.

Tomich, Dale. 1979. "The Dialectic of Colonialism and Culture: The Origins of the Negritude of Aimé Césaire." *Review of Fernand Braudel Center* 2(3): 351–85.

TransAfrica. 2005. "TransAfrica Forum Mission." February 4. https://web.archive.org/web/20050204062659/http://transafricaforum.org/mission.html.

Trouillard, Stéphanie. 2020. "Commemorating the Abolition of Slavery in France: 'This Is Our History.'" France 24. May 10. www.france24.com/en/20200510-commemorating-the-abolition-of-slavery-in-france-this-is-our-history.

Tsujiuchi, Makoto. 1998. "Historical Context of Black Studies in Japan." *Hitotsubashi Journal of Social Studies* 30(2): 95–100. www.jstor.org/stable/43294431.

Tulloch, Headley. 1975. *Black Canadians: A Long Line of Fighters*. Toronto: NC Press.

Turner, Lorenzo Dow. 1949. *Africanisms in the Gullah Dialect, by Lorenzo Dow Turner.* Chicago, IL: University of Chicago Press.

UCLan (University of Central Lancashire). 2020. "Institute for Black Atlantic Research." https://ibaruclan.com/.

USCB (University of California at Santa Barbara). 2020a. "Journal of Haitian Studies: About Center for Black Studies Research." https://cbsr.ucsb.edu/journal-of-haitian-studies/about.

USCB (University of California at Santa Barbara). 2020b. "Kosanba: Center for Black Studies Research." https://cbsr.ucsb.edu/research/haitian-studies/kosanba.

UNIA (Universal Negro Improvement Association). n.d. www.theunia-acl.com/.

University of Massachusetts Amherst. n.d. "Remapping Black Germany Conference." www.umass.edu/germanic/remapping/. Accessed October 31, 2020.

University of Oxford. 2020. "BME Staff Network: Information on the Black and Minority Ethnic Staff Network." *Equality and Diversity Unit.* https://edu.admin.ox.ac.uk/bme-staff-network.

University of the West Indies. n.d.a. "The Reggae Studies Unit." www.mona.uwi.edu/humed/ics/rsunit.php. Accessed October 31, 2020.

University of the West Indies. n.d.b. "African and African Diasporean Studies." www.mona.uwi.edu/programmes/view/1668. Accessed October 31, 2020.

University of the West Indies. n.d.c. "The Institute of Caribbean Studies." www.mona.uwi.edu/humed/ics/about.php#ics. Accessed October 31, 2020.

Urban, Wayne J. 1992. *Black Scholar: Horace Mann Bond, 1904–1972*. Athens, GA: University of Georgia Press.

Van Sertima, Ivan. 1994. *Blacks in Science: Ancient and Modern*. New Brunswick, NJ: Transaction.

Van Sertima, Ivan. 2003 (1976). *They Came before Columbus: The African Presence in Ancient America*. New York: Random House.

Vargas-Ramos, Carlos. 2018. "Puerto Ricans Keep on Growing! The Puerto Rican Population in the United States Grew at a Rapid Pace between 2016 and

2017. Centro de Estudios Puertorriqueños." *Center for Puerto Rican Studies*, September 17. https://tinyurl.com/yynyj9tm.

Wada, Kayomi. 2008. "Black Studies Association (Kokujin Kenkyu No Kai) of Japan." *Black Past*, December 29. www.blackpast.org/global-african-history/black-studies-association-kokujin-kenkyu-no-kai-japan/.

Walker, James W. St. G. 1982. *A History of Blacks in Canada: A Study Guide for Teachers and Students*. Ottawa: Minister of State Multiculturalism.

Walker, Margaret. 2016. *Jubilee*. Boston, MA: Houghton Mifflin.

Walmsley, Anne. 1992. *The Caribbean Artists Movement, 1966–72: A Literary & Cultural History*. London: New Beacon Books.

Walter Rodney Foundation. n.d. "The Walter Rodney Foundation: Sharing the Life and Works of Dr. Walter Rodney." www.walterrodneyfoundation.org/. Accessed October 31, 2020.

Walters, Ronald W. 1993. *Pan Africanism in the African Diaspora: An Analysis of Modern Afrocentric Political Movements*. Detroit, MI: Wayne State University Press.

Webster, J.B., A. Adu Boahen, and H.O. Idowu. 1973. *History of West Africa the Revolutionary Years—1815 to Independence*. Washington, DC: Praeger.

Wesley, Charles Harris, and Richard Allen. 1969. *Richard Allen, Apostle of Freedom*. Washington, DC: Associated Publishers.

White, Sarah, Roxy Harris, and Sharmilla Beezmohun. 2005. *A Meeting of the Continents: The International Book Fair of Radical Black and Third World Books—Revisited: History, Memories, Organisation and Programmes, 1982–1995*. London: New Beacon Books.

Wikipedia. 2020a. "Alain LeRoy Locke." https://en.wikipedia.org/wiki/Alain_LeRoy_Locke.

Wikipedia. 2020b. "Olivette Otele." https://en.wikipedia.org/wiki/Olivette_Otele.

Wikipedia. 2020c. "The Walking Dead." https://en.wikipedia.org/wiki/The_Walking_Dead_(TV_series)#Critical_reception.

Wikipedia. 2020d. "Firestone Natural Rubber Company." *Wikipedia*. https://en.wikipedia.org/w/index.php?title=Firestone_Natural_Rubber_Company&oldid=946044165.

Wikipedia. 2020e. "Mark Hanna Watkins." *Wikipedia*. https://en.wikipedia.org/w/index.php?title=Mark_Hanna_Watkins&oldid=978064461.

Wikipedia. 2020f. "Jean Sagbo." *Wikipedia*. https://en.wikipedia.org/w/index.php?title=Jean_Sagbo&oldid=981371981.

Wikipedia. 2020g. "American Colonization Society." *Wikipedia*. https://en.wikipedia.org/w/index.php?title=American_Colonization_Society&oldid=985513965.

Wikipedia. 2020h. "Afro-Russians." *Wikipedia*. https://en.wikipedia.org/w/index.php?title=Afro-Russians&oldid=986127655.

Wikipedia. 2020i. "Black Panther (Film)." *Wikipedia*. https://en.wikipedia.org/w/index.php?title=Black_Panther_(film)&oldid=986135803.

Wilderson, Frank. 2020. *Afropessimism*. New York: Liveright Publishing.

Wilford, Hugh. 2009. *The Mighty Wurlitzer: How the CIA Played America*. Cambridge, MA: Harvard University Press.

Willhelm, Sidney M. 1971. *Who Needs the Negro?* Garden City, NY: Doubleday.

Williams, Chancellor. 1987 (1971). *The Destruction of Black Civilization: Great Issues of a Race from 4500 B.C. to 2000 A.D.* Chicago, IL: Third World Press.

Williams, Ronald. 2010. "History: African American Studies." April 9. https://africam.berkeley.edu/history/.

Williams, Scott. n.d. "Mathematicians of the African Diaspora." www.math.buffalo.edu/mad/. Accessed November 1, 2020.

Wilson, Charles Morrow. 1971. *Liberia: Black Africa in Microcosm.* New York: Harper & Row.

Winks, Robin W. 2008 (1971). *The Blacks in Canada: A History.* Montreal: McGill-Queen's University Press.

Wint, Eleanor, and Carolyn Cooper. 2003. *Bob Marley: The Man and His Music: A Selection of Papers Presented at the Conference Marley's Music, Reggae, Rastafari, and Jamaican Culture, Held at the University of the West Indies, Mona Campus, 5–6 February 1995.* Kingston: Arawak Publications.

Wipplinger, Jonathan. 2013. "Germany, 1923: Alain Locke, Claude McKay, and the New Negro in Germany." *Callaloo* 36(1): 108.

Wright, Richard. 1995 (1954). *Black Power.* New York: Harper.

X, Malcolm. 1965. *Malcolm X Talks to Young People.* New York: Young Socialist.

X, Malcolm, Herb Boyd, Ilyasah Shabazz, Haki R Madhubuti, and James H Cone. 2013. *The Diary of Malcolm X, El-Hajj Malik El-Shabazz, 1964.*

X, Malcolm, and George Breitman. 1989. *Malcolm X Speaks.* New York: Pathfinder.

X, Malcolm. 1965. *The Autobiography of Malcolm X: As Told to Alex Haley.* New York: Ballantine Books.

Year to Pull the Covers Off ImPerialism Project. 1975. "Report from National Planning Conference: Year to Pull the Covers off Imperialism Project." *The Black Scholar* 6(5): 54–56.

Yelvington, Kevin A. 2001. "The Anthropology of Afro-Latin America and the Caribbean: Diasporic Dimensions." *Annual Review of Anthropology* 30(1): 227–60. https://doi.org/10.1146/annurev.anthro.30.1.227.

Yelvington, Kevin A. 2018. "'A Conference That Didn't': African Diaspora Studies and an Episode in Anthropology's Identity Politics of Representation." *Critique of Anthropology* 38(4): 407–32. https://doi.org/10.1177/0308275X18806574.

Yette, Samuel F. 1972. *The Choice: The Issue of Black Survival in America.* Berkeley, CA: Medallion Books.

Young, Herman A., and Barbara H. Young. 1977. "Science and Black Studies." *The Journal of Negro Education* 46(4): 380–87. https://doi.org/10.2307/2966958.

Young Historians. 2020. "Young Historians Project." Younghistoriansproject. www.younghistoriansproject.org.

Zamalin, Alex. 2019. *Black Utopia: The History of an Idea from Black Nationalism to Afrofuturism.* New York: Columbia University Press.

Zaslavsky, Claudia. 1973. "Mathematics in the Study of African Culture." *The Arithmetic Teacher* 20(7): 532–35.

Zaslavsky, Claudia. 1999. *Africa Counts: Number and Pattern in African Culture.* Chicago, IL: Lawrence Hill Books.

Zhu, Zhenxing. 2018. "Pilgrimage for Revolutionary Spirit : African American Activists, the People's Republic of China, and Chinese American Leftists in the Cold War-Civil Rights Era." International Institute of American Studies, Doshisha University. https://doi.org/10.14988/pa.2018.0000000106.

Index

Page numbers in italics refer to figures or tables.